1984

1984
INDIA'S GUILTY SECRET

PAV SINGH

KASHI HOUSE

Published by KASHI HOUSE CIC 2017

A CIP catalogue record for this book is available from the British Library

ISBN: 978 1 911271 08 6

Cover design: Paul Smith Design (www.paulsmithdesign.com)
Layout, typesetting & reprographics: Tia Džamonja, PRÉSENTATION ET
REPRÉSENTATION S.P.R.L. (tiadzamonja@gmail.com)
Maps © Pav Singh

Printed and bound by CPI Group (UK) Ltd, Croydon, CR0 4YY

KASHI HOUSE CIC
27 Old Gloucester Street, London WC1N 3AX

kashihouse.com
facebook.com/kashihouse
twitter.com/kashihouse

To the victims of *Churasee* ('1984') and the many individuals,
of all faiths and none, who offered shelter and relief,
and continue to fight for justice

'On the contrary, war hysteria is continuous and universal in all countries, and such acts as raping, looting, the slaughter of children, the reduction of whole populations to slavery... are looked upon as normal, and, when they are committed by one's own side and not by the enemy, meticulous.'

'The past is what the records and the memories agree upon. And since the party is in full control of all records, and in equally full control of the minds of its members, it follows that the past is whatever the party chooses to make it.'

George Orwell, *Nineteen Eighty-Four*

Contents

Illustrations

1. 'The Iron Ladies': Prime Minister Indira Gandhi in her Delhi office with her British counterpart, Margaret Thatcher, April 1981. John Downing/Hulton Archive/Getty Images.

2. Operation Blue Star: the aftermath of Mrs Gandhi's highly contentious military assault on the Golden Temple complex in Amritsar on 6 June 1984. Photo by Gurmeet Thukral.

3. Assassination: Arun Nehru MP (left) arriving at the All India Institute of Medical Sciences (AIIMS) in New Delhi with President Zail Singh (right) on the evening of 31 October 1984, the day of Mrs Gandhi's assassination. Photo © Ashok Vahie.

4. The day after: Mrs Gandhi's body lying in state at Teen Murti House, New Delhi, 1 November 1984. Flanking her open casket are her son and successor, Rajiv Gandhi (in white, right) and Arun Nehru MP (also in white, left). Photo © Ashok Vahie.

5. H. K. L. Bhagat MP (left) in discussion with Prime Minister Rajiv Gandhi (right) outside Teen Murti House, New Delhi, 1 November 1984. Photo © Ashok Vahie.

6. Violence erupts: a mob attacks a Sikh man in the streets of Delhi, November 1984. Photo © Ashok Vahie.

7. Arson and looting: people look on as Sikh businesses are targeted by the mobs, Delhi, November 1984. Photo © Ashok Vahie.

8. City ablaze: the Hotel Marina in Connaught Place, New Delhi, November 1984.

9. Roasted alive: four Sikh brothers, the owners of the burning Sahni Paints, are burnt alive by mobs in Paharganj, 2 November 1984, New Delhi. Photo courtesy *India Today*.

10. Nowhere to hide: a burnt-out Sikh-owned taxi, November 1984. Photo © Ashok Vahie.

11. Charred remains: a body left burning on the streets of Delhi, November 1984.

12. Left for dead: children peer at two dead Sikhs on a train, November 1984.

13. Commuters walk past two bodies on a parked luggage trolley on the platform at New Delhi Railway Station, November 1984. Photo © Ashok Vahie.

14. The killing lanes: destroyed Sikh homes in Trilokpuri, East Delhi, in the aftermath of some of the most concentrated and vicious pogroms that occurred between 1 and 2 November 1984. Photo courtesy *Hindustan Times*.

15. Blood-drenched corpses litter a Delhi courtyard, November 1984.

16. Reduced to ashes: in a gutted residence in the capital, the charred legs of a victim can be seen, November 1984. Photo © Satish Sharma.

17. A widow and her children, survivors of a devastating massacre in the Kalyanpuri colony in East Delhi, sit amidst the rubble of what was once their home in Sector 13, November 1984. Photo © Ram Rahman.

18. A mother holds her son's shorn hair and identity card, November 1984. Photo © Ashok Vahie.

19. A survivor of a massacre in East Delhi is comforted, November 1984. Photo © Ram Rahman.

20. Women from the doomed Trilokpuri colony in East Delhi, November 1984. Photo © Ashok Vahie.

21. A mother from Trilokpuri, East Delhi, holds a dismembered finger, the only remaining part of her butchered son, November 1984. Photo © Ram Rahman.

22. Manjit Singh, Delhi, October 2009. From the 1984 notebooks © Gauri Gill.

23. Taranjeet Kaur, Delhi, October 2009. From the 1984 notebooks © Gauri Gill.

24. Gopi Kaur, Delhi, September 2014. From the 1984 notebooks © Gauri Gill.

25. Bhaggi Kaur, Delhi, September 2014. From the 1984 notebooks © Gauri Gill.

26. Refugees in their own country: a Sikh family in a school yard are served by a *langarwalla* in one of several makeshift relief camps in Delhi, 5 November 1984. Bettmann/Bettmann/Getty Images.

27. A group of women and children, survivors of the violence, find safety in a relief camp in Delhi, November 1984. Photo © Ashok Vahie.

Maps

INDIA

(areas affected 1 - 4 November 1984)

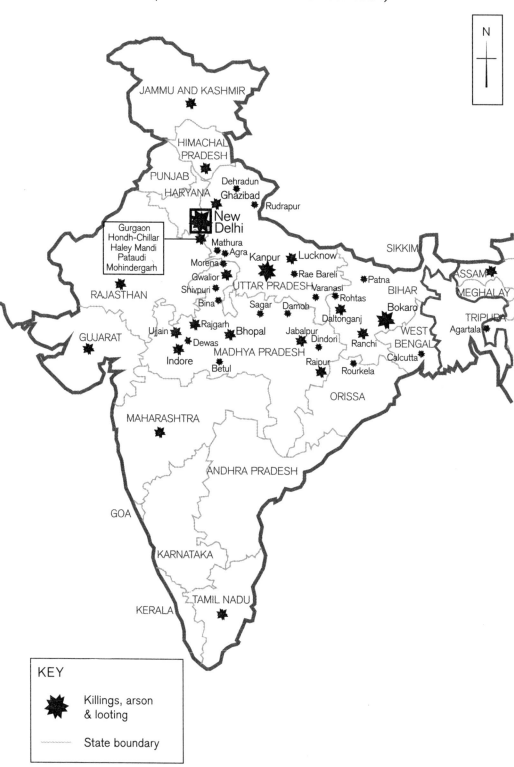

KEY

Killings, arson
& looting

State boundary

Not to scale

DELHI

(areas affected 1 - 4 November 1984)

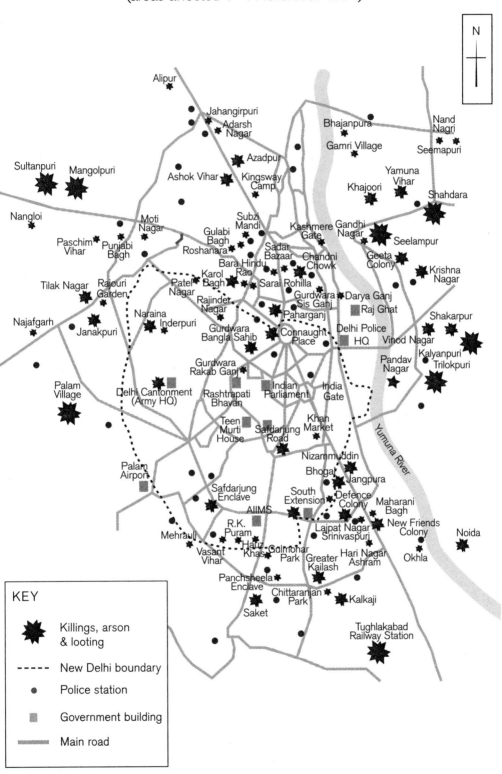

N

KEY

✹ Killings, arson & looting

- - - - New Delhi boundary

• Police station

▪ Government building

▬ Main road

Not to scale

Preface

Sikh houses and shops were marked for destruction in much the same way as those of Jews in Tsarist Russia or Nazi Germany... for the first time I understood what words like pogrom, holocaust and genocide really meant.

One of India's best-loved authors and journalists, the late Khushwant Singh, wrote these harrowing lines about the India of November 1984. He was describing his own experiences of being caught up in the wave of genocidal killings that swept through the capital, Delhi, and further afield following the assassination of the prime minister, Indira Gandhi, by two of her Sikh bodyguards.

Over four days, an estimated 8,000 Sikhs, possibly more, would be slaughtered by rampaging mobs in the world's largest democracy. To put the sheer scale of this destruction into perspective, the figure cited is broadly equivalent to the civilian death tolls of the Northern Ireland conflict, Tiananmen Square and 9/11 combined. The eminent British lawyer and campaigner Geoffrey Robertson QC rightly calls it 'India's guilty secret' – a phrase that so succinctly sums up the crimes that it lends itself to the title of this book.

At the time, the authorities projected the violence as a spontaneous reaction to the tragic loss of a much-loved prime minister.

But evidence points to a government-orchestrated genocidal massacre unleashed by politicians – with the trail leading to the very heart of the dynastic Gandhi family – and covered up with the help of the police, judiciary and sections of the media.

The Indian government of the day worked hard on its version of events. Words such as 'riot' became the newspeak of an Orwellian cover-up, of a real 1984. To protect perpetrators, the most heinous crimes have been obscured from view: evidence destroyed, language distorted and alternative 'facts' introduced. The final body count is anyone's guess. As the celebrated author and essayist Amitav Ghosh, another witness to the scenes in Delhi in 1984, has stated: 'Nowhere else in the world did the year 1984 fulfil its apocalyptic portents as it did in India'.

And yet what may well go down in history as one of the largest conspiracies of modern times is hardly known of outside of India. At the time, Western governments toed the line of their Indian counterparts and downplayed events – arguably for fear of losing trade contracts worth billions – to the misnomer of 'communal riots'.

Global reaction to other atrocities such the killings in Chile by the Pinochet regime, China's Tiananmen Square massacre and the large-scale, post-World War Two genocides of Cambodia, Rwanda, Darfur and Syria has rightly been firm and unequivocal. Each received considerable global attention and international condemnation from governments, human rights organisations and high-profile campaigners.

By way of comparison consider how the International Criminal Tribunal for the Former Yugoslavia recognised the Srebrenica massacre of 1995, in which 8,000 Bosnian Muslims were slaughtered, as a genocide. But for the innocents of November 1984, there has been a deafening silence, a lack of comparable international concern or consideration of the nature of the violence which has allowed the guilty to evade justice and crimes to go unrecognised for what they actually were.

~

As the events of November 1984 were unfolding, I was a teenager living at home in Leeds, England. My family's initial shock on hearing that Mrs Gandhi had been killed turned to anxiety and concern for relatives in Delhi, for others in the capital and for how India would react. A maternal aunt, Sukhdev Kaur, lived with her family in Janakpuri, an area in West Delhi that had fallen prey to the organised violence. We rang countless times a day, our worry increasing every time the phone remained unanswered.

A full week later our fear turned to relief when my mother spotted my uncle, Tara Singh Brar, whilst watching a BBC TV news report – my uncle, aunt and their four children had managed to escape to the safety of one of the many refugee camps that had sprung up across Delhi to house thousands of displaced and victimised Sikhs.

Years later I would learn how, in order to survive the ordeal, the family had taken shelter with their Hindu neighbours who themselves had risked everything by harbouring them. In their neighbourhood the Sikh-owned Janak Cinema and *gurdwaras* (Sikh places of worship) had been attacked by the mobs, which were becoming an ever closer danger. To survive, they had had to resort to extreme measures – the men removed their turbans and cut their long hair, symbols of their faith. My oldest cousin, Ishar Singh, managed to smuggle his father from Janakpuri to the safety of the camp on his motorbike, revolver in hand.

~

By the late 1980s I became politically active as an undergraduate studying in London. I was involved in various human rights and social justice causes, joining the Anti-Nazi League and campaigning against apartheid rule in South Africa. It was on this latter issue that Rajiv Gandhi, Indira Gandhi's son and successor as the prime minister of India, rose to global prominence, emerging as a crusader against the regime and a proponent of sanctions. Here was the face of modern India – liberal, dynamic and a serious actor on the world stage. But every time I saw him on TV or read his name in the papers, my stomach churned at the thought of the outrageous contradiction between his words on apartheid and his role in the sickening crimes that were perpetrated against his fellow countrymen under his watch.

After building my own career, some two decades after 1984 I decided to take a year-long sabbatical. I moved to India in 2004 with hopes of writing a travel book but instead I became embroiled in something much bigger and far more personal. On a visit to Delhi, Uncle Tara Singh took me to areas that had been affected by the violence. I heard story after story of unspeakable horror from survivors that still haunt me to this day. But they also motivated me to seek answers – what could possibly have driven thousands of Indians to commit such unbelievable acts of brutality on their fellow citizens, including the elderly, women and children? Left out in the cold – used as election pawns by India's political elite and denied justice – few of these victims have been able to move forward. The young among them who had borne witness to the barbarity were inflicted with an inter-generational trauma with enduring and very real negative consequences.

I also spent time in Punjab, mainly in the bustling holy city of Amritsar and in my ancestral village, Talvandi Bhangeria near Moga. Here I also came across families devastated by the Delhi pogroms and the subsequent, and often brutal and indiscriminate, suppression by the Punjab state machinery of what it considered to be a dangerous Sikh insurgency.

Near the end of my sabbatical year, in August 2005, the Indian government released the long awaited report of the Nanavati Commission. It was a shameful whitewash that ensured the guilty remained untouched. Dr Manmohan Singh, India's first Sikh prime minister, spoke for many at the time when he confessed that 'years have passed and yet the feeling persists that somehow the truth has not come out and justice has not prevailed'. But for many, his plea to forget the past and move forward fell far too short of an acceptable solution. The mass protests that followed the report's release inspired me to act. What could I do, if anything, to further the cause of justice? I decided that I had to tell the story of how an entire state apparatus was utilised to commit a heinous mass crime and to ensure decades of subsequent cover-up.

~

On my return to Britain, I kept a close eye on the series of court cases in India that exonerated the key politicians accused of complicity in the killings. I tried to raise awareness of November 1984 with human rights groups, political parties and trade unions but faced a wall of bewilderment – nobody was aware of the events I was describing. My frustration began to mount, not only with the apathy of these organisations but also with rabble-rousing Sikh groups, whose blustering made little tangible difference to the status quo.

As late as 2011, important new evidence was still coming to light. A series of high-level court cases involving some of the accused MPs led to further revelations. A WikiLeaks cable leak revealed that even United States diplomats considered them as being complicit in the killings and that a wider conspiracy to protect the guilty was at play.

Amidst all of this, incredibly, in a village just outside Gurgaon (an urban sprawl southwest of Delhi), a mass grave was accidentally unearthed. Locals knew the village as the 'deserted village of the Sardars' (*sardar* being an honorific synonymous with Sikhs). Even this ghoulish discovery was met largely with indifference by the Indian media, with barely a ripple being created globally. At some level I wasn't surprised given the years of denial, inaction and impunity.

However, in 2012, India and the world were shocked by the gruesome gang-rape and murder in Delhi of Jyoti Singh. The country's arcane attitudes towards rape and sexual assault became the subject of global scrutiny. Condemnation from all quarters was immediate, tourism took a hit and changes were rightly made to the Indian legal system regarding how rape was to be reported and treated.

As welcome as the attention and changes were, I couldn't help thinking how this monstrous act had been repeated thousands of times in November 1984 but the rapists were walking free, immune from justice, due to a dangerously corrupt political system masquerading as a democracy.

A year later, in 2013, nearly a full three decades on from the massacres, I was working at the publishing house, Bloomsbury. There, I met the Canadian writer, Jaspreet Singh, who had witnessed the violence in Delhi as a child. By sheer coincidence, he had just finished writing a fictional account of his experiences. In his novel, *Helium*, we meet Nelly Kaur, the wife of a professor who is burnt alive in November 1984. In her private library in Simla, she is secretly creating an archive of first-hand material relating to the anti-Sikh pogroms. Unwittingly, this fictional woman of conviction, and the realisation that original witness testimonies were beginning to disappear from the public sphere and that police had begun to destroy their own records, would become the catalysts for my own book.

~

For the Indian authorities, it was not enough that thousands of innocent people had been killed in 1984 in what have misleadingly been labelled as 'riots'. They had to be falsely remembered as traitors, having 'celebrated' the prime minister's death or 'supported' the secessionist movement in Punjab. The distortions of a true-life Orwellian plot of nightmarish proportions had worked, and for most people it has stuck.

In this book, I have attempted to join a series of obscured and murky dots by making extensive use of often harrowing victim testimonies, official accounts, eyewitness statements and media reports.

Collectively they reveal not only the extent of the genocidal massacres and rapes that took place over those four hellish days, but they also lay bare the conspiracy of silence, censorship and impunity offered to the guilty that has persisted for well over three decades. The former is covered in Part I, which takes the form of reportage. Part II, examines in detail the nature of a cover-up that continues to this day. The role of Western governments, in particular that of the Conservative Party under Margaret Thatcher, the media and academia are also considered.

If India is truly to live up to its democratic credentials, it has to find a way to address the serious failings of its past to achieve closure for the victims of 1984. The accountability of those wielding power, the justice system, women's rights and the position of minorities in India are problems that persist to this day, blighting the lives of ordinary Indians from all walks of life who deserve far better.

The violence described in this book is graphic and I make no apology for that. I owe it to the victims and survivors of the pogroms to give as clear and unflinching an account as possible, in order to help change the narrative, bring about an end to the impunity and to ensure justice for the survivors of India's guilty secret.

Acknowledgements

There are many people to whom I am indebted for their involvement in this endeavour. The team at Kashi House, my UK publisher, have created a book out of my research. I would especially like to single out Harbakhsh Singh and Dr Bikram Singh Brar for their superbly diligent efforts in shaping its narrative. They were ably supported by Parmjit Singh, Naina Singh, Sukhdeep Singh, Y Kaur, L Kaur, D Shastri and Daniel Scott. I was fortunate to have the book expertly designed by two talented designers, Tia Džamonja (layout, typesetting and reprographics) and Paul Smith (cover).

Thanks also to Shambhu Sahu of Rupa Publications, my Indian publisher, and my agent Mita Kapur from Siyahi, both of whom believed in the project at every step.

Finally, I consider it an honour to have received support, encouragement and feedback from the following who excel in the fields of academia, law, medicine, human rights advocacy, literature and art:

UK: Professor Philip Spencer, Geoffrey Robertson QC, Dr. Paul Moore, Professor Swaran Preet Singh, researcher Phil Miller, Aisha Rahman, Rebecca Wright and my cousin Ishar Singh Brar.

INDIA: feminist and historian Dr Uma Chakravarti, Senior Delhi Advocate H. S. Phoolka, journalists and authors Sanjay Suri, Aseem Shrivastava, Hartosh Singh Bal and Manoj Mitta, contemporary artist Arpana Caur, and photographers Gauri Gill, Ashok Vahie and Ram Rahman.

NORTH AMERICA: US human rights advocate Jaskaran Kaur and Canadian author Jaspreet Singh.

Introduction
A Deadly Spark

On the morning of 31 October 1984, renowned British actor, comedian and writer, Peter Ustinov, sat waiting for Prime Minister Indira Gandhi in her New Delhi office adjacent to her official residence. Both buildings were in the same compound in a broad, leafy boulevard in one of the capital's most elegant areas. With the camera set up on the lawn of the extensive garden, the film crew were ready to record an interview for a new series entitled *Peter Ustinov's People*. The serene, fair-weathered Indian morning belied the ensuing bloodshed that would consume the nation.

On that fateful day, the Mrs Gandhi had a typically busy agenda. In the afternoon she was due to host former British prime minister, James Callaghan, for tea. The evening was reserved for a private dinner with Her Royal Highness Princess Anne, who was in India in her capacity as the president of the Save the Children charity.

Elsewhere in the city the England cricket team, led by its captain David Gower, was landing at the airport for a hotly anticipated cricket series with India – one that would be played against a backdrop of unfolding violence, terror and disaster.

~

Less than forty years after Britain's rushed exit from the Indian subcontinent, the relationship with her former colonial master was cordial. India appeared to all intents and purposes to have established itself as a fully integrated member of the international community, albeit an occasionally faltering one. As a mainly functioning democracy, it could, and did, lay claim to being the world's largest.

The journey to becoming the world's most populous democracy began in August 1947, when India was released from nearly two centuries of domination by the British. But it came at a staggering cost for millions of ordinary people. The border dividing India and the newly created Islamic republic of West Pakistan cut through the heart of the northern state of Punjab. In what is believed to be one of, if not the, largest migrations in human history, up to twelve million Hindu, Muslim and Sikh refugees poured across the border over a three-month period seeking sanctuary on their chosen side. Families were torn apart from their kith and kin, their ancestral homes and the lands they had tilled for generations.

The birth pangs of the two new nations culminated in unprecedented bloodshed. In an explosion of sectarian violence, armed groups of Hindus, Muslims and Sikhs roamed the countryside in search of the 'other', terrorising city dwellers and village folk alike. Massacres, arson, abduction and rape were rife. Women in particular were targeted – 'ghost trains' full of dead bodies with their breasts severed rolled into stations, fuelling the fury of the mobs. Up to 100,000 women are estimated to have been kidnapped and raped, and the final death toll is believed to have exceeded a million.

The reverberations were also felt far away in Delhi where pogroms targeting local Muslims resulted in the death of approximately 25,000. On hearing of the carnage, Jawaharlal Nehru, the Cambridge-educated barrister who became Independent India's first prime minister, is said to have rushed to Connaught Place in disgust. Grabbing a baton from a policeman, he began to pummel the mob that had gathered.

Nehru's only child, Indira Nehru (who would become a Gandhi after marrying Feroze Gandhi, no relation to Mahatma Gandhi) followed her father into politics. Having grown up in a political household she was well versed in state affairs and had gone on to serve as the widowed prime minister's unofficial first lady. Two years after being elected to parliament in 1964, the year Nehru died, she became the country's first and only female prime minister.

~

As their countries' respective prime ministers, Indira Gandhi and Margaret Thatcher were two of the world's most powerful women. Despite being on opposite ends of the political spectrum, they shared similarities that gave rise to a cordial and often intimate relationship. Both were alumni of Somerville College at Oxford and had held several important ministerial roles before serving as prime minister. They had won decisive victories in major wars against Pakistan and Argentina respectively and were perceived as nothing less than liberators by the people of Bangladesh and the Falkland Islands. In recognition of their reputations as unwavering conviction politicians, both had been nicknamed 'Iron Lady' by the press. However, the two leaders had also exhibited authoritarian tendencies, with neither afraid to confront the 'enemy within'.

Indeed, just a few years earlier, Mrs Gandhi had declared a state of emergency in India. When, in June 1975, the Allahabad High Court disqualified her from parliament for electoral malpractice, Gandhi's response was unequivocal. She used her extraordinary powers to launch a crackdown on civil liberties, arresting thousands of political opponents and dissenters (Narendra Modi, the current prime minister of India, avoided arrest by disguising himself as a turban- and beard-wearing Sikh). With the media censored, elections suspended and laws rewritten to allow her to rule by decree, Gandhi became the *de facto* dictator of India.

The Sikhs of Punjab were firm opponents of the Emergency. Led by the Akali Dal Party, the largest and most influential Sikh political party, they began a nationwide protest styled the 'Campaign to

Save Democracy'. Faced with arrest, some Sikh leaders took refuge in the complex containing the Sikhs' holiest shrine, the Harimandir Sahib – popularly known as the Golden Temple of Amritsar. Out of an estimated 140,000 arrested and held without trial over the twenty-one-month-long Emergency, Sikhs numbered some 40,000 or 30 percent of the total – something Mrs Gandhi would neither forgive nor forget. When elections were finally called in 1977, Gandhi was heavily defeated. She lingered in the political wilderness until 1980, when she staged a remarkable return to power.

~

For both Mrs Thatcher and Mrs Gandhi, the challenges of leadership and their somewhat confrontational styles led to very real threats to their lives. For Mrs Thatcher, this took the form of an Irish Republican Army bomb that detonated at a Brighton hotel on 12 October 1984. The blast took the lives of five people and came within a whisker of claiming her as its sixth victim.

A mere nineteen days later, Mrs Gandhi would undertake the short stroll from her official residence to her office. Accompanied by a small contingent of aides, officials and bodyguards, she walked through well-manicured gardens to meet Mr Ustinov: 'Everything was ready, the tea was poured, she was coming towards us (from her nearby house),' he would later recollect.

The serene morning atmosphere was abruptly shattered by what one of the Indian cameramen at first dismissed as firecrackers. The sound of birdsong gave way to a deafening burst of machine gun fire. Struck by over thirty rounds, the prime minister dropped to the ground where she lay, bleeding profusely.

To the surprise of everyone, her assailants were not intruders lurking behind bushes but two of her own bodyguards – both turbaned Sikhs. She was rushed to hospital at 9.30am but, after sustained attempts to save her life, she was pronounced dead later that day.

The assassins claimed their actions were in retaliation for Operation Blue Star, the prime minister's contentious decision to send the

Indian army into the Golden Temple of Amritsar earlier that year to bring to heel Sikh dissidents who had occupied fortified parts of the temple precincts. Military commanders had assured her that the operation would be a relatively simple exercise aimed at ridding the complex of the alleged terrorists; but it proved to be anything but.

The attack took place on 6 June, one of the shrine's busiest days. The number of civilian deaths ran into the hundreds, possibly thousands, as innocent Sikh pilgrims lost their lives in the bloody military action, in which tanks were used to fire a barrage of explosive shells at the temple complex, undertaken without warning or evacuation. True to form, Gandhi drew upon many of the same tactics she had used during the Emergency. A media blackout was imposed in Punjab for Indian and foreign journalists. With constitutional rights suspended, human rights abuses inevitably followed.

~

After concluding their deadly mission the two bodyguards dropped their weapons and surrendered, with the senior of the two, Beant Singh, claiming he had done what he needed to, and it was up to others to do with him as they saw fit. He was killed extra-judicially minutes later by some of his fellow bodyguards whilst the surviving assassin, Satwant Singh, would later be tried and hanged (along with Beant Singh's uncle, Kehar Singh, who had given his nephew counsel) for his part in the killing.

As news of the shooting spread, a group of distinguished Sikh military veterans hurriedly convened a meeting. They included Lieutenant-General Jagjit Singh Aurora, the hero of Mrs Gandhi's war of liberation in East Pakistan – the region that would become the nation of Bangladesh. In an attempt to prevent retaliation against the minority Sikh populace, they issued the following condemnation of the assassination:

> No society, least of all a society like ours with its long traditions of spiritualism, scholarship and humanism,

can allow black deeds of murderous folly to destroy its civilized fabric. We condemn in unequivocal terms the dastardly attempt on the life of the Prime Minister, Mrs Indira Gandhi, to which she tragically fell victim. We consider such an act, and what it is likely to trigger off, a grave threat to the country's integrity and unity.

The statement failed to make the news bulletins. By nightfall, Mrs Gandhi's son, Rajiv, was hurriedly installed as the country's sixth, and youngest ever, prime minister. As scion of India's pre-eminent political dynasty he had reluctantly given up his career as an airline pilot to fulfil the role of his mother's heir apparent after his younger brother Sanjay, the natural successor, had died in a plane crash in 1980. As of November 1984, Rajiv Gandhi was very much a political novice, untested and unprepared to steer a divided nation in such turmoil to a position of stability. His greatest leadership challenge up to that point had come from being a member of the 1982 Asian Games organising committee.

With a new prime minister quickly in place it may have appeared that any prospect of violence would now dissipate. However, in hindsight, ominous signs of what was to come had been apparent in the immediate hours following the assassination.

As rumours spread of Indira Gandhi's killing, followed by confirmed reports, the atmosphere across the capital and the country began to change. Whilst crowds had gathered outside the hospital where Mrs Gandhi lay and surgeons battled to save her life, the first sporadic attacks on Sikhs began.

A young trainee surgeon named Swaran Preet Singh was one of the first to be attacked whilst working at the hospital before escaping by rickshaw. He later recounted the developing mood:

> People spoke in hushed whispers, the crowd swarmed anxiously, senior government figures arrived with blaring alarms, police and security guards were

everywhere. There was an ominous foreboding in the humid air.

Amidst the understandable public shock and sadness at the loss of a woman regarded by many as their 'Mother India', a deadly spark had been ignited, a spark that rapidly grew into a raging fire, engulfing all whom it touched.

Part 1

THE CRIME

Instigation & Preparation

Rajiv Gandhi reportedly learned that his mother had been gunned down on the BBC World Service, which one of his aides had been listening to on a transistor radio. Cutting short a political tour of the state of West Bengal, he flew back to New Delhi on an air force jet from Calcutta. After seeing his mother's bullet-ridden body, he emerged from the hospital later in the afternoon, flanked by two members of parliament. Amidst an ugly mood, cries for revenge began to emanate from a vengeful crowd. One of the MPs tacitly incited those present to take matters into their own hands by proclaiming: 'What is the point of assembling here?'

Amidst this strained atmosphere, among the first Sikhs to be attacked was India's president, Zail Singh. A political heavyweight who had served as chief minister of Punjab in the 1970s and joined Mrs Gandhi's cabinet as minister of home affairs a decade later, he was the first Sikh to hold the presidential office.

As his motorcade approached the hospital early on the evening of 31 October, it was greeted by a mob chanting anti-Sikh slogans and pelted with stones. Although his bulletproof car was relatively unscathed, a bodyguard's turban was forcibly removed. In a second vehicle, his press officer fended off a vicious attack by staff-wielding thugs with a seat that had been ripped out of his car. On reflection, the assailing of the president and his staff was a clear warning shot in the one-sided battle to come, orchestrated in this instance by supporters of a local metropolitan councillor.

A bystander had earlier witnessed Delhi's senior Congress leadership – comprising of H. K. L. Bhagat, Lalit Maken, Sajjan Kumar, Dharam Dass Shastri and Arjan Dass – leaving the hospital around 4pm. Soon afterwards, the attacks on Sikhs in the area began. A journalist witnessed what may well have been the very first retaliatory death just north of the hospital near the INA market. In an attack in broad daylight, a Sikh man was brutally battered with bricks.

It would take another three decades for evidence to emerge as to what these Congressmen were planning. According to information collected by Zail Singh himself, they had decided on a chilling slogan to underpin their plans: 'Blood for blood'.

That evening, another clandestine meeting took place, this time at the home of the minister of information and broadcasting. Also in attendance were senior police officers. They formulated and finalised elements of a deadly plan that would commence the next morning, engulfing towns, cities and villages right across the vast swathe of northern India, but especially concentrated right in the heart of the capital city of the world's most populous democracy.

A concerted effort was made to create a heightened atmosphere of fear and hatred to facilitate the violence to come. Lies cloaked as 'truths' began to circulate. This disinformation was coordinated and overseen on the ground primarily by the local police.

On the night of 31 October, rumors began circulating that Sikhs across Delhi were celebrating Mrs Gandhi's assassination. They were said to be distributing sweets, dancing and lighting Diwali lights in their households.

Sikhs were also alleged to have poisoned the city's drinking water. Swaran Preet Singh recalled how two police officers, from my local police station, went around our colony with a megaphone: 'Don't drink water. The Sikhs have poisoned it.' I challenged them: 'Do you think taps know the religion of a household? Would Delhi Sikhs be able to avoid being poisoned? What nonsense is this?' One of them pushed me aside.

A civil rights worker also heard one of these announcements being made by the police over their public address system: 'Your water supply has been poisoned. Please do not drink the water'.

Meanwhile, scenes were broadcast on the state's Doordarshan TV channel of Mrs Gandhi's corpse alongside the continuous naming of the assassins and, significantly, an emphasis on their faith. In a clear incitement, the predetermined chilling phrase, 'blood for blood', was aired and repeated over state-controlled airwaves. Swaran Preet Singh recalled the moment clearly:

> The killings started late that evening. National television had a continuous broadcast of footage of Indira Gandhi's body, surrounded by crowds shouting *'Khoon ka badla khoon'* ('Seek blood for blood'). The Wikipedia entry for the riots states that the first Sikh was killed on 1 November 1984. I know of an elderly Sikh man who was killed on 31 October around 9 pm. Truth is hard to establish in a state of total anarchy.

~

Eventually morning came and with it, perhaps a sense that the firestorm had subsided or blown itself out. Alas, it was not the case.

To those responsible for directing the mob's fury, it was imperative that certain images 'had to be burned into the [Sikh] psyche' forever. This necessitated the systematic targeting of Sikh places of worship known as *gurdwaras*, which had a centuries-old tradition of providing free food and sanctuary to the poor and the persecuted.

False rumours continued to be propagated to underpin and incite people to carry out attacks. Lies were spread that every gurdwara was an arsenal, apparently evidenced by the discovery of weapons kept under the temples by sympathisers of Sikh separatists – though no such weapons were ever found – and that Sikhs armed with swords were preparing night-time attacks against Hindus in which they would kidnap children.

The morning of 1 November ushered in the attacks on gurdwaras, several of which were burnt down. In Delhi alone, more than 330 Sikh places of worship are believed to have been damaged. Hundreds more across northern India were hit in a manner chillingly reminiscent of the burning of synagogues during the 1938 *Kristallnacht* ('Night of Broken Glass') pogroms in Germany.

Also targeted were volumes of the Sikh scripture, the Guru Granth Sahib, hundreds of which were desecrated in public displays of hate. The renowned author and historian Khushwant Singh witnessed how copies of this sacred text raided from a house adjacent to his central Delhi apartment were thrown onto a bonfire in the street and ignited with cigarettes.

When a Sikh priest was later interviewed about the burning of his shrine, his interviewer poignantly noted how 'his deep hurt at finding that someone had urinated on the Sikh scriptures has perhaps not been captured in our translation'. This is hardly surprising given the reverence in which the Guru Granth Sahib is held by Sikhs, who consider it their Eternal Guru, and primary source of enlightenment, direction and spiritual knowledge.

The parallels with the desecration of Jewish Torah scrolls in Germany during the 1930s were disturbingly apparent. A century before the rise of the Nazis, the radical German poet Heinrich Heine had predicted that 'where they burn books, they will in the end burn people too'. His prophecy was fulfilled a second time by the mobs in 1984. One man who came across the dead corpses of both his uncle and the local Sikh priest described how 'the hair of both had been tied together and one volume of [our] holy book was lying on their bodies in a burnt condition'.

Word spread that Sikhs were gathering *en masse* to retaliate. The Delhi police were mobilised to disarm any Sikhs who held licensed firearms, supposedly under the pretext of public safety. For which 'public' they did not specify.

By 2 November, as trains began to arrive into Delhi overflowing with the bodies of dead Sikhs, rumours were spread claiming Hindus had been killed in Punjab and it was their corpses that lay on the Jhelum Express. The scene was set for what was becoming ever more apparently a pre-planned act of disturbing magnitude and horror.

2

Execution & Direction

The ensuing attacks on the Sikh community – a perennial minority outside of the state of Punjab – were shocking in both their ferocity and their coordinated nature. The wave of violence spared little. Sikh temples, businesses and entire neighbourhoods were put to the torch.

A definitive pattern began to emerge within twenty-four hours of Mrs Gandhi assassination on 31 October. Whilst sporadic, seemingly spontaneous, violence was initially confined mainly to areas around south Delhi and the New Delhi hospital where the prime minister's body lay, by the next morning a new *modus operandi* – initiated in what can only be described as state-sanctioned, large-scale organised terror unleashed on innocent citizens – had spread to all four corners of the capital and surrounding rural areas.

Early on the morning of 1 November, organised mobs were transported in buses from outside Delhi and began descending on Sikh neighbourhoods. They were equipped with firearms, iron rods, knives, clubs and an abundant supply of kerosene. Sacks of white phosphorous powder had also been procured and provided.

The perpetrators roamed in huge gangs, sometimes hundreds strong but they were not alone or acting on impulse. They were directed by men in white *kurta pajamas* – simple garments often worn by Indian politicians to indicate an often false sense of piety. Along with lower-ranking Congress Party officials, they made no attempt to hide their presence. The distinctive white Hindustan Ambassador cars of politicians were sighted driving alongside the mobs as the police looked on, taking no action.

With all the pre-planning and coordination in place, what followed was equally highly organised. Armed and with clear intent of purpose, the crowds operated as death squads in a manner redolent of Himmler's *Einsatzgruppen*: the SS paramilitary death squads that operated in Eastern Europe during the Second World War, hunting down previously identified Jews who they had marked for execution.

Eyewitnesses would later report on the meticulous manner in which the mobs operated. When their initial attack was repulsed, they would retire briefly only to return, again and again, hunting for their prey. Rape and killing-by-incineration were central elements of the violence, with even children not being spared.

Just as in the Rwandan genocide ten years later – where Hutu militias were provided with carefully-prepared lists of Tutsis – the killers went from door to door, working their way down the lists. Sikh gurdwaras voter records were used to identify Sikh homes and businesses. To ensure none were missed, school registers, ration lists and electoral rolls were used for cross-referencing.

Crucially, on the preceding night of 31 October, Sikh homes had been carefully identified by 'surveyors'. One witness saw as many as twenty-five people involved in this operation: 'They were carrying a list showing the houses in which Sikhs were staying. I saw them put marks on the houses of Sikhs'. One was seen operating in a market town, going 'from door to door of Sikh houses marking them with an 'S', ready for the arson, looting and murder'.

The usually bustling New Delhi shopping area of Connaught Place was described by one reporter as looking 'like a battlefield'.

Columns of black smoke rose high into the sky as local Sikh businesses were torched along with Sikh-owned taxis and trucks.

During the carnage, a masters student at the Delhi School of Economics witnessed how Sikh properties were so easily identified:

> The streets were empty except for a few motorcycles that were running back and forth. The men on them seemed to be ferrying the oil to the people doing the arson. I then noticed that the pillion riders on at least two bikes had sheets of paper in their hands. When they stopped I looked over someone's shoulder to see that they were holding in their hands a list of houses to be burnt! The list had the house number and the name of the head of the household, usually a 'Singh'.

Every name on the death lists had to be accounted for. A Sikh, who was being sheltered by his Hindu friends, overheard the conversation between his protectors and members of the death squad: 'Look, his name has not been struck off from the list and his dead body has not been taken away'. In one of the capital's central districts, mobs came on four separate occasions, over two days, until they found those in hiding. One extended family in Palam Village, a major suburb in South West Delhi and home to the capital's international airport, was left with twenty-one widows.

A survivor would later explain how a gang, four- or five-hundred strong, marched to her home and began to hurl stones at both of her parents. Her father fell down injured but she told the mob that he had died. They left, seemingly satisfied with their work, but returned the next day on six separate occasions. By the seventh visit, they found her wounded father. Brandishing an axe, one of the mob leaders struck him in the abdomen. 'Others also hit him and his brain came out,' recalled the daughter. 'Kerosene was sprinkled on him and he was burnt alive.'

3

Butchering & Burning

Over four days, unimaginably sickening horrors were systematically inflicted on the innocent in Delhi and elsewhere. As gangs swarmed into Sikh houses, they often began their barbaric violence with a calculated physical and psychological gesture: the severing of male victims' hair.

For observant Sikh males, their long, unshorn hair and beard stand as sacred markers of their faith, identity and history. Comparisons can be drawn with the plight of European Jews in the 1920s and 30s, whose beards and side-curls were also targeted in anti-Semitic attacks by both Polish and German troops. And yet, many German Jews had won their stripes in the trenches of the Kaiser's army.

Even more strikingly, India's Sikhs were renowned for their martial history and significant role in the struggle for, and defence of, independent India. The act of effectively 'scalping' their victims was intended to inflict maximum suffering and humiliation:

> While their hair was cut, the mob jeered and mocked at them, chanting 'mona mona mona' [a person with short hair]; [the Sikhs] were ordered to keep dancing while the mob laughed wildly.

Frenzied assailants butchered people without remorse. One twenty-eight-year-old woman recounted how, in front of her son and three small daughters, the killers 'dragged her husband, by his genitals, and hacked him to death'. Veteran Indian journalist, Pranay Gupte, reported that some Sikh children were 'castrated and their genitals stuffed into the mouths of their mothers and sisters'.

Others were decapitated. In a statement submitted to a government inquiry three years later, a woman described how she saw the heads of her two dead nephews separated from their bodies and placed on dinner plates.

Peter Ustinov, who had earlier been planning to interview the prime minister, would later recall that the air was full of a stench reminiscent of the Blitz. Germany's raids over London during the Second World War had released bombs containing the chemical agent, phosphorus. He was not far from the truth – in many areas, the murder squads had used the phosphorus that had been supplied to them to incinerate their victims. A highly inflammable agent, it quickly burnt human flesh down to the bone.

A favoured method of killing used repeatedly on adults and children alike was 'necklacing'. In this form of execution, a rubber tyre filled with fuel is placed over a victim's chest and arms before being set aflame. For some, watching necklaced Sikhs being burned alive would become the day's spectacle.

John Fear, Delhi correspondent for a gospel-inspired radio station operated by the Far East Broadcasting Associates, was an eyewitness to the religious fury and communal hatred that had engulfed the city.

Writing to a colleague just days after the attacks, he told of how several colleagues who lived in the suburbs and housing settlements around the capital had seen horrific things during the height of the pogroms. One studio technician spoke of gangs relentlessly beating, stabbing and burning alive over a hundred Sikh men in his district, and the chopping off of the fingers of women and children.

Next door to Fear's hostel room in New Delhi an armed gang attempted to storm a gurdwara. There was a constant sound of explosions and the night sky was illuminated by huge flames as shanty towns burned. In his opinion, the words 'genocide' and 'holocaust' were not too strong descriptions for what had actually occurred.

Many Sikh men suffered the indignity of having to discard their turbans, cut off their long hair and beards, all acts of sacrilege that were enough to traumatise some for life. Some families desperately attempted to save their adolescent boys by disguising them as girls. This meant plaiting their long hair into two plats and dressing them in *salvar-kameez*, the traditional loose trousers and dress suit worn by women.

~

On the morning of 1 November, a huge bloodthirsty crowd roamed through the Trilokpuri colony in East Delhi, one of the poorest parts of the capital that bore the brunt of its casualties. The worst massacres took place in Block 32 along two narrow alleys, just 150 yards long, in which hundreds of Sikh residents inhabiting single-room tenements were casually butchered over several days.

When the historian William Dalrymple visited the colony many years later, he spoke with an elderly Sikh couple about this terrifying ordeal. Initially, around 150 local Sikhs were able to fend off the stone-throwing mob numbering several thousand. Two hours later the local police suddenly intervened. To the relief of the besieged Sikhs they escorted the marauders away, only to return to relieve the Sikhs of their staffs and swords – their only means of defence. After instructing the Sikhs to return to their homes, the police allowed the killers to return:

> Once they shouted: 'Send out the men and we won't harm them.' A couple of doors opened and some of our neighbours gave themselves up. They took them away. It was only later that we discovered they had

taken them to the edge of the block, made them drink kerosene then set them alight.

In a calculated manner, and with the connivance of the police, the mob sealed off and guarded all exit points from the area to ensure that no Sikh could escape but the police could enter. Armed with rudimentary weapons – cleavers, scythes, kitchen knives and scissors – they got to work, only taking breaks for meals. Within just a kilometre from two police stations, the violence recommenced, the mobs splitting victims' skulls and filling the gashes with kerosene before setting them alight.

The following evening, on the eve of Indira Gandhi's funeral, three Indian reporters were among the first outsiders to enter Trilokpuri. They walked into a ghastly scene of utter depravity created by killers who had 'toiled for 30 long and uninterrupted hours'. The entire area, awash with blood, was described by one of the reporters:

> Two lanes, an area of around 500 square yards are littered with corpses, the drains choked with dismembered limbs and masses of hair. Cindered human remains lie scattered in the first 20 yards of the first lane. The remaining 40-yard stretch of the street is strewn with naked bodies, brutally hacked beyond recognition. Lifeless arms hang over balconies; many houses have bodies piled three-deep on their doorsteps.

Surveying the carnage they came across the harrowing sight of a two-year-old girl who, 'unmindful of the bodies, walked lazily over to us holding out her arms asking to be taken home. Unfortunately, she was already home; but one littered with the bloated bodies of her parents and siblings killed two nights earlier'.

Two of the reporters who attempted to inform the police on the morning of 2 November about the massacres at Trilokpuri were laughed out of the control room.

When a Sikh lady finally dared to come out of the shelter afforded her and her children by a Muslim neighbour, she later recalled seeing the lifeless bodies of Sikh children scattered across the streets, still burning like wood. A senior police officer was overheard casually comparing the scene to the burning of garbage.

The grizzly aftermath was also seen by a former minister of law & justice, who ventured into the colony with some of his colleagues from the Supreme Court:

> As we turned, an unidentified body was lying across the road. A Sikh had been shaved and burnt. We made our way further. Charred bodies were visible in the lane, unmistakably of the Sikhs, their long hair had been cut and was lying around the bodies; iron rods had been pierced through their backs and they had obviously been burnt by kerosene or petrol. A male corpse was lying in the veranda of every house.

~

In several other poor districts in the east of the capital across Delhi's main river, the Yamuna, babies were snatched from the arms of their mothers and butchered – the bodies of some were casually tossed onto makeshift bonfires. Men were dragged to the rooftops of their houses and hurled off. Children were lynched in front of their parents. Holy sites were burnt to the ground, sometimes with worshippers still inside them.

In Vinod Nagar East, a few kilometres north of Trilokpuri, a truckload of men from nearby villages first razed Sikh shrines to the ground before moving on to people's homes. The local postmaster's house was set ablaze with his children inside. A local cinema owner's home was also torched despite being just a stone's throw away from a police station – four policemen were present at the time of the attack in which all eleven family members, including women and children, were roasted alive.

Nightfall allowed no respite from the onslaught. The police in Old Delhi were reported to have spread the ominous slogan: 'The nights are ours, the days are yours'. The barbarity continued unabated into the night. One woman later described how her husband, who was discovered hiding in a trunk, was dragged out and cut to pieces. She also witnessed a sixteen-year-old boy and a small child he was carrying both killed without remorse.

As the massacres progressed, a further disturbing revelation began to emerge. In several areas, the killers were not all politically-directed thugs. A twenty-two-year-old man, the sole survivor of an attack, in which his entire family was slaughtered, recalled how his Hindu neighbours had initially assured them that they would be safe and protected. Hours later, the very same neighbours returned with weapons and forced the doors open:

> Immediately when we came out they pounced upon us like blood-thirsty animals. The first blow hit my mother. She was so dazed by this sudden and unprovoked attack that she did not even scream and fell down on the ground. The chopper caused a deep cut on her shoulder and she bled profusely. The attackers did not stop after she had fallen but all of them gave her blows with their weapons causing grievous injuries and thus killed her. The next to be attacked was my younger sister, aged seventeen. A long knife was thrust into her neck, which caused a deep cut and a stream of blood flowed from it. She instantaneously fell down but the criminals continued to hit her till they were sure that my helpless sister was dead.

Sometimes neighbours would recognise boys who had been disguised as girls and point them out to the baying crowds. One survivor witnessed a harrowing attack from the safety of their hideout:

> We saw a child of about ten, dressed in a salvar-kameez, who was moving on the road. The child was walking quite normally down the street. He was actually a young boy in the process of fleeing to safety and had been dressed as a girl. Something about the

child's appearance made the mob suspect that the child was a boy and someone shouted '*he must be the son of a Sikh*'. The child panicked and started running but the mob pursued him and caught him. They asked him where the other members of his family were. The boy was really frightened and he pointed in a certain direction and said that his father was lying there and that he was dead. To my horror the mob dragged the boy up to the father's body, threw the child on him and burnt him, saying '*this is the son of a snake, finish him off too*'.

~

However, even at the height of the unbridled barbarity, ordinary Hindu and Muslim citizens came to the aid of their Sikh neighbours, undoubtedly saving countless lives while risking their own.

Six hundred Sikhs were saved by the Hindus of Trilokpuri. According to an army officer posted in Shahdara, of the Sikh families he rescued from different parts of the area at least seventy per cent were sheltered by Hindus. In Yusuf Sarai market, Hindu shopkeepers laid down in front of Sikh shops and told the mob they would have to burn them first before touching any Sikh-owned businesses. In Vinod Nagar East, a Hindu dragged a Sikh and his children out of a burning taxi. In Sadiq Nagar, Sikhs were reassured by their Hindu neighbours that they would be protected. When a Sikh tried to rescue his niece in West Delhi he was stunned to find that a group of Hindus were protecting her. A Hindu family in Shakurpur saved three families by keeping them hidden in their house. While protecting three women, Prabhu Dyal, a Hindu employee of a Sikh-owned factory, caught fire himself and died. The leader of the main Sikh political party, the Akali Dal, would later attend a ceremony in honour of his ultimate sacrifice.

Reports also emerged in colony after colony of people forming their own protection squads as the cousins of this author did in their Janakpuri neighbourhood in West Delhi. Whereas the neighbours of their D-block banded together to ensure the protection of the area and its inhabitants, the neighbouring B- and C-blocks were hit hard by attacks.

In the Govindpuri area of South Delhi, men from both the Sikh and Hindu communities set up patrols to deter the mobs from entering their neighbourhoods. Elsewhere voluntary groups organised vigils in areas like Tilak Nagar, Hari Nagar and Shiv Nagar. Residents, both Sikh and Hindu, informed reporters that none of the people who came to loot and kill appeared to be local.

In Trilokpuri, five Muslim houses in Block 32 stood as a buffer between the mobs and the Sikhs. A Muslim risked his life saving his Sikh neighbour. Muslims also saved a Sikh lady and her children in Shahdara.

Human rights workers would come across Sikhs in the refugee camps who told them that but for their neighbours, they would have been butchered. A team of lawyers who later visited five affected colonies heard similar stories from local Hindus who had wanted to protect Sikhs but were helpless in the face of highly organised mobs that were far superior in numbers.

Both during and after those four tragic days, many ordinary citizens from all walks of life resolutely upheld their humanity and did what they could to help the innocent in the absence of any official response. They volunteered in the refugee camps, set up peace committees, organised peace marches, helped file police complaints and documented what had happened.

4

Terror Spreads

The violence was not just confined to the capital. Attacks were soon unleashed on the outer colonies around Delhi and further afield, wherever Sikhs were concentrated throughout the 'cow-belt' states of northern India and beyond.

The second most affected place after Delhi was the cosmopolitan city of Kanpur in the northern state of Uttar Pradesh. The attacks started at 7am on 1 November with groups from the south-eastern suburb of Jajmau vandalising Sikh shops and ransacking their homes. The rapes and killings began in earnest when local Congress leaders took control. It was not until 4 November that the administration – whose district magistrate was accused of complicity in the violence – finally imposed a curfew to give relief to the beleaguered Sikhs.

Equally intense was the violence that erupted in Bokaro Steel City and the Chas area in the Bokaro District of the eastern state of Bihar (now in Jharkhand). The small colony inhabited by Sikhs, many of whom were employed as technicians in steel plants, was razed to the ground by gangs made up mostly of local shanty-town dwellers. They were indiscriminate in their decimation of Sikh men and women. As in Delhi, Kanpur and elsewhere, Congress workers led the operation – their trademark white Ambassador cars were sighted alongside frenzied mobs, distributing supplies to them before and after the massacres.

Similar attacks occurred in states right across India. From Jammu & Kashmir and Himachal Pradesh in the north-west, violence spread across the central northern states of Uttar Pradesh and Madhya Pradesh, where close to forty towns were affected by the organised violence. Rajasthan and Gujarat in the west, and Bihar and West Bengal in the east saw outbreaks of violence, as did Maharashtra in the south. The barbarity even reached Assam in the remote north-east of the country.

A young girl from Bihar recounted how on the morning of 1 November, a large crowd, including some neighbours, marched to her house chanting anti-Sikh slogans. Armed with iron rods, axes, spears and firearms, they managed to break open the front door and dragged out her parents and three brothers, aged sixteen, twenty-five and thirty-two. She watched helplessly from a window in another neighbour's house as her family members were each butchered in turn.

The state of Haryana surrounds Delhi on three sides and shares its capital city, Chandigarh, with Punjab, the traditional homeland of the Sikhs. Waves of violence swept across the state, most notably in Pataudi, a town in the Gurgaon district lying approximately seventy kilometres south-west of Delhi. Mobs mobilised in the same fashion as elsewhere, following the sickening blueprint. On the evening of 1 November the local gurdwara building was attacked. The following day, they targeted the Sikhs. Seventeen people were burnt alive in one incident. In another, two teenage sisters were dragged out into the street, stripped naked, beaten and urinated on before being incinerated alive. A witness to this ghastly scene was the Sikh gatekeeper of the local gurdwara, who had taken cover to save his life: 'What role did these girls have in Mrs Gandhi's assassination? Were we all responsible?' He went on to lament over the injustices inflicted upon his kinsfolk:

> I want my children to see what was done to us at the
> hands of our own people, in our own country. Before

1984, there were close to thirty Sikh families in Pataudi, but today there are only five. We, who chose to stay back, were forced to rise out of the sewers to rebuild our lives.

Nearby, the small community of Sikhs in the village of Hondh-Chillar, 100 kilometres south-west of Delhi, were attacked on 2 November by approximately 500 armed men transported from outside the locality in trucks. Yelling, 'Sikhs are traitors, we will wipe them out', they were again commanded by local Congress leaders, who coordinated with the police to cordon off the area before the violence began. Sikh men, women and children were torched alive in their homes and, according to survivors, several women were gang-raped during the ordeal.

Yet it was not until January 2011, over twenty-seven years later, that the incident hit the headlines in India. The press reported how an engineer stumbled across the village, which had been deserted since 1984. At first, he did not know what to make of the bones that were lying scattered around. One of the burnt-out buildings displayed quotations from Sikh scripture on its walls, indicating that it had once been a gurdwara. The grim realisation soon struck him - he was standing amongst the remnants of skeletons in what was a mass grave. After the story hit the airwaves, the engineer was sacked by his employer – they denied their decision had anything to do with his discovery.

A month after the waves of attacks on Sikhs, the UK's Channel 4 sent a film crew to report on the situation in East Delhi, one of the poorest areas to be affected. They followed the local Sikh community leader from house to house as he described how the massacres affected every Sikh family in the area:

> In this house lived a scooter driver. He was beaten with sticks, his belongings were taken. Afterwards, he was brought out and set alight here. In this house, one man was killed. He used to be a porter at the local railway station. In the next house, another man was killed.

He also used to be a railway porter. Here, his young brother was killed. He used to be a rickshaw driver. Finally, this is where my own brothers were killed, both set alight.

~

Beyond Sikh neighbourhoods, India's sprawling railway network became an easy hunting ground for murderers – just as it had during Partition. According to records obtained from the railway authorities, there were at least forty-six unauthorised train stoppages in the first two days of November. Once stopped, Sikhs were identified, dragged out and executed, their bodies left on platforms or thrown onto the tracks.

On 1 November, a day after the assassination, a doctor travelling to Delhi from West Bengal was a witness to how the mobs operated with the connivance of railway police and officials. Her train was frequently stopped to allow the mobs to hunt down Sikh passengers. Several were dragged off the train and killed, despite protests from the other passengers, who could hear the nightmarish sounds of the beatings and stabbings from inside their compartments. The doctor was able to give refuge in her top sleeping bunk to two young Sikhs.

The mobs boasted that all Sikh travellers into the capital had been killed. A former railways minister who was travelling from Mumbai to Delhi on the Rajdhani Express heard people shouting: 'No Sikh will be allowed to leave the train alive'. When two were discovered on board, they were thrown on the platform and set on fire while police stood idly by. The mob then spotted a Sikh railway employee, wearing his distinctive blue uniform, leaving the station master's office. He was immediately surrounded and killed on the spot. Three more dead Sikhs were found lying in various train compartments.

A booking clerk at Tughlakabad railway station in south Delhi witnessed attacks by villagers armed with iron rods: 'They searched the entire train and dragged out Sikh passengers and started beating them mercilessly. Those men had kerosene oil with them. Twenty-five to thirty were burnt'.

On the Bombay-Amritsar Deluxe train, eight corpses were recovered. In the reporting of the crime, a statement of chilling simplicity asked the police to 'please arrange to remove twelve dead bodies lying on [the] platform'.

Of this period, future prime minister, I. K. Gujral, recorded in his diary: 'Delhi is burning. There are reports of trains arriving with corpses. It is like 1947. Gen Aurora spent the night with us. The hero of 1971 could not sleep in his own house in Delhi'.

~

The trauma for survivors did not end with the cessation of violence. In times of major crises, hospitals and medical centres are naturally the first to open their doors to the injured. Yet so well-orchestrated was the anti-Sikh prejudice and hatred during those calamitous few days that those doors remained, more often than not, firmly shut.

Unbelievably, several government-run hospitals refused to admit injured Sikhs. A man whose son was shot in the head and refused treatment at Orsale Hospital Parade in Kanpur died the next day. A widow, whose husband had just been killed, sought medical aid for her daughter-in-law who had been raped. Doctors at two hospitals in Kanpur and Delhi refused to admit her, ultimately resulting in the girl being paralysed from the waist down. A child suffering burns was refused treatment at Hindu Rao Hospital in north Delhi. His father took him to Lok Nayak Jai Prakash Hospital, six kilometres away, where he succumbed to his injuries. The doctors refused to even conduct an investigation into his death.

At a Public Health Centre in south-west Delhi, Sikhs who had come for treatment were set upon, leaving eight murdered. A journalist related stories of several Sikhs with burn injuries being turned away by medical staff in Delhi hospitals. Indeed, some hospital burns units were closed exactly at a time when multiple burns were the most common cause of injuries. Several of these horribly wounded and vulnerable Sikhs would fall victim to the mobs waiting outside.

A lawyer, Ram Jethmalani, who with his colleagues tried to help the beleaguered victims, stated hospital authorities at the All India Institute for Medical Sciences (AIIMS) – where Mrs Gandhi was taken after being shot – refused to admit them. Kuldip Singh, a Sikh civil rights activist who was attacked on a train, had to wait forty-eight hours for treatment at Daltonganj Hospital in Bihar. He was only treated when his non-Sikh friends threatened the doctors. Another victim at the Guru Nanak hospital in Kanpur was told to cut his hair or leave the hospital.

It would be thirty years before a leading surgeon, Dr A. K. Banerji, now at the Indraprastha Apollo Hospital in Delhi, admitted to former trainee surgeon, Swaran Preet Singh, his shame over his staff's refusal to treat Sikhs in Delhi's hospitals following the massacres.

~

By 2 November, leaders representing a hundred nations had arrived for Mrs Gandhi's funeral the next day. These included the UK's prime minister, Margaret Thatcher, the premier of the Soviet Union, Nikolai Tikhonov, and the United States secretary of state, George P. Shultz. In total, fourteen presidents attended the funeral. Whether the gathered world leaders had any idea of the scale of the retribution taking place just outside their guarded compound is not known. However, Princess Anne's personal protection officer would later recall how they could hear the sound of violence emanating from beyond the walls of the British High Commission. Having come to India to help promote the work of Save the Children, the Princess was now unwittingly surrounded by scenes of unremitting barbarity against children and their families.

The killings had a further two full days to run their course. Alongside the murders came the rapes. Once again, children would not be spared.

5

Mass Rape

Rape and sexual assault are a recurring aspect of genocide and ethnic cleansing. The Armenian Genocide, for example, was characterised by the rape of women and children by Turkish mobs, often in the presence of male family members, with the intent to demoralise and humiliate.

In India in 1984, rape was similarly central element of the violence from the onset. However, the relative lack of attention that has been paid to it in both unofficial and official accounts stems largely from the social stigma attached to sexual violence in India. Furthermore, the intensity and horror of the massacres were such that they have largely overshadowed the sexual assaults that, in themselves, amount to a mass crime against humanity.

In 2006, filmmaker Reema Anand recorded testimonies that confirmed not only the targeted killing of men and boys but also of mass rape and killing of women and girls. Some suffered horrific injuries from being cut up or burnt. Witnesses spoke of seeing naked bodies dumped in trucks and driven away.

Harrowing testimonies from survivors speak of their unimaginable horror. Cases were reported of women being stripped and raped while their husbands and sons were forced to watch. Children were often present while their mothers and sisters were being repeatedly brutalised. Some of the sexual violence was committed in the presence of the still smouldering corpses of murdered family members.

The gang rapes were efficiently organised and planned. Much of the sexual violence was carried out on the instructions of local Congress leaders. Sikh men were also subject to sexualised humiliation, being forced to watch their wives, daughters, and sisters raped before they themselves were killed.

On 1 November, one forty-five-year-old woman was with her husband and three sons at their home in Block 32 of the Trilokpuri colony when they were viciously attacked around noon by a gang of approximately eight teenagers. That morning the family had been watching the television coverage showing scenes outside Teen Murti House, the former residence of Jawaharlal Nehru, where Mrs Gandhi's body had been brought to be kept in state until her funeral. Hearing the mob at work outside, the father ran outside with the two eldest sons. They came under attack and were burnt alive. The woman's youngest son, who had remained inside with her, pre-emptively cut his own hair and shaved his beard to avoid being identified as a Sikh. But when the gang entered the house he was still targeted. As his mother tried to shield her only surviving son, she was herself violently stripped naked and raped by boys she would later describe as being no older than fourteen or sixteen. Her son tearfully begged for them to stop, pleading that they should look upon her as they did their own mothers, but they carried on regardless.

When they finally left, the woman still feared for her son's life and so she decided to look for sanctuary away from the house. They went outside and sat among a group of women. But the son was soon recognised and dragged away to a street corner where he was beaten with staffs before being sprinkled with kerosene. As he reeled from the blows the mobs set him alight. The mother tried to save her son but she was beaten back, sustaining knife wounds and a broken arm.

Also, in Trilokpuri, a gang comprising mainly of teenagers taunted a group of Sikh women by insisting that their menfolk were dead so they should present themselves outside in a group or they too would be killed. The women and girls helplessly huddled together and were offered some water. As they were drinking the girls were dragged away, one by one, to a nearby mosque and gang-raped. Some returned from their ordeal, others did not. One young girl said that she was raped by fifteen men. Another woman who tried to intervene to save her children was gang raped by around a dozen men and spoke of being bitten all over her body.

At the height of the Trilokpuri massacres, in which no Sikh man was left alive, some thirty women and girls were abducted and held captive in Chilla, a village two kilometres to the west of the capital. When the army eventually arrived on 3 November, some of the women were returned but many were not – they were either killed or remained as captives, their fate unknown.

~

A woman, whose family had moved to Delhi from the newly-created Pakistan at the time of Partition in 1947, would later identify the leader of the mob that killed her eighteen-year-old son as 'the Congress-I block *pradhan*' or neighbourhood leader. Some of the killers were from the same area and others from nearby villages. She recounted her ordeal:

> The women were horded together into one room. Some of them ran away but were pursued to the nearby *nallah* [alley] where they were raped. Their shrieks and cries for help fell on deaf ears. From among the women held in the room, the hoodlums asked each other to select whomsoever they chose. All the women were stripped and many dishonoured.

The woman who related this account was herself raped by ten men. Their savagery satisfied, they told the women to leave, still naked to add to their shame.

In Sultanpuri in the west of the capital, another woman identified local Congress leaders spearheading the mobs on 1 November.

In an affidavit she stated that after her menfolk had been killed, they grabbed hold of her daughter and stripped her naked. This took place on the eve of her wedding day. She was abducted and returned home only after being violated for three days. In another case, a young girl was unable to remember who she was, so brutal was the attack she endured. One survivor testified that girls as young as nine to ten were raped.

On 2 November, a medical officer from Guru Nanak Hospital in Kanpur visited a relief camp. She came across at least thirteen cases of girls and women aged between sixteen and twenty who had been gang-raped on the orders of the local Congress leader. In another incident in that city, two sisters, one of whom was pregnant, were raped in the street. Before leaving, their assailants poured acid over their bodies. Interviews recorded by human rights activists at other relief camps revealed a similar pattern. The trauma led to several of the victims taking their own lives, either during their stay at the camps or in the months and years to come.

Elderly women were also subjected to sexual assaults in front of their families, especially in Trilokpuri. In Nand Nagri, an eighty-year-old woman informed a social worker that she had been raped. As in all such situations, the major purpose of these vile attacks was clearly to inflict maximum humiliation in order to completely destroy the victims' morale.

In a complete dereliction of duty, the government provided no physical protection to the victims, nor did it make any arrangements for them to reach safety. Furthermore, the local administration did little to create an environment where victims of rape could record their ordeal or testify. Many, if not most, cases went unreported – those who suffered wanted their shame to remain buried deep within the cinders of their homes.

The impact of the hideous crimes committed against these women would remain forever more, with devastating consequences not only for their life outcomes but also those of their surviving children. A culture of lifelong and intergenerational suffering had been born.

6

The Body Count

It will not come as a surprise that a government intent on committing acts of terror against its own people will have an incentive to hide the truth. From the outset, the dead of November 1984 were never properly counted. Indeed, there was a deliberate strategy to hide the extent of the massacres such that, in the words of leading Indian author Amitav Ghosh, who was in Delhi in 1984, the 'total death toll may never be known'.

One thing we do know is that the official declarations of deaths were nothing short of farcical. On 1 November, the home secretary stated that the number of people killed in the entire country was just *ten*, including five in Delhi. This was the same day that journalists had stumbled across the corpses of 400 Sikhs in East Delhi.

The next day, the capital's police commissioner asserted that 'fifteen, maybe twenty people have died in violence during the day'. To this, the governor added his voice, saying that 'things are under control'. These words of reassurance came at a time when the likely number of deaths was already running into the thousands.

Five days later, the home ministry released a revised figure of 599 dead. According to the journalist Romesh Thapar, the home secretary 'spent his active hours minimising what had happened and criticising "exaggerated accounts"'. On 11 November, the *Hindustan Times* published a table giving the official number of those killed in Delhi as 325.

It took three years for the Delhi Administration to conclude the official death toll – of 2,733 – when the Ahuja Committee submitted its report in August 1987. But even this would prove to be an understatement.

The official count overlooked the attacks committed on trains, buses and in taxis, let alone the wider massacres across India. Journalists who were present at the kill zones of Kanpur, Lucknow and Ghaziabad estimated that thousands were murdered in those cities alone. Also unaccounted for were those butchered in remote villages far from any media gaze.

The destruction of evidence has also obscured the real figures. Targeted incinerations would have resulted in more deaths than injuries. And in cases where whole families and communities were wiped out, no one would have been left to record their deaths, let alone file criminal cases or make a claim for recompense.

Victim testimonies also indicate a division of labour amongst the gangs, whereby people not involved in the killings were tasked with disposing of what was left of the dead. One survivor reported seeing bodies being collected up, doused in oil and set ablaze in the streets. Another saw half-burnt corpses being unceremoniously shoved into gunny sacks and taken away in three-wheeler auto rickshaws. In some parts of the capital, street sweepers removed the dead. Witnesses observed bodies piled up amongst the city's garbage and hauled away in trucks.

Maxwell Pereira, one of the few police officers who actually saved Sikh lives during the atrocities, told a reporter that he saw 'a mountain of bodies' when at a Delhi morgue. There were 'half-burnt [and] fully burnt bodies piled one on top of the other'.

Shyam Bhatia, a staff reporter at *The Observer*, received an anonymous phone call at his hotel on the night of 1 November informing him that dead bodies were being dumped at Subzi Mandi, a vegetable market in Old Delhi. He and his colleague, Robin Lustig, jumped into a taxi provided by the hotel and headed off into the deserted streets to investigate. When they arrived they noticed a makeshift mortuary adjacent to the vegetable market. Peering through the high metal railings they saw scattered about its grounds small bundles of rags. Bhatia climbed over the metal railing to take a closer look. Proceeding further he tripped over some burnt tyres, a portentous sign of what he was soon to discover – the bundles were charred Sikh corpses. Some still donned partially burnt turbans. Bhatia managed to count 119 bodies before being overwhelmed by the smell of smoke and burnt flesh. The journalists then noticed what appeared to be a green army lorry parked nearby with its back open. On closer inspection he found approximately thirty Sikh bodies piled up. 'It was impossible to sleep the rest of that night,' he would later recount, 'and despite repeated hot showers, the stench refused to leave.'

Little or no doubt remains that the police were complicit in this gruesome logistical process. Evidence suggests that they helped transport bodies in trucks and vans to the outskirts of the capital and other cities to be done away with in mass cremations. One survivor claimed that the police had collected bodies from different parts of the city using up to 120 trucks in which they 'piled them [the bodies] one on top of the other and took the bundles to the forests on the outskirts of Delhi and Aravalli Hills surrounding Delhi to set the lots on fire with the help of petrol, diesel or other chemicals'.

~

Several non-governmental organisations (NGOs) conducted their own investigations into the death toll. Their findings ranged from 3,870 in Delhi alone to a national death toll exceeding 3,000, with the proviso that the actual toll was likely double this figure.

In 2013, an article in *The Economist* stated that at least 8,000 Sikhs were killed nationwide, half in the capital. But even this may be an understatement – a US-based NGO, Sikhs for Justice, quoted official Indian government figures showing a staggering 35,000 claims filed by the victims (albeit they may include injuries and damage to properties in addition to deaths).

Within weeks of the massacres, Maneka Gandhi, Indira Gandhi's estranged daughter-in-law, made several damning statements in an interview with *Time* magazine's South Asia correspondent. The widow of Sanjay Gandhi who was raised in a Sikh family, she reportedly laid the blame for the bloody aftermath of the assassination on her brother-in-law, Rajiv. She went on to dismiss what was then the official death toll of 601 as utter nonsense – in her estimation up to 10,000 had been slaughtered, with entire villages cleansed of Sikhs. She went further, claiming that in New Delhi and elsewhere, secret mass cremations had been conducted to hide the truth.

While the figures will continue to be debated, the atrocities that gave rise to them are beyond contention. And the methodical manner by which the dead were disposed of could not possibly have been organised within a day of Mrs Gandhi's assassination on 31 October. As with the other harrowing aspects of the attacks, it is impossible not to contend that they must have been organised weeks, possibly months, in advance.

7

The Aftermath

By 4 November, just four days after the outbreak of the vicious and widespread bloodletting, the violence appeared to have subsided almost as quickly as it had erupted. In its wake remained thousands of wounded and distressed, among them countless widows and orphans. Entire communities, particularly in the outer suburbs of Delhi, had been burnt, looted, tortured, executed, raped and essentially erased from the ground up, leaving nothing but charred human remains amongst the dying embers of their temples and towns.

The immediate aftermath saw survivors relocate to 'relief camps' or simply flee. It is estimated that up to 50,000 became internally displaced. Many heads turned towards Punjab, while others who could chose to leave the country altogether. Entire swathes of villages, towns and the capital city itself were essentially ethnically-cleansed on a scale not seen since the Partition of 1947. Thirty-seven years on from the monumental horrors of the division of the subcontinent, a beleaguered community was once again on the move by any means necessary in order to reach safety.

In those first few crucial days the Congress government made little or no attempt to help the victims, who barely clung on to life. Thousands went hungry and many died of their injuries as hospitals and medical staff continued to refuse to administer much-needed treatment.

In stark contrast to this callous and pernicious negligence, voluntary organisations such as the Citizens Unity Forum and the gurdwaras that still remained standing stepped in to fill the vacuum. Relief in the form of food, clothing and medicine was organised for victims. They also organised peace marches despite opposition from the police.

By the time the government had managed to set up ten relief camps, at least eighteen established by voluntary groups and located mainly in gurdwaras had sprang up in Delhi alone. They were soon bursting at the seams – one that had been set up in a school swelled at its peak to around 18,000 internal refugees. Incredibly, the authorities did not recognise these unofficial relief centres and therefore, officially, the victims in them simply did not exist.

For some of the camps' residents, it seemed as if all hope had evaporated. Victims told and retold their terrible stories to one another. Traumatised women and children spoke of witnessing the carnage and burnings carried out by stranger and neighbour alike. One young man, a witness to his friend's murder, described the absolute powerlessness felt by the survivors in these camps: 'There were all these grieving people. Some had lost their families, some their businesses, and some even their sanity. It was surreal'.

~

The survivors knew exactly who was behind the violence. They were, after all, first-hand witnesses to the organised massacres by death squads, which had been aided and abetted by a number of politicians and police.

At the camp at Janakpuri, a residential neighbourhood in west Delhi populated predominantly by Punjabi settlers after Partition, the survivors took a stand against the perpetrators. Unwilling to be silenced by threats, they erected a signpost at the camp entrance with the declaration: 'Sorry, no Congress politicians allowed'. It was placed next to another sign that stated: 'No stray dogs allowed'. Both were later removed by the police.

Realising the camps were politically inconvenient – drawing attention as they did to the enormity of the crime – and anxious to proclaim the restoration of normalcy, the Congress government incredibly began the process of shutting them down. Commencing on 10 November, survivors were removed and sent back, some forcibly, to the areas that they had fled from only days earlier. It was within these shattered communities that they had watched loved ones being hacked, raped and engulfed in flames. Now they were expected to return to the burnt-out, empty shells that were once their homes, compelled to live amongst the very murderers who had looted and killed their families.

Heart-rending pleas, to not be abandoned and left defenceless at the mercy of their tormentors, proved futile. Having been handed the pathetic sum of 50 rupees (equivalent to just over £3) and some dry rations, survivors were herded into Delhi Corporation Transport buses – the very same that had brought the killing squads into their neighbourhoods days earlier – and sent on their way.

~

While the government's energies at this time were focused on covering up and reducing the visibility of the crimes through the deliberate destruction of reports, Dr Uma Chaktravarti, a historian at Miranda University in Delhi, and her student, Nandita Haksar, were able to record and preserve a great number of crucial victim testimonies.

All the while, stray incidents of looting and murder continued, despite the presence of the army. In an interview recorded two decades after the massacres, the then trainee surgeon, Swaran Preet Singh, described his experience of visiting the west Delhi suburb of Hari Nagar, which became home to many of the Sikh widows. A few days after the pogroms he came across a young girl who had been raped and molested:

She was taken to the hospital but, like so many other victims, refused treatment. A few weeks later, in another incident, an elderly woman was brought by the police. She had explained that her son was being held at a police station for a minor offence before the killings. As rumours were rife that Sikh prisoners were being killed, she decided to go herself to see if her son was safe. The station house officer shouted at her 'yes we have killed him, now fuck off'. She started wailing and tried to hit him. They arrested her and badly beat her up. When she was brought to the hospital and complained to the doctors of her treatment, the police told them she was lying. She was in a bad way, beaten all over her body, with bruises covering her face, breasts and thighs. With further probing she admitted that they had stuck a baton into her vagina.

Although the events of November 1984 had shaken him, Swaran Preet Singh decided to put his skills to use as a volunteer doctor. However, he was ill-prepared for what was to come:

The widows were in a perpetual state of mourning, so absorbed in their own grief. Yet nobody was paying attention to the children... When I started working with the child victims, I saw and heard things that haunted me for years. I couldn't sleep at night. I left Delhi, never wanting to come back.

One of the boys in his care was so psychologically scared that he would ascend to the rooftops and threaten to jump, screaming in desperation for the man who killed his father to be found. For many of the widows life became too much to bear. Some gave up their lives by plunging into the Yamuna River, while others simply became destitute.

What saved many Sikhs was the community's 'spirit of optimism' or *chardi-kala* – positivity in the face of seemingly insurmountable odds. Those who made it through the bloodshed relatively unscathed provided succour to others who had lost everything. Volunteers serving free food, the *langarwallas*, not only ensured that no one went hungry, but they also provided emotional support to the widows, whom they affectionately referred to as their sisters in an attempt to give them a sense of identity and belonging once again.

~

Despite accusations beginning to mount regarding the involvement of his Congress Party colleagues in the violence, Prime Minister Rajiv Gandhi cynically seized upon the death of his mother in the belief that his government would reap the rewards of a heightened state of tension. While initially calling for calm and the reinstitution of law and order in his first radio broadcast to the nation on 31 October, within a fortnight he was announcing immediate parliamentary elections. The calculation relied on the nation's Hindu majority casting their votes in sympathy for his mother as a means of venting their anti-Sikh feelings – feelings that had been stirred from the outset of the planning of the violence and which now would become shockingly overt in their manifestation.

An anti-Sikh backlash formed the central theme of the election campaign. The demonisation of the Sikh community that underpinned the massacres was now projected via mainstream media. Huge billboards went up around India showing posters of Sikhs brandishing automatic weapons over the bullet-ridden body of the former prime minister. Their message to voters was simple – unite against sinister forces (namely Sikh separatists in Punjab and their Pakistani backers) that threatened the integrity and security of the beloved mother land. There were even sightings of advertising hoardings showing two Sikhs in uniform gunning down a blood-stained Mrs Gandhi against the backdrop of a map of India.

The general election was slated to take place at the end of December 1984, up until which time the government offensive against Sikhs continued relentlessly in the national print media. Newspapers carried full-page advertisements employing alarming imagery of barbed-wire with the splash headline: 'Will the country's border finally be moved to your doorstep?' Posters of Congress candidates prominently displayed in Delhi asked: 'Would you trust a taxi driver from another state? For better security, vote Congress.' Given that a significant proportion of Delhi's taxi drivers were Sikhs with their roots in Punjab, the insinuation was abundantly clear.

With the constant barrage of attacks on the Sikh community in local, state and national discourse, it was only inevitable that members of the general public would begin to openly express their hatred. In one instance, Prakash Kaur, a Punjabi teacher at Delhi University, described how children threw rotten food into her home while her work colleagues joked about the massacres; chillingly they also expressed their feelings on how Sikhs should be treated: 'These people should be grabbed by their top knots, whirled around and beaten up thoroughly'.

Others shamelessly gloated about seeing Sikh gurdwaras consumed by flames and how they had 'taken out the Guru Granth Sahib, spat [on] it, and urinated over it'. Prakash Kaur recounted how a fellow Sikh bus passenger was humiliated with cigarette smoke – tobacco being a prohibited substance according to Sikh tenets:

> The other day I was in a bus, which three young college students got into. One of them lit a cigarette and made sure that the smoke went right into the face of a middle aged Sikh travelling in the bus, blowing directly on to his face. The man sat there looking quietly sullen, choking his anger in the face of such a flagrant abuse.

Days after the killings, the stench of burning flesh still in the air, the situation was a source of amusement for some. A retired foreign office civil servant remembered his friend's children telling him about the jokes that were doing the rounds in some of the elite Delhi schools: 'What is a burnt Sikh? And the answer is - a seekh kebab'. In Germany after the war, many Germans would claim they knew nothing about the death camps. Disturbingly, in India, the burnings were not only common knowledge, they were celebrated.

The Congress Party's caustic campaign strategy proved remarkably effective. Rajiv Gandhi achieved a massive landslide in the December 1984 elections, winning 404 out of 533 seats (267 were required to achieve a majority). His mandate was unprecedented.

In a further sickening blow to the survivors and to justice, the very politicians named by victims as spearheading the violence would see huge increases in their majorities. They would also go on to be rewarded with powerful government positions.

Not one of the accused was arrested. Indeed, journalists would witness several of the accused Congress politicians at police stations busily trying to secure the release of their supporters who had been members of the killing squads.

Part II

THE COVER-UP

8

The Planning

The Rwandan genocide of 1994 was sparked by the death of President Juvénal Habyarimana, a member of the majority Hutu ethnic group, when his plane was shot down. His demise was blamed on the Rwandan Patriotic Front, a group comprised predominantly of the minority Tutsi ethnic group. But doubt remains as to whether they were ever involved, with some evidence and testimony suggesting rogue Hutu elements being responsible.

Whoever it was, the murder was used as the overt trigger to commence mass killings – the execution of a premeditated plan, the 'final solution' to kill Rwandan Tutsis *en masse*. This had included the Rwandan government importing thousands of machetes from China and the compilation of hit lists of 'traitors', as well as the broadcasting of anti-Tutsi propaganda via a new television and radio station.

Were the massacres of November 1984 similarly planned? Would the waves of violence have transpired even if the prime minister had not been assassinated? Was there a wider conspiracy and plan behind the killings? These are important questions that successive Indian governments and official inquiries have largely chosen to ignore.

~

Prime Minister Rajiv Gandhi downplayed the notion that the violence was organised, characterising it instead as 'riots' that were to be expected from an angered Indian populace that had just learnt of Indira Gandhi's assassination. Echoing this causal link two decades later former Indian diplomat and national security adviser J. N. Dixit asserted that the violence was provoked by some Sikhs who had killed the prime minister.

As recently as 2016, Pranab Mukherjee, former president of India and the most senior Congress leader in November 1984, though not implicated in the massacres sought to deflect blame away from his own party by claiming that the death of Mrs Gandhi gave way to a grief-stricken nation, and that in such a climate 'miscreants' had carried out the murders and acts of looting.

This explanation has remained the Indian establishment's rationale for the massacres for the past three decades. Yet within a month of the events occurring, the media and human rights organisations began to speak of a chilling premeditated conspiracy that implicated the upper echelons of the Congress government.

~

One of the first to air their suspicions was the veteran human rights activist, Amiya Rao. During the Emergency she and her husband had released clandestine publications in opposition and would go on to co-author the controversial report *Oppression in Punjab* in 1985. In an article published on 8 December 1984, she suggested that a well-planned and well-organised orgy of anti-Sikh violence would have 'burst forth even if Indira Gandhi had been alive':

> People in Shivaji Park, a middle-class colony in East Delhi, told me long before October 31, for weeks they would hear a voice, at midnight calling on Hindus 'to wake up, to arise and destroy'... Many have told me that Indira Gandhi's assassination had merely advanced the date of violence.

From information personally gathered from 'influential officials' by human rights activist Ram Narayan Kumar, it has been suggested that the original plan was actually to commence the massacres on 8 November, a national holiday commemorating the birth of the first Sikh Guru:

> The plan and its methodology had been worked out independently, immediately after Operation Blue Star, to be quickly implemented at the first possible occasion, as it was done. One retired bureaucrat from Delhi said that the original plan was to instigate a riot on Guru Nanak's birth anniversary, which falls in November, and to carry out the anti-Sikh pogrom.

A Sikh lady, whose father was highly placed in Mrs Gandhi's entourage and two other close relatives held senior government posts, had been warned beforehand that something was amiss. She was later advised to remove her children from school and get them to safety before the violence began. She suspected that 'a plan to create communal violence in the capital had been in place for some time', which was pushed up 'to take advantage of the conditions created by the assassination'.

According to a Sikh medical student, his father had received word from a contact in the home ministry that 'the plan was for the violence to continue for three days before being curtailed'. On 3 November, a retired Sikh chief justice of the Punjab and Haryana High Court was advised by a Sikh friend to wait until the following day before going out into the streets as he had been 'informed by a Congress friend that this programme was only for three days'.

~

According to Tarlochan Singh, the president's press secretary, Zail Singh had discovered that a meeting of Congress leaders – including Arun Nehru, H. K. L. Bhagat and Jagdish Tytler – had taken place on 31 October, prior to Rajiv Gandhi's arrival at the hospital where his mother lay. It is believed that the official go-ahead for the plan was given at this meeting, with 'blood for blood' chosen as the rallying cry.

That evening, a secret meeting at the home of Bhagat, Minister of Information and Broadcasting, was attended by senior police officers, among them the additional commissioner of police, Hukum Chand Jatav, who had command over the capital's Central, East and North districts. According to Shoorveer Singh Tyagi, Station House Officer in charge of Kalyanpuri police station, it was decided upon that officials 'down the line [were] to let the killings take place and then erase all traces of the crime'.

At another meeting near the Trilokpuri colony, this time at the home of the local Congress Party *pardhan* (leader) Rampal Saroj, instructions were verbally given to the Congress leaders present that 'the entire Sikh community had to be taught a lesson'.

The foundations of their plan had, however, been laid well in advance and were in part the outcome of years of suspicion, misgivings and disagreements between the centre and the state: between the Congress central government and the latter's political, economic and social demands as framed by the Akali Dal, the governing Sikh-centric party in Punjab. Greater autonomy, the supply of electricity and better deals on river rights to improve the lot of farmers in a predominantly agriculture state were just some of points of contention that would drive a wedge between New Delhi and the Sikhs of Punjab.

~

It is believed that key players in the Congress government used the increasingly volatile situation in Punjab to blur the perception of the Sikh community in the eyes of their fellow citizens. Potent propaganda helped created an atmosphere of distrust between Sikhs and Hindus, especially in the North. These poisoned sentiments gathered such deadly momentum that the execution of Operation Blue Star in June 1984 was regarded by some as 'inevitable'.

Released a month after the bungled military operation, the government's *White Paper on the Punjab Agitation* set out its rationale for sending tanks and troops into the Sikhs' most revered sacred space. The paper referred to the 'secessionist and anti-national movement' among the Sikhs, accusing the Akali Dal party as 'unwilling to negotiate a settlement'. The narrative cast the Congress government and its agencies as guardians of the nation's integrity, and the Sikhs as 'anti-national' elements intent on ripping the country asunder. In reality, however, it was the Congress government that would renege on a deal in February 1984 at the behest of the chief minister of neighbouring state of Haryana. According to the journalist and part-time political consultant, Kuldip Nayar, the Congress leader 'took an intransigent stand' on the issue of the status of Chandigarh, the joint state capital and was in no mood to compromise on the issue. Soon after the talks were aborted, violence against Sikhs flared up in two major cities in Haryana, Panipat and Jagadhari, resulting in nine dead and three gurdwaras destroyed. Reports suggested the authorities did 'very little' to protect Sikhs.

Among those who had taken part in the negotiations with the Akali Dal six months prior to the November massacres was H. K. L. Bhagat. Kuldip Nayar met Bhagat at his residence in April 1984 to help iron out a formula that both sides could agree on to settle the stalemate that existed between the Akali Dal and Congress. The formula made its way to the prime minister but nothing came of it and Nayar had no further contact from Bhagat. Ostensibly, the government was keen to be seen to be doing everything possible to arrive at an agreement, but behind the scenes it was more interested in painting the Akali Dal as the intransigent party. The cost of this cynical double-game would escalate with deadly consequences.

To bolster the insinuation that the Sikhs' desire for regional autonomy posed a national threat, the government commissioned a series of documentaries in early 1984. Mani Shankar Iyer, Joint Secretary to the Government of India, was said by an associate to have claimed that 'he was given an unpleasant job of portraying Sikhs as terrorists. He was there on some special duty with Minister of Information and Broadcasting'. The minister in question was none other than Bhagat.

It is believed that in the aftermath of Operation Blue Star, several thousand video cassette copies were made of a documentary for overseas viewing. They were posted anonymously to individuals and organisations in the Indian diaspora with a view to polarising opinion and quash any sympathy harboured for the 'terrorist' Sikhs of Punjab.

The footage included scenes showing a large cache of Pakistani and Chinese armaments that the military had allegedly found inside the Golden Temple. However, this assertion was sensationally contested in a cover story in *Surya* magazine. Quoting a highly placed (and apparently disillusioned) source in the Research and Analysis Wing (known as RAW), India's foremost foreign intelligence agency, the article claimed the majority of the arsenal recovered from inside the shrine had been smuggled in under the supervision of a special covert agency, created by RAW operatives and run by the director of the prime minister's secretariat. A week before the army action, the Punjab police had intercepted two truck-loads of weapons and ammunition but allowed them to go on their way to the Golden Temple at the behest of the covert agency.

In an article published a month after the army action, Subramaniam Swamy, President of the Janata Party (which became the first non-Congress government in India's history after the cessation of the Emergency in 1977), asserted that the Congress government had been peddling a campaign of misinformation in an attempt to legitimise Operation Blue Star. At its heart was the desire to show that 'the Golden Temple was the haven of criminals, a store of armoury and a citadel of the nation's dismemberment conspiracy'.

Sikhs were also vilified as a group. In anticipation of the backlash that was expected to erupt in the wake of the attack on the Golden Temple, the following official army bulletin vilifying initiated Sikhs (*Amritdharis*) was circulated amongst the Indian Army in July 1984:

> Any knowledge of the Amritdharis who are dangerous people and pledged to commit murders, arson and act of terrorism should immediately be brought to the notice of the authorities. These people might appear harmless from [the] outside but they are basically committed to

terrorism. In the interest of all of us their identity and whereabouts must always be disclosed.

~

The successful execution of the planned mass assault on Sikhs nationally was entirely dependent on ensuring the logistical support for those who would carry out the killings was in place beforehand. The synchronisation of its various components could not have been possible without significant advance planning – India's infastracture and bureacracy is often disorganised at the best of times, but in November 1984, it somehow swung into action almost immediately. Even the largely discredited Nanavati Inquiry concluded as much in 2005:

> But for the backing and help of influential and resourceful persons, killing of Sikhs so swiftly and in large numbers could not have happened. The systematic manner in which the Sikhs were thus killed indicates that the attacks on them were organised.

In Delhi, civilian targets were identified using gurdwara voter lists – according to a former government secretary, the gathering of this type of detailed information was undertaken in the lead up to Operation Blue Star, under the auspices of Arun Nehru (a key advisor to the Gandhi family) in anticipation of a Sikh backlash. In a matter of hours, thousands of weapons were distributed to the murder squads, with buses made available to transport them into Sikh neighbourhoods. Sacks of phosphorous powder – an inflammable chemical not normally accessible to the public – were procured from chemical factories. A number of petrol depots belonging to Congress Party members and their supporters were used as a central point to access stocks of kerosene oil. Promises of financial reward were satisfied with cash payments to the killers on the conclusion of their grim work. The disposal of corpses was carefully coordinated by the authorities to ensure the body count was kept as low as possible and evidence obliterated from crime scenes.

But why?

Why would the government of the most populous democracy in the world invent and circulate propaganda designed to portray a minority group as a dangerous enemy, and meticulously plan such barbaric acts of violence against them?

9

The Motives

On 2 November whilst attending meetings to organise peace committees and safety patrols, university student Aseem Shrivastava noted how the mobs had dissipated from his neighbourhood in the New Friends Colony of affluent South Delhi.

The sudden halt to the violence was inexplicable until a young Congress worker, who lived in the badly hit area of nearby Bharat Nagar, advised Aseem's father that there was no point in holding the meetings as their property would not be touched. 'If you lose even a pin,' the man boasted, 'you can get it from me'. He revealed that 'they' had planned on teaching the Sikhs a 'small lesson' but matters had 'got out of hand'.

Putting aside his blatant understatement, the comment tallied with the assessment of many of the survivors interviewed in Delhi's relief camps: the 'aggressive' Sikh community had to be taught a lesson. This was in reference to decades of increasingly embittered political relations between the beleaguered Akali Dal Party in the northern border state and the Congress Party at the centre.

Yet in Delhi, the Sikh victims of November 1984 could hardly be said to have had a stake in the volatile affairs that had gripped Punjab effectively since Partition – in the hardest hit areas of the capital, the majority of victims were poor and originally hailed from Rajasthan or pre-Partition Sindh, one of the provinces that became part of Pakistan. Needless to say, neither did they have anything to do with the assassination of Mrs Gandhi – indeed many would have been staunch supporters of her Congress Party.

~

The roots of the issue lay in the distant past – in the Sikh Empire, its annexation by the British and ultimately in the rise of an independent India. Despite, or perhaps because of their prominent role in the military, political and economic life of the subcontinent, Sikhs have sometimes been regarded as over-achievers, perhaps too successful, strident or demanding for their own good.

And for a community that had, two centuries earlier, forged its own powerful empire that had stretched from the Khyber Pass across the vast plains of Punjab to the Tibetan borders, and almost as far south as Delhi – which had briefly submitted to the Sikhs in 1783 – the formation of an independent India in 1947, with the partitioning of its traditional homeland of Punjab, had been a particularly difficult episode.

A century earlier, the brief but prosperous Sikh Empire had brought about peace and stability in a region that had been beset by centuries of foreign invasions and rulers. A prosperous economy emerged and ongoing development of its army, in part trained by ex-Napoleonic officers, gave rise to a tradition of military success. However, its ambitions for expansion southwards were quashed by the machinations and military might of the East India Company. Ultimately in 1849, after two bitterly-fought wars, the power of the Sikh Empire was extinguished as its territories were annexed by the British, who projected themselves as the rightful successors to the Mughals in the subcontinent.

Despite this, the Sikhs largely reconciled with their conquerors and within a generation would become stalwarts of the British Raj. This was particularly true in the armed forces where they were disproportionately represented – despite comprising only around one per cent of the population of British India, Sikhs made up nearly twenty per cent of the Indian Army at the start of the First World War. In the Second World War, six battalions of the Sikh Regiment fought on the battlefields of El Alamein, Burma, Italy and Iraq.

Conversely, the Sikhs would also become standard bearers of the independence movement before, during and after the World Wars. They agitated in large numbers to push for an end to colonial rule, as well as for greater autonomy in their own religious and social affairs.

In these endeavours they often paid the ultimate sacrifice: out of 2,175 Indian's who were martyred for freedom, 1,557 (70%) were Sikh. Of the 2,646 Indians subjected to life imprisonment on the penal colony on the Andamans Islands, 2,147 (80%) were Sikh, as were ninety-two (70%) of the 127 Indians who were hanged. They also made up 12,000 (60%) of the 20,000-strong Indian National Army under Subhas Bose.

With the Second World War over, the new Labour government in Britain decided that India was strategically indefensible, and financially burdensome, and decided to withdraw.

As independence approached, Indian politics became fiercely sectarian. Caught between the Muslim League and the mainly Hindu Congress Party, the dominant Sikh political party, the Akali Dal, threw their support behind Congress, spurred by Congress leader Jawaharlal Nehru's assurances that Sikh control over their territories would be respected – Sikh political leaders having moved for an autonomous Azad ('Free') Punjab in 1942 as a counter to Muslim demands for Pakistan.

The Akali Dal re-floated the idea of an independent Sikh state in 1946 but the departing British showed little interest in their self-styled utopia, variously referred to as 'Sikhistan' and 'Khalistan'. At the All India Congress Committee meeting in Calcutta in 1946, however, Nehru offered assurances that their desire for autonomy would be satisfied:

The brave Sikhs of Punjab are entitled to special considerations. I see nothing wrong in an area set up in the north of India wherein the Sikhs can also experience the glow of freedom.

Later that year, the possibility that the Sikhs would be granted greater federal control was broached when a resolution passed by the Indian Constituent Assembly in December 1946 gave its support, predicting that the new state of India would be an independent sovereign republic, comprising autonomous units with residuary powers.

When independence finally came the following year it ripped Punjab apart. The Land of the Five Rivers, the homeland of the vast majority of Sikhs, was bifurcated. The majority of its fertile territory went to the newly-created Pakistan. Millions of Sikhs and Hindus crossed over the new border into eastern Punjab in Independent India. The final death toll is believed to have exceeded a million. Up to 100,000 women are estimated to have been kidnapped and raped.

The new reality proved problematic for Sikh political interests. In 1949, a new article in the country's constitution concerned many Sikhs who took offence at being categorised as 'Hindu' for the purposes of defining religious freedoms. Having already lost an empire, they now feared the loss of identity in the suffocating grip of the Hindu 'boa constrictor'.

However, this was followed in 1955 with a government proposal to reorganise states on a linguistic basis, rather than on caste or religious lines. This step was welcomed by Sikhs as Punjabi was predominantly spoken by them. But their hopes were dashed when central government under Nehru reneged on the grounds that states formed on linguistic lines could pose a threat to the secular fabric of the country and thus, national unity. The issue persisted well into the 1960s, leading to protracted talks and protests by the Akali Dal.

But in 1966, Indira Gandhi, the new prime minister who was grateful for the Sikhs' support during the Indo-Pakistani war in 1965, granted what her father had refused to do. Whilst the decision was hailed a victory for supporters of the Punjabi language, it actually resulted in the further carving up of their state since on the eve of the 1951 census the majority of Punjabi-speaking Hindus actually chose to officially identify with Hindi rather than their actual mother-tongue. They had been persuaded by a pro-Hindi campaign led by Congress leader, Lala Jagat Narain, who was head of the influential *Hind Samachar* newspaper group.

As a consequence, the majority Hindi-speaking state of Haryana was etched out of the south-eastern districts of post-Partition Punjab. It shares its northern border with Punjab and Himachal Pradesh (also formerly a part of post-partition Punjab but declared as union territory, under central government control, in 1956), and borders Delhi on all but its eastern side.

Since the emergence of this Hindu-majority state, acrimony has existed between it and the much reduced Punjab, the only Sikh-majority state in India. Two of the prickliest issues were the distribution of Punjab's river waters and the sharing of Chandigarh as state capital.

The former was problematic for a state whose farmers relied heavily on irrigation in order to produce the wheat and rice the nation depended on – at the time, 60% of the country's wheat stockpiles originated from Punjab, which was regarded as the 'breadbasket of India', having been the first state to take advantage in the green revolution of the late 1960s.

The latter issue originated when Punjab's traditional capital city, Lahore, had been allocated to Pakistan in 1947. A new city named Chandigarh, designed by the renowned Swiss-French modernist and architect, Le Corbusier, was to be the state's new capital. Located on the border between Haryana and Punjab, it was under the jurisdiction of neither. Instead, it was classified as a union territory, meaning its administration was solely in the hands of central government.

These issues would come to form the bedrock of Akali Dal demands in the coming years. In 1972, abysmal results in state and national elections saw the Congress Party take control of Punjab. Forced into a period of introspection, the Akali Dal came up with an inspired solution in 1973 – the Anandpur Sahib Resolution. This contained a series of policies that appealed to Sikh economic and religious sentiments to secure votes. On its release, the battle for resources and perceived injustices reached a new intensity as the demands, which included greater devolution of federal power, better allocation of Punjab's waters and the abolishment of the limit for the recruitment of Sikhs in the army, were given little consideration in New Delhi.

When Indira Gandhi imposed a state of emergency two years later, the Akali Dal in Punjab offered a sustained resistance to her decision to suspend the constitution.

On the restoration of democracy in 1977, Mrs Gandhi greatly misjudged her own popularity with a resentful electorate and was roundly defeated. In Punjab, her Congress Party was trounced by the Akali Dal, putting the Anandpur Sahib Resolution firmly back on the table. Some argue that she and her closest political ally, her eldest son Sanjay, never forgave the Sikhs for the losses they suffered, or indeed for their fierce resistance during the Emergency.

~

The desire to regain power in Punjab (as well as in other states where Congress lost at the ballot box) saw Sanjay devise a plan to discredit and disrupt the Akali Dal. Key to the strategy was to divide the Sikh vote, and cause consternation to the Akali Dal. Along with Zail Singh, who had recently suffered defeat as Congress's chief minister of Punjab, Sanjay spotted the potential in an enigmatic holy man or *sant*.

Sant Jarnail Singh Bhindranwale was a tall, wiry Sikh preacher with a fiery oratory. Coincidentally also in 1977 he had been selected to head his traditional Sikh seminary, the Damdami Taksal. He had been passionately campaigning from village to village in an effort to uphold Sikh orthodoxy, in particular rallying his audiences against the evils of the caste system and the dangers of alcohol consumption and illicit substances, which had blighted the Sikh peasantry.

His star was on the rise and the Congress Party saw their chance to capitalise on his growing popularity.

Though not officially inducted into the Congress Party, and with Zail Singh as his effective handler, Bhindranwale was carefully positioned (unknowingly according to some commentators) against the Akali Dal. The seemingly rustic, plain-speaking preacher 'seemed too uneducated, too unsophisticated to pose any threat' to those who had sought to direct and utilise him. However, as he gained an increasingly larger following, power and influence came but so too did the violence, including murders, bombings and even a plane hijacking in protest against his arrest in connection with the murder of the highly critical newspaper baron, Lala Jagat Narain, on 9 September 1981. Although a warrant was issued for his arrest in 12 September, such was his power that Bhindranwale chose when and how to hand himself in to police. He was released a month later without charge – something that could not have been done without the intervention of the recently appointed home minister, Zail Singh. With the police still keen on arresting him, he was by August 1982 living within the sanctuary of the Golden Temple complex.

By mid-1983, Bhindranwale was clearly no longer under any control by Congress and was the most influential religious figure in Punjab. As part of a wider front of Sikh groups agitating for greater religious, political and economic demands, no political settlement was likely without his agreement. Tension between central government and the varying Sikh factions including the Akali Dal were at a high and Punjab was engulfed in violence, which threatened to tear it asunder.

Indira Gandhi, who had returned as prime minister in 1980, finally took action. She dismissed the ruling Congress Party in

Punjab and declared president's rule – as Zail Singh had become President in 1982, in theory, this meant Bhindranwale's former advocate was now back in charge. But by then, Bhindranwale and his militarised followers were already ensconced in the temple complex. If anything, the violence was only set to escalate. The scene was set for an ever-growing escalation of hostilities. The potential for military action was high and, by early 1984, Indian Army commandos were poised to invade the Sikhs' holiest site.

~

The breakdown in law and order in Punjab during the early 1980s, which saw a rise in sectarian violence, has been used to justify what took place in November 1984. In one typically gruesome attack that is often cited, a bus was hijacked in Punjab in October 1983. Six Hindu passengers were separated out from the Sikhs and shot dead on the spot. Akali Dal leaders condemned these atrocities but they received little media attention. One writer later noted how an overwhelming majority of Delhites felt that the killings and arson in November 1984 were, in some way, a justifiable response to what was happening to their kinsmen in Punjab.

With the 1984 elections drawing near and a right-wing opposition increasingly using *Hindutva* (Hindu nationalist) rhetoric to gain support, Congress sought to capture the votes of the Hindu majority. In time-honoured political fashion, in order to accomplish this they sought to juxtapose the majority against a minority by establishing a narrative that the latter was sabotaging the country.

In May 1984, anti-Muslim pogroms broke out twenty kilometres north-east of Mumbai in the town of Bhiwandi. Hindu right-wing activists were transported into Muslim areas after a saffron flag, which was being used as the battle standard for a resurgent far-right Hindu movement, was placed atop a mosque. The consequent looting, violence and killings were systematic, foreshadowing what was to occur in Delhi six months later. The violence spread rapidly to the suburbs of Mumbai and continued for ten days. Official figures reported nearly 300 killed and over a thousand injured. The violence quelled, Mrs Gandhi held a campaign rally in

Mumbai. Pandering to the Hindu right, she declared: 'Majorities too have their rights'.

~

When talks between the Akali Dal and central government eventually broke down, there was an increase in violent incidents in Punjab. The peasantry, who were becoming increasingly disillusioned with the centre's agricultural policies, staged mass protests. Tens of thousands of farmers were mobilised for civil disobedience. In late May 1984, the Akali Dal called for a boycott of the Food Corporation of India, whereby farmers would withhold their harvests.

Adding to the increasing sense of foreboding was Bhindranwale's occupation of the Golden Temple complex, which was being fortified by his men. Realising that she may need to act, Mrs Gandhi had ordered the army to remain on high alert months earlier – a replica Golden Temple was constructed in the foothills of the Himalayas to aid preparations for an assault. Recent revelations from secret government papers unearthed in the UK's National Archives show how the Indian government had asked the British government for military advice on a possible military operation as early as February 1984.

With the pressure mounting, Mrs Gandhi decided to act. On 3 June 1984, the Indian Army was ordered into the Golden Temple complex on the pretext of removing Sikh dissidents led by Bhindranwale.

Taking place on one of the busiest and holiest days in the Sikh calendar – the anniversary of the martyrdom of the shrine's founder, the fifth Sikh Guru, Guru Arjan – and without due warning or any evacuation of pilgrims, the military assault resulted in thousands being wilfully trapped.

The outcome of Operation Blue Star was a bloodbath. The Akal Takht, the Sikhs' temporal seat of authority situated in a courtyard opposite the main entrance of the Golden Temple, was severely damaged. So too was the Sikh Reference Library, which contained priceless manuscripts. One commentator spoke of this unprecedented act in post-independent India as one 'not to eliminate a political figure or a political movement but to suppress the culture of a people, to attack their heart, to strike a blow at their spirit and self-confidence'. Official figures put the death toll at 575 but unofficially, the casualties were believed to run into the thousands.

~

As was expected, the Sikh community was stunned and outraged. Protests erupted in Punjab, Delhi and around the globe. At least 4,000 Sikh soldiers mutinied across India, resulting in several pitched battles as they attempted to make their way towards Amritsar. Sikh dignitaries resigned their positions and honours in protest. Captain Amarinder Singh, the former maharaja of the pre-independence state of Patiala, resigned his parliamentary seat and membership of the Congress Party as did others. The former parliamentarian, historian and journalist Khushwant Singh, who had authored *Train to Pakistan* about the horrors of Partition, handed back a cherished civilian award in disgust.

For some Congress members, however, further attacks were needed against this troublesome minority. Targets ranging from homes, commercial establishments and places of worship were identified in preparation for the massacres to come.

10

Killers in Uniform

On 21 April 2014, Indian media company Cobrapost aired an undercover investigative report, 'Chapter 84', which featured the unwitting confessions of eight former Delhi police officers snared in a sting operation. Several of them had been responsible for a number of the capital's police stations during the massacres of November 1984. They described how the police force willingly colluded with the Congress government of the day to 'teach the Sikhs a lesson'. Twenty-nine years after the carnage, members of the state apparatus had finally provided damning testimony of their own guilt.

The policemen – among them Station House Officers Shoorveer Singh Tyagi of the police station in Kalyanpuri, Rhotas Singh of Delhi Cantonment and S. N. Bhaskar of Krishna Nagar – emphasised how they had acted on orders from above. The police were commanded not to file First Information Reports (FIRs, the documents used to register crimes). As police control rooms were flooded with messages of violence and arson, only two per cent of them were actually logged. Logbooks were subsequently amended to obscure evidence of inaction by senior officers, who forbade their subordinates from upholding the law.

Prevented from taking action against perpetrators or to protect victims, they were instead to assist in the covering up of crimes, which included the removal of mutilated Sikh corpses from where they were killed and dumping them elsewhere.

It is beyond doubt that this atrocious dereliction of duty was a key factor in the mass crime against Sikhs. Thousands of lives may well have been saved if the Delhi police force had upheld their motto – *Shanti, Seva, Nyaya* or 'Peace, Service, Justice'. In reality, it was inverted in sickening fashion: instead of ensuring peace, they facilitated violence; instead of service, they abdicated from protecting the city's citizenry; and instead of justice, they serviced the perpetrators of mass murder, particularly through the wilful destruction of evidence.

~

Policing had effectively been curtailed across the capital, with very few exceptions. Nonetheless, crowd movements were continually being reported and recorded over the police's wireless network, offering them every opportunity to deploy their resources to trouble spots. But as the violence began to erupt in East Delhi, the state's initial response was to muster just *three* policemen.

Of the high-ranking officers who were duty-bound to take control of the unfolding lawlessness that was rapidly spreading across the capital, the majority felt their presence was better suited at Teen Murti House where Mrs Gandhi's body lay.

Gradually, as more of Delhi's policemen began arriving at flashpoints, it became clear to observers that they were acting in a contrary manner. Methodically and systematically, they engaged in a variety of complicit roles, fluidly shifting from one to another as required by the ever-changing context.

Police undertook reconnaissance to pinpoint Sikhs in hiding, coaxing them out on the pretext of offering protection. One widow from the doomed Trilokpuri colony, Vidya Kaur, witnessed this type of collusion. She described how police had reassured some Sikhs in hiding that they would help them. Once they had revealed their location, this information was duly passed on to the would-be killers. As the police watched on, some of the women pleaded with the gang members, calling them brothers and begging for their lives to be spared. 'We are not your brothers,' taunted the attackers. 'We are your husbands. We will kidnap you tonight.' And that is exactly what they did.

Delhi's finest also spent the first day after the assassination disarming Sikhs of any weapons that they could use to defend themselves – even those legally owned. On the morning of 1 November, mobs alleged to have been led by local Congress leader Dr Ashok Gupta, descended on Block 11 of Kalyanpuri in East Delhi. But they were forced to retreat when the Sikhs there opened fire. Within minutes the police arrived and ordered the Sikhs to surrender their weapons under promise of protection. Those who refused were threatened at gunpoint. Twenty-five Sikhs were arrested – perversely, these were the only arrests to figure in police records on that first day – and sent to Tihar Prison. Having seized their licensed weapons, the police left the remaining, unarmed, Sikhs of Block 11 at the mercy of the death squads who were waiting in the wings.

Elsewhere, policemen implicitly condoned acts of violence through inaction. The Delhi Fire Services (DFS) later claimed that the police refused to escort their teams into the most severely affected areas, which meant that fires continued to rage across the capital until 5 November. Of the 174 gurdwaras that were subject to arson attack, they were only able to extinguish fires at four, leaving the remaining 170 burning.

While mobs were burning down every Sikh house in Block C-4 in Sultanpuri in northwest Delhi and immolating the inhabitants, the police simply waited in nearby lanes. On a flyover between the villages of Bhogal and Ashram in South Delhi, twenty policemen watched as six Sikhs were beaten to death. A resident of East Vinod Nagar who was harbouring her Sikh neighbours was shocked to see how, after a group of would-be assassins were about to retreat when some policemen arrived, they were reprimanded by these guardians of the law and encouraged to continue on their rampage. Their colleagues elsewhere cheered from their police jeep when a Sikh taxi driver was burnt to death in his vehicle.

In the aftermath of one of the massacres in East Delhi, a journalist asked Nikhil Kumar, the additional commissioner of police (the fourth highest rank in the Indian police service equivalent to the UK's assistant chief constable) about the gruesome practice of 'necklacing', which had become the primary method for murdering Sikh men. His reported responses, that 'Hindus are just burning garbage' and 'how could police stop the madding crowd?', spoke volumes. Kumar would later become the governor of Nagaland.

Little surprise, then, that murderers were heard to brag that 'the police are with us'. In this vain, some policemen went even further, taking an active role in the killings.

In one incident in Block C-3 of the Sultanpuri colony, a policeman was reported to have shot a local Sikh leader, his accomplices being two other constables.

After the first wave of killings, police attached themselves to roaming death squads in the hunt to chase down as many surviving Sikhs as possible. Several people testified that the police were instrumental in repeatedly giving killers free passage into colonies to ensure that those on murder lists had been accounted for, even though a curfew had been imposed – which effectively only applied to the Sikhs. Some police responded to survivors' pleas for help with the sinister retort: 'Don't worry; we are coming to burn you too'.

~

One shocking revelation was the discovery of the deployment of police personnel from a police-training centre in Haryana 'to create chaos, lawlessness and destruction'. A survivor who later testified at an inquiry described how he had managed to get hold of one of those indulging in the violence and recovered an identity card proving he was from the Madhuban Police Training Centre. Scores of Sikhs were killed in his neighbourhood, though no investigation has ever made of the involvement of the training centre.

Like Dutch bounty hunters during the Second World War, the death squads were recompensed in cash directly in proportion to the number of kills they had totted up. A Sikh lady was privy to a revealing conversation between a local police inspector and a mob. Even though the police were 'otherwise apprehending and killing Sikhs,' this particular inspector had taken pity on her and her two sons. He was berated by the ringleaders for not handing over the boys, which would be 'putting them to a loss of 500 [£34] rupees each'.

Policemen also acted as conduits between senior colleagues and the gangs, passing on information and instructions. On the morning of 1 November in Jahangirpuri in the north of the capital, the police were overheard explaining to mobs: 'You have thirty-six hours. Do whatever you wish to do'. Residents testified that it was the police themselves who burnt down the local gurdwara.

When police officers arrived at one housing block in Yamuna Vihar in north-eastern Delhi, they reportedly informed the mob that they 'had the rest of the evening and the night to kill the remaining Sikhs'. Similar instructions were given to death squads unleashed in other areas where they were permitted three days to finish off any lingering Sikhs. On 3 November, police officials from Khajori police station in the north-eastern part of the capital actually reprimanded the mobs for not having 'completed the job' of slaying all the local Sikhs despite being given three days to do it.

~

The Delhi police force boasted thousands of Sikhs in their ranks so the question arises: 'Where were they?' The answer is simple – they were all ordered to stand down. A radio order from headquarters in New Delhi on the morning of 1 November required all Sikh police officers to 'lay down their arms'. In such a defenceless state some were murdered en route to their homes or later on with their families.

Sikhs were however still able to rely on some police officers who were intent on fulfilling their duty. On 1 November, Maxwell

Pereira, the additional deputy commissioner of police based in the north district of the capital, had that morning been pulled out of his area and sent to Teen Murti House. When he heard over the radio that disturbances were taking place at the historic Gurdwara Sis Ganj near the Red Fort in the northeast of Delhi, he rushed to the spot.

When he arrived he saw hundreds of people marching towards the shrine. The Sikhs inside responded by coming out brandishing their swords. At that point, Pereira intervened by convincing the Sikhs that he was responsible for their safety and that they should remain within the gurdwaras premises. He also escorted several Sikhs who had been hiding in nearby lanes to the shrine.

With twenty or so policemen, Pereira managed to keep the two groups separated. On hearing that Sikh-owned shops in Chandni Chowk to the west of the gurdwara were being torched, he headed off to disperse the arsonists. But they lingered, becoming increasingly menacing and continued to burn properties. Pereira ordered a colleague to open fire and one person dropped dead, which had an immediate impact on the crowd. Potentially hundreds of people had been saved by Pereira's actions.

When he reported the firing to the police control room, no one responded. When he attempted to bring the matter to the attention of his superiors, Additional Commissioner Hukum Chand Jatav and Commissioner Subhash Tandon, their 'pin-drop silence' troubled him.

Another non-Sikh officer who helped significantly was Inspector Ranbir Singh, the station house officer Karol Bagh. He held looters back and kept Sikhs in his area safe, even to the point of rushing on foot to disperse a crowd as his jeep had engine issues. Next to no Sikh shops were attacked in his district because of his vigilance.

One of the few policemen who risked his career in pursuit of his duty was Jugti Ram, duty officer at Kalyanpuri police station. He rescued Sikh women who had been abducted to nearby Chilla village in the eastern part of Delhi and sent a radio message to his superiors informing them about the large-scale massacre that had taken place in Block 32 in Trilokpuri. He recorded the same in his logbook. He was subsequently suspended and a case of criminal negligence filed against him as punishment for defying the order to not record the killings of Sikhs. In stark contrast, officers who acted in accordance with the directives not to log crimes against Sikhs were subsequently promoted.

~

For the small proportion of crimes that were logged, the police did their utmost to ensure that any cases that were heard would have little chance of success.

Evidence was manipulated, major offences reduced to minor ones, paper trails destroyed, and eyewitnesses threatened and forced to sign affidavits placing the police in a favourable light. Of the crucial FIRs that were completed, they were done so inadequately. The names and addresses of alleged perpetrators were left out even when they were known. To downplay the stats that would clearly prove the extent of the violence, they merged hundreds of cases of murder and violence into a single 'vague and generally worded omnibus' FIR and counted them as one crime. Nearly half of the cases lodged were closed on the grounds that the culprits were purportedly 'untraceable'. They refused to register FIRs against police officers and government officials but instead registered them against Sikhs who had defended themselves. Several policemen even wrote false affidavits after pretending to be victims to absolve Congress leaders who had been seen inciting mobs. It came as no surprise therefore when an official commission found in 2005 that police investigations had been 'absolutely casual, perfunctory and faulty'.

In illustration of the impact of police connivance, human rights lawyer Vrinda Grover, who represented several victims, summarised the judgements in 126 court cases that had had their day in court by 2002. A staggering 118 cases ended in acquittals. Of the eight that resulted in convictions, two were later overturned by the Delhi High Court. Her assessment of the police's role was damning:

> It is clear that a combination of grave lapses of investigation, shoddy investigation, inordinate delays, insufficient collection of evidence and non-compliance with legal procedures by the police led to a majority of cases concluding in acquittals. The acquittals were to a very large extent a direct consequence of the incompetent, unprofessional and casual investigation by the police.

Beyond the police stations, in the killing fields of Delhi's streets, policemen collaborated in the concealment of the number of dead. Corpses that had been left partially incinerated were promptly disposed of – in some cases, the ashes were merely swept away. Relatives who complained that the bodies of their loved ones were not handed over were victims of a deliberate operation to ensure only minimal numbers of deaths were reported. There was no dignity for the dead and no denying who was, in part, clearly culpable.

~

Virtually all attempts to investigate the police's role in 1984 have been curtailed. The first official inquiry into their role began in 1985 and was headed by Ved Marwah, who was an inspector general of Special Branch. Early on, attempts were made to halt Marwah's investigation in the High Court by several police officers, including the deputy commissioners of police in South and East Delhi, Chander Prakash and Sewa Dass. They failed to stop him and Marwah continued with his probe into the actions of his colleagues.

In an arduous three-month process, documents were gathered from individual police stations, the police control room and the commissioner's control room, and the interviewing of eyewitnesses undertaken. But when Marwah was about to question senior officials – namely the capital's lieutenant governor and its police commissioner at the time of the massacres – he was ordered to stop by his superior, Police Commissioner S. S. Jog. No explanation was given but Marwah claims it was 'due to political pressure as the report would have been an embarrassment for the Congress government'. His findings clearly pointed to the police being culpable of shielding the mobs in a cataclysmic failure of duty.

In 2013, Marwah was summoned to appear in court for defamation against police officers, including Chander Prakash. Although his was an official inquiry, the government has failed to defend Marwah or show any support.

A second inquiry into the role of the police was set up in 1987. The Kusum Mittal Committee identified seventy-two police officers involved in the violence. They found both Station House Officer Shoorveer Singh Tyagi of Kalyanpuri police station (who was described as a 'living shame') Deputy Commissioner Sewa Dass (similarly described as a 'slur' on the police) were responsible for the mass murders and destruction in the killing lanes of Trilokpuri due to their actions – firstly, by disarming Sikhs who had gathered together, and secondly, by standing by while the mobs went on the attack.

While recommendations were made for further investigations, none of the accused Kalyanpuri police officers were ever brought to justice, despite overwhelming evidence submitted by victims and journalists. Instead, the key suspects actually went on to gain higher office. Dass was promoted to special commissioner of Delhi police, and Tyagi stepped into the shoes of assistant commissioner of police.

Other senior officers shrouded in guilt were also rewarded for their fealty to their political masters. Nikhil Kumar, Additional Commissioner of Police, later become head of the National Security Guard before taking on the governorships of Nagaland and Kerala. Hukam Chand Jatav was accused by the station house officer of Patel Nagar police station of refusing to act even after being alerted to the murders and arson taking place in Karol Bagh by journalists.

The Kusum Mittal Committee summed up his role as 'questionable, partisan and inexcusable'. Despite this, he was allowed to remain as additional commissioner of police until July 1985.

I I

Where was the Army?

As the fourth largest army in the world, and with its headquarters in Delhi, India's army was more than capable of dealing with the failing law and order situation compounded by a complicit police force.

India retains clear operational procedures in times of civil unrest. Curfews are declared and military units deployed as the situation demands – nowhere are such standards more keenly adopted than in the nation's capital.

The military had previously taken to the streets to quell communal violence following independence in August 1947. As police forces came under extreme pressure to cope, India's first Prime Minister, Jawaharlal Nehru, acted swiftly to try to reduce the impact of the disturbances. He deployed the army and issued a 'shoot-to-kill' policy against rampaging mobs. For Nehru, communalism was as dangerous to India as fascism; the violent actions conducted by dissidents and agitators were a threat to the cohesion of the new country and he was keenly aware that his Congress Party was not immune to this threat. In the face of similar threats to human life four decades later, his grandson's government would act in a very different way.

~

As the violence spiralled out of control in Delhi and across northern India, calls for the army came repeatedly and from several quarters. By the evening of 31 October it became increasingly apparent to South Delhi's deputy commissioner of police, Chander Prakash, that the use of military force would be necessary. The additional commissioner of police, Gautam Kaul (a cousin of the prime minister) refused the recommendation on the grounds that 'a meeting had already taken place sometime earlier in the prime minister's house, where the home minister was also present, and a decision had been taken not to impose curfew and call out the army at that stage'.

That same evening, Home Minister P. V. Narasimha Rao (who would himself become prime minister in the early 1990s) appeared 'indifferent' according to two senior lawyers who urged him in person to act to prevent a looming massacre. The home minister left them with an uninspiring assurance that he would be 'looking into this matter'.

The next day an opposition MP rang both the home minister and Shiv Shankar, a minister in the new cabinet who was also a confidante of the Gandhi family, to inform them of the increasingly worrying situation and the need for a military response. The ministers reassured the caller that the army would be summoned imminently and that a curfew was to be imposed.

A Sikh brigadier, A. S. Brar, who was then commandant of the Rajputana Rifles Regimental Centre in Delhi, described the unwillingness of the civilian authorities to deploy the army that was under the command of Major General J. S. Jamwal, General Officer Commanding of Delhi area. As a precaution he had ordered 1,600 men of the 15th Sikh Light Infantry back to the capital from Meerut the previous day. They arrived at their Dehli barracks at 11pm. Of the total of just over 6,000 soldiers now at Jamwal's disposal, just over half were controlling Teen Murti House, where Indira Gandhi's body lay in state, or surrounding the route to the cremation ground. The remainder were theoretically available for duty at flashpoints across the capital. Jamwal's orders to deploy came the following morning but were initially limited to only the central and southern districts of the capital. This left Delhi's four other districts without military coverage until that order was given to patrol them on 3 November.

In charge of military patrols in South Delhi was a Sikh major whose troops soon became involved in an altercation with a man who identified himself as a senior intelligence officer. He questioned why the army was there and warned them that they had no authority to intervene. The individual was chased away but, within an hour, the major was ordered to back to the cantonment where his men were confined to barracks. No investigation has ever been conducted as to the identity of the intelligence officer.

Brigadier Brar was also facing problems. Repeated requests to army headquarters to send out the 3,000 troops at his disposal – in order to deal with the 'distress' calls that were continuously being made to his office – were largely met with a wall of indifference. The reason appeared to be due to a lack of core logistical support – in a a clear breach of protocol no effort had been made to set up a joint control room at any point during those crucial first days. Consequently, coordination was made impossible between the commissioner of police, the army commander and the lieutenant governor (who held joint responsibility for law and order in Delhi with the home minister). This would in part explain how it was possible for the commissioner of police, Subhash Tandon, to later feel able to directly contradict Brigadier Brar by claiming that there were not enough army personnel available to deal with the situation.

Recalling this period of utter confusion, celebrated war veteran Lieutenant General Aurora, himself a Sikh, expressed bewilderedment of the fact that the home minister failed to make any attempt either to contact Major General Jamwal in order to 'draw a plan for controlling the violent situation prevailing in the city'. According to Aurora, Rao knew Jamwal was in Delhi and was therefore 'grossly negligent in his approach,' and his inaction 'clearly reflected his connivance with perpetrators of the heinous crimes being committed against the Sikhs and their families with impunity'.

Brigadier Brar's soldiers complained to him about the lack of information from, and coodination with, the police. They were being sent to places where little violence had occurred, or where the murderers had already left death and destruction in their wake. One army officer had even been handed a pre-1974 map of the city, which excluded the resettlement colonies in East Delhi where the most horrific acts of violence were taking place.

Brar did manage to extend a helping hand to some families by utilising his regiment's mess hall as a refuge but was 'unceremoniously' transferred out of Delhi as a result. He later regretted how his 'biggest crime was that I was stupid enough to interfere with state-sponsored terrorism'.

~

It was on 2 November that the Indian press began reporting on the army's deployment, and the introduction of a curfew and the implementation with immediate effect of a shoot-at-sight policy. In reality, the deployment was lacklustre and ineffectual. In South Delhi that afternoon, an army convey was seen passing through a road block on a main road guarded by a hundred armed men. As the convoy approached, the mob temporarily retreated a short distance to allow it to pass through before regrouping to intimidate a peace march that had just arrived.

The next day, activists from prominent human rights groups and opposition MPs descended on the prime minister's residence to plead for army protection for the survivors of the Trilokpuri massacre in East Delhi. The delegation met with Arun Nehru who gave the go ahead for a military deployment, but being limited to patrolling the streets it fell short of what was required. This was in sharp contrast to how the situation was being managed at around the same time on the streets of Amritsar in Punjab. Soldiers and policeman were posted at every street corner, in every bazaar and neighbourhood and curfew was imposed every night until dawn. Veteran journalist Pranay Gupte witnessed the Indian army roaring down the city's streets, soldiers walking with their semi-automatic weapons 'pointed warily at passers-by'.

One senior official who was in no doubts as to why the army wasn't deployed sooner was the lieutenant governor of Delhi, P. G. Gavai. He later claimed that he asked Police Commissioner Tandon to call in the army in the morning of 1 November, just as the carnage was beginning. But he knew the government had deliberately delayed the order: 'The sequence of events clearly tells a tale. Political authorities purposely wasted time in keeping with their nefarious design to teach Sikhs a lesson'. As a non-Congress, lower caste official, Gavai was resigned to the strong possibility of being 'made a scapegoat to shield the higher-ups'.

~

Sikhs in the armed forces also came under attack – their proud military tradition and years of distinguished service for the motherland failing to shield them from the fury of the murderous attack.

On 1 November, a young officer Bhupinder Malhi was travelling on the Jhelum Express to Delhi when a mob stormed the train. Armed men began a methodical search for Sikhs in each compartment. Malhi and other army officers tried in vain to reason with them. They attacked several Sikh officers, stabbing to death a Captain Gill of the 89th Armoured Regiment and pulverising another, who was found hiding under his berth, with iron rods. A young officer with his newly-wed wife narrowly escaped becoming a target by shearing his hair and cutting his beard before he had been spotted.

Attacks on both junior and high-ranking Sikh officers also occurred at Tughlakabad and Nangloi railway stations en route to Delhi. The FIR detailing these attacks noted that the victims to the mayhem were 'serving Sikh defence personnel'. The Railway Protection Force, though present during the incidents, failed in its duty to protect the servicemen.

Retired Sikh officers also found themselves caught up in the carnage. On 1 November in the heart of Delhi, a mob several-thousand strong laid siege to the property of a decorated war hero. Manmohan Bir Singh Talwar had been a wing commander during the Indo-Pakistani war in 1971, in which he successfully led five airborne missions deep behind enemy lines. For his services to the country he was awarded India's second highest award for gallantry, the Maha Vir Chakra.

When violence broke out that morning, Talwar and his two sons prepared to defend themselves armed with a shotgun and hockey sticks against what was initially a small group of stone-throwing arsonists. Talwar appealed to their sense of patriotism by informing them of his military service. The gang was eventually persuaded to disperse by several of Talwar's Hindu neighbours, who stood firmly by the family throughout the ordeal.

However, it wasn't long before a second, larger, crowd formed outside of Talwar's gates. They had just set fire to a shop opposite and were now intent on continuing their rampage. Some tried to break into his ground-floor shop below his house while others incited Talwar to shoot at them. Again, the retired officer kept his cool and attempted to placate them by shouting nationalistic slogans: 'Long live Indira Gandhi', 'May Indira Gandhi live forever', 'May India remain undivided'. Incredibly, the crowd was persuaded to disperse once again by the Hindu neighbours.

But in the early afternoon two Delhi Transport Corporation buses parked up outside the property and dropped off several men who reorganised the mobs who now targeted the Talwar family and property with heightened intensity, raising the now-familiar chant: 'We will take blood for blood'. By 4pm the crowd had swelled to several thousand. They taunted the Hindus who were helping shield their Sikh neighbours with screams of 'Bring out the Sikhs'. Several men managed to break into the house and struck at Talwar with iron rods – that was when he fired his first shots into the crowds, who dropped back.

Amidst the baying mob Talwar noted the unmistakable presence of several policemen. Armed with pistols and rifles, they took occasional shots at him. Some even clambered up onto the neighbours' roofs from where they attempted to throw fireballs into the property.

The attack continued for several tense hours into the night until a senior police chief, Amod Kanth, turned up and told Talwar to surrender in exchange for police protection. He accepted the offer but was thrown into prison on a trumped up murder charge, while the mob was allowed to disperse. While incarcerated, the war hero who had acted in self-defence was forced to do menial work.

~

It took the authorities a staggering twenty-four years to finally admit that thirty-four Sikh soldiers had been killed in the immediate aftermath of Indira Gandhi's assassination. In the absence of an official investigation this figure has been disputed, with one retired army officer estimating that up to 200 Sikh soldiers fell victim. He accused the Congress government – which had prevented the army from revealing the names of the dead – of having dishonoured those unaccounted for as deserters.

12

The Big Lie

At the heart of New Delhi stands India Gate, the national memorial to the 70,000 soldiers of undivided India killed in action from 1914–21 primarily in the Great War. Adjacent is the Delhi Boat Club, which had become a hub for political rallies in the post-colonial era. In his first public rally as prime minister, Rajiv Gandhi spoke to thousands of his supporters here on the anniversary of his mother's birth – 19 November – just a fortnight after the massacres:

> Some riots took place in the country following the murder of Indiraji. We know the people were very angry and for a few days it seemed that India had been shaken. But, when a mighty tree falls, it is only natural that the earth around it does shake a little.

From his podium, the prime minister presented his casual justification for the mass murder of thousands of his fellow citizens: it was a natural phenomenon, spontaneous and tragic but only to be expected and nothing of any greater consequence.

Who was to blame? Well, according to the prime minister, it was those who were so stirred by the loss of a much beloved public figure that they let their anger get the better of them – it was, after all, these people who went to the streets and 'rioted' for four continuous days in villages, towns and cities spanning the world's largest democracy. It was they who somehow arranged to bus themselves into Sikh neighbourhoods, procure plentiful supplies of tyres, kerosene and phosphorus, colluded with the police and delayed the calling in of the army. And it was of course these very same people who chose not to subsequently investigate the crimes.

There were no words of comfort to the victims or to condemn the crimes inflicted upon them. Instead, the prime minister commended the mobs for ending the violence, which somehow demonstrated to the world that India was a genuine democracy.

His incongruous choice of language was not only designed to point the blame as far away from his Congress party as possible, it also helped reinforce the official narrative that would be repeated for years to come.

~

When he turned on the television on the morning of 1 November, retired chief justice of the Punjab and Haryana High Court, Ranjit Singh Narula, watched the live scenes outside Teen Murti House where the former prime minister lay in state.

He had tuned in to the state-owned television station, Doordarshan – the only TV channel then available in India – and noticed two conspicuous men, Youth Congress workers, amidst the clamouring crowds spewing hate-filled slogans – 'We will take blood for blood!', 'Sikhs are the nation's traitors!' – as high-ranking government and police officials looked on. At one point during the day a forty-second segment of footage showed the 'blood for blood' slogan being repeated eighteen times. According to the former chief justice, no one present stopped the chanting of these inflammatory slogans, which were well within earshot of the new prime minister, Rajiv Gandhi. These highly-charged scenes seemed to continue to be aired throughout the day.

A similar point was made by Aseem Shrivastava, then a university student:

If someone had relied only on TV news and coverage in those days they couldn't possibly believe that almost 3,000 innocents were murdered in 4 days, most of them in broad daylight, in India's capital city. Not one image of the looting and arsoning, let alone of the killing, was ever shown on TV.

Radio was little better – broadcasts aired on the state-owned All India Radio emphasised how Indira Gandhi's killers had been Sikhs. Initial reports on both television and radio painted the attacks as an 'exchange of fire', giving the erroneous impression that there was fighting between two communities.

The potential impact of this kind of skewed reporting was significant. Audiences nationally for Doordarshan and All India Radio at the time were around 250 million and 35 million respectively. What they transmitted as news to a population with a high rate of illiteracy was hugely significant. They held the power to shape the nation's mood, particularly when wielded as a tool of propaganda.

The Congress government had previously employed state media to spread their biased narrative during the Emergency, when civil liberties were curtailed and the press heavily censored. Mrs Gandhi had instructed her minister for information and broadcasting to monitor the scripts for all radio and television news bulletins.

Newspapers also had their coverage strictly controlled in order to present the prime minister's government positively. When it came to the reporting of opposition rallies, severe restrictions were imposed.

By controlling the airwaves and press in that pre-internet age, the government had the power to dictate the official story with its own barrage of propaganda to shape the perceptions of millions.

That same desire to control the narrative was evident in the lead up to Operation Blue Star in June 1984. Shortly before the Indian army began its offensive, all foreign journalists were escorted out of Punjab. A media blackout was imposed and the Indian press corps ordered out of the area. As the tanks rolled back from the rubble-strewn precincts of the Golden Temple complex, Mrs Gandhi imposed a two-month ban on reporting within Punjab. During that period her government's *White Paper on the Punjab Agitation* took centre stage in the battle for the hearts and minds of an agitated Indian populace.

Released on 10 July 1984, it entirely absolved the government of blame. The decay in law and order, it surmised, was owing to a toxic mix of weak local political leadership, secessionist agitations, terrorist groups, the stockpiling of arms and ammunition in Sikh places of worship (most prominently the Golden Temple complex in Amritsar), the committing of acts of murder, sabotage, arson and loot, and evidence of the influence of external forces that harboured a deep-rooted desire for the disintegration of India. Also given a dishonourable mention were criminals, smugglers, Naxalites and other 'anti-social' elements that took advantage of the situation for their own ends.

In essence, the *White Paper* served as a bulwark against the spread of public sympathy for the Sikh cause in the wake of an unprecedented attack on their most holy and frequently visited shrine.

~

On the whole, India's newspapers adopted their government's stance during November 1984. Although they did report on the violence, they focused on Indira Gandhi's death, the happenings at Teen Murti House where she lay in state and her cremation. They also self-censored their stories and unquestioningly adopted government briefings.

Only *The Indian Express*, which had a reputation of acting as a champion of the truth, stood alone, devoting special attention to covering the impact on the Sikh victims during and after the violence. Viewed as pro-victim, several of its employees were in fact beaten up by the mobs.

The Indian Express had refused to fall in line, along with *The Statesmen*, when the media was heavily censored during the Emergency. By way of protest against the imposition of emergency rule, they had left the first edition of their editorial pages blank. In the face of strong government censure, *The Indian Express*'s continued its anti-establishment stance with its coverage of Operation Blue Star. By early June 1984, it had racked up twenty-seven registered censorship violations.

It was first alerted to the massacres in Trilokpuri in East Delhi on 2 November when a survivor, Mohan Singh, escaped and made it to *The Indian Express* offices. The next day, its journalists were also dispatched to find out about the horrific killings at Sultanpuri in the north-western part of Delhi.

With reporters on the ground, they were able to counter one of the most outrageous narratives spun by the government – the mounting death toll.

A key figure in this deception was the home secretary, M. M. K. Wali. At a press conference on 1 November, he insisted that most of the violence consisted of arson and that few personal attacks had occurred – in what seems an outrageous statement he even claimed that only two people had been confirmed killed in New Delhi.

On 4 November, soon after he had been sworn in as Delhi's new lieutenant governor, he revised the number of deaths to 458. *The Indian Express* had already contradicted these pitifully low figures, reporting on 2 November that in two incidents in Delhi alone there were already over 500 dead including '200 bodies lying in the police mortuary at Tis Hazari' and 'at least 350 bodies on one street in Trilokpuri'.

However, many years later one of its reporter's, Sanjay Suri, would acknowledge that jounalists including himself had got it badly wrong, reporting in the hundreds when at least 3,000 had already been killed in the capital alone.

The government vehemently dismissed the coverage, as well as allegations of Congress involvement, as 'opposition' propaganda. Congress Party headquarters published a statement on 6 November stating that the allegations that their members were involved in the violence was 'utterly malicious'. On the same day, most likely anticipating further bad press, the government banned both Indian and foreign journalists from entering the relief camps.

But when it came to reporting the mass rapes, even *The Indian Express* was silent, despite journalists having heard victims' accounts first-hand. According to Suri, his editor decided not to print anything on the rapes to avoid an already tense situation becoming worse.

In this regard, the paper was, in effect, toeing the government's line, which was to clamp down on the reporting of what it deemed 'inflammable material' that could 'excite passions in the country'. When Wali addressed a gathering of international journalists, he gave the following rationale for the government's tough stance: 'You have your right, but if you are doing something that is sensitive, we have a right to prevent it'.

Meanwhile despite the national clampdown, word of the astonishingly brutal mass killings was being reported across the globe. In the UK, Michael Hamlyn's front-page article in *The Times* of 3 November described how Sikhs were 'butchered in mob attacks on trains to Delhi' and recorded that the number of deaths from 'intercommunal incidents' had risen to 500. On 8 November, the paper ran his sensational story, 'Congress Party for violence against Sikhs', which quoted opposition leaders in India who had identified Congress MPs as being behind the carnage.

But these graphic accounts of Congress complicity could do little to dent the official story. The morning after this story was run, Geoffrey Howe, the UK's foreign secretary, spoke in parliament of the 'the senseless, cowardly assassination of the Indian Prime Minister, Mrs. Indira Gandhi', yet completely neglected to mention the massacres. Instead, he voiced his disgust at 'the tiny minority of people here who have sought to exploit, and—still more shocking—to rejoice at, this evil deed'. It was left to the Liberal MP, Russell Johnston, to point out that the 'tragedy' of Mrs Gandhi's death had led to 'a ghastly series of riots and murders'. This description of the situation was almost identical to Rajiv Gandhi's as articulated ten days later at the Boat Club.

~

The term 'riot' to describe the massacres soon gained currency and has been used – sometimes in its modified form of 'anti-Sikh riots' – almost exclusively by the media, politicians, activists and academics ever since.

A riot, though, is normally defined as a violent disturbance of the peace by a crowd. In the Indian context it is usually framed as a communal clash between two or more communities resulting in damage to property and loss of life, as in the predominantly Hindu-Muslim riots during Partition.

But in the events of November 1984, only Sikhs were looted and murdered. Where the violence was at its most fierce, the attacks were systematic and organised, aimed at wiping out Sikhs and Sikh neighbourhoods. In these instances, the perpetrators made their intentions known through public pronouncements calling for the eradication of as many Sikh males as possible. The level of physical and sexual violence inflicted ensured that even those who survived would be damaged for years to come.

Some commentators indeed went as far as classifying the violence as genocidal in nature, as the victims were only targeted because they were Sikhs. According to one academic who had studied the Punjab situation in the 1980s, a clear pattern was evident:

> Both the explicit targeting of *amritdhari* [initiated] Sikhs as traitors following Operation Blue Star and the clear earmarking of Sikh residences and businesses in the post-assassination carnage speak to an incipient genocidal campaign.

Differing from the Holocaust and more recent internationally recognised genocides such as in Cambodia and Rwanda, smaller scale atrocities aimed at exterminating a section of a group, whether men, women or children, in a given area, have come to be defined as genocidal massacres. When unleashed by a state to deal with a 'troublesome' minority, they become devastating weapons.

Thus, the use of the word 'riot' appears to have been deliberately chosen by the Congress government to absolve itself from any responsibility for the organised violence. Simultaneously it helped draw attention, including from the international community, away from the catastrophic level of one-sided violence that was unleashed, in what was in effect an anti-Sikh genocidal massacre.

~

The Indian government was quick to apply its powers of censorship against material deemed politically too sensitive. One of the earliest targets was monthly political magazine, *Surya*. It had been founded Maneka Gandhi, Mrs Gandhi's Sikh daughter-in-law, in the late 1970s and was widely regarded as having helped positively re-brand the Gandhi image after Congress's post-Emergency election losses. When it published a stark front cover of three burning Sikh corpses, the Home Ministry ordered the removal of all copies from newsstands the day they appeared.

On 12 November, the government, increasingly worried about the reaction in Punjab, decided to ban all periodicals, newspapers or leaflets carrying any news of the killings and rapes in the capital and the rest of the country. When journalist James Mann of *The New York Times* travelled to Punjab to interview people, he was arrested, threatened with lengthy imprisonment and his equipment confiscated.

Within a fortnight of the massacres, two human rights organisations, The People's Union for Democratic Rights and the People's Union of Civil Liberties, published a damning report based on their joint investigations. *Who are the Guilty* catalogued witness testimonies highlighting the Congress Party's involvement in the crimes.

It was later translated into Punjabi and released by the Association for Democratic Rights. When a second Punjabi edition was released in February 1985, it was duly banned in Punjab, which was then under president's rule. Its publisher, Professor Jagmohan Singh, was charged for 'waging war against the nation'. It remained a banned publication as late as 2014.

The world's largest film industry was also not immune. Bollywood audiences had to wait two whole decades before depictions of the events could be shown in cinemas. *Amu* by Shonali Bose (who had worked in relief camps following the massacres) told the fictional story of a young woman discovering how her own family had suffered during the massacres. The release was initially delayed for three months while the Indian Censor Board went through it with a fine-tooth comb, finally passing it for release in December 2004. However, five lines of audio referring to the complicity of politicians and police were cut from the film and a member of the censor board, the actor Anupam Kher, was reportedly dismissed for initially passing it. The film was eventually given an 'A' (adult only) certificate by the censors, who argued that 'young people do not need to know' about what took place in November 1984.

~

The year 2004 was also one in which the octogenarian Sikh historian and journalist, Khushwant Singh, wrote a heartfelt article reflecting on the aftermath of the violence he had witnessed two decades earlier. He recalled the heavily-biased reporting in the Indian press, opining how N. C. Menon, who succeeded Singh as editor of *The Hindustan Times*, had asserted that Sikhs 'had it coming to them'. Equally extreme, thought Khushwant Singh, was Girilal Jain's editorial in *The Times of India*, in which he was able to rationalise the violence, since 'the Hindu cup of patience had become full to the brim'.

Jain was well-known as an ardent follower of Indira Gandhi, even during the Emergency. He expressed sympathy towards Hindu nationalism and became a vocal supporter of the Hindutva, or Hindu hegemony, movement, as shown by his welcoming of the construction of a Hindu temple on the site of a mosque at

Ayodhya. Hindu nationalists eventually demolished the mosque in 1992, an act that led to an outbreak of local communal violence that spread to other parts of India, resulting in over 200 deaths. Before Jain retired in 1988, Khushwant Singh had accused him of demonstrating an increasingly 'anti-Muslim, anti-Christian and anti-Sikh bias' in his editorials.

In spite of these strong personal beliefs, in his editorial on 2 November 1984 entitled 'Quelling the flames', Jain could not deny what was happening in Delhi and across India. The mobs that were 'systematically burning' Sikhs were made up of 'mostly educated people' alongside 'anti-social elements'. 'The people know the truth,' he said, 'they do not depend on newspapers to tell them the facts.'

Jain followed this with an even more powerfully worded editorial on 7 November: 'Identify and Punish'. In it, he referred to the 'victims of the communal holocaust' and hinted at the power of propaganda that was driving a wedge between Hindus and Sikhs: 'Some of us have been known to have "seen" things which have never existed... Many of us have a predisposition to believe what we are told and to circulate these things'. The police, he argued, had to be pressured into doing their duty by Rajiv Gandhi yet were facing interference from Congress councillors and MPs. In addition, some members of the Youth Congress were to blame for the violence, which contained 'lumpens who recognise no moral law and tend to go berserk at the slightest opportunity'. Jain concluded that the onus was on Rajiv Gandhi to be courageous and not 'allow gangsters to seek asylum in his party... [or] to meddle with the enforcement of law and order'.

~

In 1987, Mumbai-born author Salman Rushdie was in India to make *The Riddle of Midnight*, his 'State of the Nation' documentary to coincide with country's 40th anniversary since independence. His interviews with India's 'Midnight's Children' – people who were themselves born at the same time as the new nation and shared its fortieth birthday – included a Sikh widow who had witnessed the murder of her husband and children at the hands of the mobs. They had, in Rushdie's words, exacted 'revenge' upon 'the entire Sikh community' for the assassination of Mrs Gandhi.

During the production of this particular segment, Rushdie was taken aback by the behaviour of the Indian authorities – they went to great lengths to prevent his crew filming any of the widows or any scenes related to the massacres that had so blighted their lives. Fortunately, an audio recording was made and used in the final cut. In lieu of video footage, a series of still images of several widows was used in a montage, which Rushdie felt was, if anything, 'even more powerful than the moving image would have been'.

When the Indian High Commission in London realised that Channel 4 were planning on airing the documentary which included the widow's testimony, it reacted angrily and attempted to prevent the broadcast. At the time, the commission was headed by none other than P.C. Alexander, former principal secretary to Mrs Gandhi and her son, Rajiv. Channel 4 stood its ground and the broadcast went ahead without any cuts.

The segment began with Rushdie's narration:

> The massacre of Delhi's Sikhs in November 1984 and the government's subsequent failure to prosecute the killers did more to alienate the Sikh community than even the attack on the Golden Temple. Yet the Indian authorities tried to prevent us from including the Sikh woman with whom this film ends, and who is now too frightened of her government to be named. Once again, the argument was to show such things would be counterproductive. But this anonymous voice is only one of thousands, and when such grief cannot be spoken or addressed, terrorism can only increase.

Then, in what one reviewer regarded as the documentary's 'most moving moment', a woman referred to only as 'R' (for fear of reprisals) spoke out:

What kind of justice is it when these government-supporting killers go free? They're not arrested, even those whose names have been reported. I say that those who have done this should be caught. Be they Sikhs, Muslims, Untouchables or whoever. They should be punished, but the government's dogs protect themselves.

I no longer have the strength to go on. I am so full of pain and sorrow. May God punish those who have done this to us. I ask the government: why do we continue to suffer?

We want justice, nothing else.

Rushdie would later reflect on how

it was astonishing that – as an aspect of the cover-up of the ruling party's involvement in the atrocities, during which many thousands of Sikhs died – the Indian government had tried to suppress the testimony, not of a terrorist, but of a victim of terrorism.

As Rushdie noted, the Sikhs had been the most patriotic of India's minorities until the trauma of 1984 changed everything.

13

The Accused (I):
All the Prime Minister's Men

One of the earliest allegations of Congress complicity was published in *The New York Times* on 4 November. The article, filed the day before by Barbara Crossette while reporting from the killing fields of Trilokpuri, noted how middle-class Sikhs and opposition politicians laid the blame on Congress Party members for inciting the killers at the local level.

On 8 November in *The Times*, Delhi correspondent Michael Hamlyn's article, 'Opposition leaders blame Congress Party for violence against Sikhs', included an interview with former prime minister Chaudhary Charan Singh. An erstwhile Congress politician who had been an outspoken critic of Nehru's economic policies and was jailed by Indira Gandhi during the Emergency, he told Hamlyn that Congress Party legislators had 'incited people they had brought in from the outskirts to burn, loot and if possible murder Sikhs'.

The names of those considered responsible first appeared in a joint report released by the People's Union for Democratic Rights and People's Union for Civil Liberties on 19 November 1984. In *Who are the Guilty*, it was claimed that activists had been informed by both Hindus and Sikhs (many of whom had been Congress supporters) that 'certain Congress (I) leaders played a decisive role' in organising the violence. The report named sixteen politicians alleged to have instigated violence or protected alleged criminals, and thirteen police officials alleged to have neglected their duty and having aided or participated in the violence.

Shortly after the Congress Party's landslide victory in the December 1984 election, social activist Amiya Rao estimated in a report published by Citizens for Democracy that at least 150 of the ruling party's members – including leaders, MPs and city councillors – had played an active role in what she described as 'not an ordinary holocaust [but] an organised orgy'. The killings, she contended, were scheduled to start on 1 November following a series of meetings held the previous night around Delhi at which Congress leaders gave the 'final touches' to the plan that had already been prepared 'with meticulous care'.

~

One of the key figures present at these clandestine gatherings was Arun Nehru, a distant cousin of Rajiv Gandhi's who had left his job in the private sector to enter politics at the behest of Indira Gandhi. In the Congress comeback in 1980 he was elected as an MP for the Rae Bareli constituency in the northern state of Uttar Pradesh, then a stronghold for his party. He became a key advisor to the Gandhi family, playing a pivotal role in developing and implementing Operation Blue Star in June 1984.

Rumours have circulated for decades about Nehru's key role in the organisation and implementation of the November 1984 massacres. A civil servant, who had the night before saved a Sikh motorcyclist and his father, went to see Nehru on 1 November. When he demanded that the army be deployed, Nehru's demeanour was 'frighteningly casual' as he explained that he and the Congress party were doing everything they could.

Darker and even more disturbing allegations were levelled by those with connections in India's defence and intelligence communities. According to one source, the massacres had perversely been codenamed 'Operation Shanti' (*shanti* being Hindi for 'peace').

It was initially planned for around 8 November to coincide with the birth anniversary of the first Sikh Guru, Guru Nanak – at such a time large gatherings of Sikhs at gurdwaras across the country would make for easy targeting.

However, the assassination on 31 October offered the opportunity to bring the killings forward. The source claimed that Arun Nehru took command of the operation and issued directives to Congress members of parliament, councillors and Youth Congress workers. Delhi police were to either stand aside or assist where needed.

The most damning revelation, though, came in 2014. The former petroleum secretary, Avtar Singh Gill, recalled how he had been warned about the violence in the morning of 1 November. A hotelier and friend of Rajiv Gandhi's by the name of Lalit Suri told him what he knew: 'Clearance has been given by Arun Nehru for the killings in Delhi and the killings have started'. He went on to describe how the gruesome plan was to be implemented:

> The strategy is to catch Sikh youth, fling a tyre over their heads, douse them with kerosene and set them on fire. This will calm the anger of the Hindus.

Suri warned Gill to remain vigilant even though his name was not on the Delhi gurdwara voting lists: 'They have been provided this list,' cautioned Suri. 'This will last for three days. It has started today; it will end on the third'. According to intelligence sources, Nehru had overseen the gathering of voting lists in the lead up to Operation Blue Star to help contain any backlash from Delhi's Sikh community once it had taken place.

~

Prior to Operation Blue Star, Nehru had discretely sounded out associates with Sikh connections about the possible repercussions of a military assault on the Golden Temple of Amritsar. Another senior Congress politician who had done the same was Hari

Krishan Lal Bhagat.

Teetotal and a strict vegetarian, Bhagat was a political big-hitter with close connections to Indira Gandhi. Following a stint as the capital's deputy mayor, his rise in the 1970s saw him become one of the most important personalities in Delhi's political scene. He held several ministerial positions, and by 1984 he was serving as the minister of Information and Broadcasting.

During the anti-Sikh pogroms, he was one of the most visible senior Congress minister involved. Eyewitnesses in his East Delhi constituency reported seeing him over the four days inciting people to commit murder, distributing money to mob leaders even leading some of the gangs himself.

On his way home after the day's work around 8pm on 31 October, a Hindu vegatable seller, Sukhan Singh Saini, joined a crowd of men near his home in Shakarpur. He recognised those present, especially Bhagat, whom he knew well. The minister was handing out bundles of rupees to the ringleaders with instructions to 'keep these two thousand rupees for liquor and do as I have told you'. Bhagat assured them: 'You need not worry at all. I will look after everything'. After warning a Sikh friend early the next morning, Saini saw Sikhs being beaten in the streets by several of the men from the night before.

One of the widows, Ajay Kaur, filed an affidavit in 1984 naming Bhagat. She stated that on the night of 31 October, she saw him telling a crowd that the police would 'not interfere for three days. Kill every Sikh and do [your] duty to Mother India.'

Later on the night of 31 October, Bhagat was seen by Wazir Singh, a boy of eleven who lived with his grandmother in Himmatpuri (not far from the Kalyanpuri police station), coming out of the house of Congress worker, Rampal Saroj. He had just held a meeting with local party members, and as he left, they raised anti-Sikh slogans. The following morning, Wazir Singh noticed Saroj leading an armed mob about fifty-strong including several Congress workers.

It was clear to the boy that Bhagat had 'given instructions in the meeting to kill the Sikhs'. Saroj also took part in the massacre in neighbouring Trilokpuri.

Bhagat was next sighted on the morning of 1 November by Gurmeet Singh, a taxi stand owner and driver from Laxmi Nagar. Singh was among of group of a hundred armed Sikhs who had assembled at the local gurdwara to defend themselves against a similarly sized mob that had attacked their homes earlier on. Just after 11am a white Ambassador car approached at the head of a cavalcade of nearly 200 armed people yelling anti-Sikh slogans on scooters, motorbikes and tuk-tuks. It parked up nearby and, to Singh's surprise, Bhagat alighted from the car. He knew the minister well as he was a strong Congress supporter – he had even hired his taxi out for free for Bhagat's election rallies. As six policemen (who had up to that point been watching the mob at work) approached the minister, Bhagat asked them and the mob how it was that 'they' – pointing towards the Sikhs – had not yet been killed? Having incited the murderers, he got back into his car and drove off.

As Shital Singh tried to make his escape after his home near Gamri Village had been torched, he was surrounded by a large group of men at a crossroads. His brother Satu Singh (who had cut his own hair to avoid detection) saw him struck by a brick and fall to the ground. It was at this point that Bhagat emerged from the crowd. Wearing his distinctive black glasses, he gave the order to kill Shital Singh, spurring on the furious crowd with the words: 'He is the child of a snake, kill him, don't spare him, if you spare him, he will give a lot of pain'. Satu Singh then saw someone throw what looked like 'some chemical' on his brother's face, which ignited instantly. Next, a truck tyre doused with kerosene was thrown over him and set alight. As the fire caught hold, Bhagat was heard taunting his victim: 'call your Guru Gobind Singh, I want to see him, where is he?' Shital Singh replied: 'Guru Gobind Singh is with me… do whatever you want to do'.

Bhagat's role shifted to one of coercion in the months after the massacres, threatening victims or promising them incentives in order to coerce them to withdraw their statements naming him. Housing was offered to the residents of Block 32 in the Trilokpuri colony on several occasions in August 1985 in exchange for two dozen affidavits stating that no Congress workers were involved in the attacks. Others, such as Satnami Bai who had named Bhagat as instigating mobs, withdrew their allegations under duress.

One of those who has held out for three decades in the hope of seeing justice served is Darshan Kaur, a survivor of the Trilokpuri atrocities. On the night of the attack, as she had crouched down to take cover inside her house, she'd heard Bhagat egging on the assailants: 'Whatever you need – chemicals, powders, anything – I will give them to you'. They discovered her husband hiding in a small landing in the attic and dragged him into the street, where he was immolated. In total, she lost twelve members of her family that day.

Besides naming Bhagat, she also identified the local Congress leader Rampal Saroj as a chief instigator of the deadly crowds who was witnessed calling out the rallying cry 'No one should be spared'. Despite other witnesses withdrawing their statements, Darshan Kaur stood her ground, even when men sent by Bhagat offered her large sums of money in exchange for her silence. She has been physically attacked and intimidated in the years since but has refused all advances.

Bhagat was also implicated in the death of a Delhi police head constable, Niranjan Singh. He had been on duty at Shahdara railway station on 1 November until he was chased down and lynched, and his body set ablaze outside his house. The next day, his teenage son and son-in-law were also killed. Niranjan Singh's widow, Harminder Kaur, survived and filed a case against Bhagat and others in 1996. While the judicial process moved along slowly, she faced constant harassment from the police. As the evidence against Bhagat was deemed insufficient the case against him was dropped in 2000. However, three other people were eventually convicted for the murders in 2007.

~

Another of the prime minister's men was Sajjan Kumar. Initially a roadside tea seller and later a bakery owner, he was said to have been handpicked by Sanjay Gandhi to enter politics. In 1984, he was MP for the constituency of Mangolpuri in North East Delhi. Kumar was named by several survivors as presiding over the pogroms in a number of Delhi suburbs.

On 31 October, Sajjan's men canvassed homes in West Sagarpur, South West Delhi, to collect fifteen rupees from each household towards the construction of a new road. At the same time they also checked the ration cards of Sikh families. Come the morning the local gurdwara and Sikh-owned shops were burnt down before Sikh residents themselves also came under attack.

In a park in Sultanpuri, adjacent to Kumar's Mangolpuri constituency, Cham Kaur heard him address a gathering of local residents: 'Sikhs had killed Mrs Gandhi; therefore, you kill them, loot their goods and burn them alive'. Kumar was next spotted the following day personally directing mobs. Several witnesses also saw him heavily involved in the violence. Joginder Singh recognised Kumar and other Congress leaders (including Jai Kishan, a former Member of the Legislative Assembly) amongst the murderers as they dragged his cousin and other Sikhs from their homes: 'Sajjan was laughing and ordering the mob to search for Sikhs and kill them,' he recalled. 'I was a clean-shaven Sikh so they were unaware of the fact that I am a Sikh'. During this attack, Kumar kicked Kamla Kaur aside as she begged him to spare her husband and son. He was also accused by Bhagwani Bai of orchestrating the deaths of her sons, who were burnt in front of her under Kumar's orders.

On 1 November at Nangloi, again not far from his constituency, Kumar was seen inciting the crowd to attack Sikh homes. One of his intended victims was Gurbachan Singh, who had taken up a defensive position on the second storey of his house with his brothers:

> About ten police officials were also present at the spot and they were encouraging the mob to kill us. I saw

Sajjan Kumar, the then Congress MP of our area
standing amongst the mob and he was directing the
mob to attack us with more and more force and kill us.

After witnessing the killing of his father and two other members of
his wife's family, he and his brothers, who were armed with swords,
managed to cut their way through. When he tried to report the
murders at the local police station two days later, he was 'made
to fill out a pre-formatted FIR. In the blanks next to who led the
mob, the word "unknown" had been written'. Kumar's name was
never entered into police records.

On 2 November, Kumar was seen in a police jeep in Palam, South
West Delhi announcing: 'No Sikh should live. If anyone gives
shelter to Sikh families, their houses will be burnt'. That evening
he was seen in nearby Raj Nagar inciting the attackers 'to kill more
Sikhs'. At least 340 Sikhs were killed in Raj Nagar, an area covered
by Delhi Cantonment police station. The diary entries of the police,
though, tell a completely different story: 'end of the day 1st and 2nd
of November: all clear, nothing to report'.

~

Three decades on from the massacres, Jagdish Tytler, another of
Sanjay Gandhi's close associates and an active member in the
Congress Party's youth organisation, was specifically named in a
WikiLeaks American Embassy cable as having 'played a particularly
grotesque role, competing with local Congress Party leaders to
see which wards could shed more Sikh blood'. Jasbir Singh, the
witness who had heard the MP for the Delhi Sadar constituency
near Old Delhi rebuke his men for the 'nominal killing of Sikhs in
his constituency', had fled to the US after he had lost twenty-six
relatives in the carnage.

The alleged scolding dished out by Tytler exposes a sickening
arrogance:

Because of you, I am ashamed to look at Sajjan
Kumar's constituency in the north or H. K. L. Bhagat's

constituency in the east. Colony after colony of Sikhs has been destroyed but in my area so few Sikhs have been killed. I had promised that maximum Sikhs would be killed in my colony.

Tytler was also seen on the morning of 1 November by Surinder Singh, a Sikh *granthi* (scripture reader) of the Pul Bangash Gurdwara in North Delhi. As he watched from the safety of the top floor, he could see that Tytler was in control of a crowd armed with staffs and iron rods. On his command, they set fire to the building and killed three Sikhs inside:

> He incited the mob to burn the gurdwara and kill the Sikhs. Some people in the mob were carrying flags of Congress. They were raising slogans like 'We will take revenge', 'Sikhs are traitors', 'Kill! Burn!' Five to six policemen were also with the mob.

Surinder Singh made it to safety that night with the help of his Muslim neighbours.

A few days later, Tytler was further compromised when he burst into the office of police commissioner, Subhash Tandon, just as he was in the middle of a press briefing with Indian and foreign journalists. Tandon had just categorically denied the allegation that Congress MPs had tried to get their men, who had been jailed on suspicion of committing acts of violence, released. Just as he had finished stating that he had never received any calls or visits by any politician, Congress or otherwise, Tytler barged in along with three followers, demanding at the top of his voice: 'What is this Mr. Tandon? You still have not done what I asked you to do?' Realising the *faux pas* he said to the embarrassed commissioner: 'By holding my men you are hampering relief work'. To the bemused reporters he boasted: 'There is not a single refugee in any camp in my constituency. I have made sure that they are given protection and sent back home'. According to one of the journalists present, the incident left the commissioner speechless and them in no doubt about Congress interference in police work.

~

Another Congress MP who made a public show of his sway over the police was Kamal Nath. Again, he had close ties to the Gandhi family, having attended the Doon School (known as the 'Eton of India') with his friend, Sanjay Gandhi. He was elected as an MP in 1980 in the constituency of Chhindwara in the central state of Madhya Pradesh.

On 1 November 1984, Nath was accused of leading an armed mob that laid siege to Gurdwara Rakab Ganj, a major shrine in the heart of New Delhi only a few hundred yards from the nation's Parliament buildings. It is historically significant as it commemorates the spot where the ninth Sikh Guru's body was cremated following his execution by order of a Mughal emperor in 1675. A member of the gurdwara staff, Mukhtiar Singh, had seen an angry crowd approach and then begin pelting stones at the shrine and those inside its boundary walls. Delhi police officers were present but showed no interest in intervening. Within half an hour the crowd had swelled in size to around a thousand-strong. At noon an attempt was made to storm the building but staff and devotees collectively managed to push the mob back. An elderly Sikh devotee then decided to appeal for peace and approached the mob with folded hands. He was dragged out of the boundary and severely assaulted with stones. While he lay on the ground, white powder – most probably phosphorus – was thrown on his body causing it to catch fire. His son ran to attempt a rescue but, like his father, was also injured and set alight. The Sikhs managed to drag them, still alive, into the safety of the gurdwara but they died a few hours later for lack of medical treatment – the shrine being surrounded on all sides and the police unresponsive to calls for assistance.

Further attacks were mounted. With the assistance of several police officers the mob eventually succeeded in entering the sacred building. Mukhtiar Singh and others drove them back again, this time pelting the intruders with the same stones that had been hurled at them. Another tactic used to hold them back was the setting off of fire crackers with a gun-like launcher, which the mob mistook for actual gunfire. Still though, more attacks followed. In desperation one of the Sikhs fired his licenced pistol into the air. It was soon after this that a much larger force approached the gurdwara, Mukhtiar Singh clearly saw Nath and other Congress men including Vasant Sathe, former minister of Information and Broadcasting, at its head. According to him, the police fired several rounds at those inside the gurdwaras after receiving instructions from Nath.

Observing from the street was crime reporter for *The Indian Express*, Sanjay Suri. He had set out that morning on his scooter and reached the gurdwara by following a combination of the columns of smoke that rose above the city and some tip-offs from police contacts. On arriving he saw Nath standing near to the front of the crowd, which was repeatedly surging forward as it attacked again and again. The police watched on, among them the additional commissioner of police, Gautam Kaul, who was carrying a bamboo shield. It was clear to Suri that the management of the crowd had been left to Nath – when he signalled, the crowd listened. This level of control led to Suri to conclude that they were Congress party workers who accepted him as their leader.

~

Lalit Maken, whose father-in-law, Dr Shankar Dayal Sharma, would later become India's president, was seen paying mob members a hundred rupees each plus a bottle of liquor during the carnage. The Delhi metropolitan councillor with a trade union background was reportedly seen giving instructions to those indulging in arson near Azadpur in North West Delhi from inside his white Ambassador car.

One of those reported to have used voter lists to identify Sikh targets was Dharam Dass Shastri, MP for Karol Bagh, a heavily commercial neighbourhood in West Delhi. One survivor who had fled to Amritsar following the attacks in Karol Bagh told a reporter for *The New York Times* that he had seen Shastri in action. 'I saw it happen, and I saw this man Shastri leading and directing the crowd,' said Jitinder Singh. 'He had lists.'

From roof of his house, Davinder Singh saw Shastri and a senior police officer provoking a mob to attack Sikhs. Nearby, electrical-shop owner Amrik Singh saw the minister ordering a large group of men to set Sikh properties and businesses on fire and to annihilate Sikh men, women and children. Their rampaging led them to also attack a local gurdwara, urinating on copies of the Sikhs' holy scripture.

A resident of Karol Bagh, Chuni Lal, overheard a local Congress worker – whom Shastri had visited at his home the night before – encouraging a group of youths to take revenge on Sikhs for the death of Indira Gandhi. He gave reassurances that the police had been instructed by Shastri not to arrest any Hindus who looted, committed arson or even killed Sikhs. Shastri was later seen in a heated exchange with police at the local police station, attempting to secure the release of 300 supporters who had been arrested for looting. The minister denied the allegation, insisting that he had 'only tried to gain the release of members of local vigilante groups that appeared across New Delhi to defend their neighbourhoods after the police failed to do so'.

One of the most high profile politicians to be embroiled was P. V. Narasimha Rao. This lawyer-turned-politician rose to prominence in the 1970s with several diverse ministerial portfolios in the cabinets of both Indira Gandhi and Rajiv Gandhi. As the minister of home affairs in November 1984, Rao was responsible for the maintenance of the nation's internal security, which included law and order. He was therefore responsible for the security of the country's citizens.

Several prominent individuals including senior politician (and later prime minister) Chandra Shekhar and Mahatma Gandhi's grandson, Rajmohan Gandhi, met Rao to personally urge him to call out the army. But his casual approach in handling the violence, repeatedly ignoring requests to deploy the army, shocked a delegation of several notable citizens – including future prime minister I. K. Gujral, war veteran General Aurora and the author Patwant Singh. As Rao played cool, nearly 200 houses in Block 32 of the Trilokpuri colony were being decimated.

Rao's decision, to choose party over duty, followed a call allegedly from the prime minister's office instructing him to do nothing about the killings that had just begun in what one commentator described as his 'vilest hour'.

Delhi's former lieutenant governor, P. G. Gavai, would later state publicly that this future prime minister of India 'hid like a rat' when the violence began to engulf large parts of the country. Throughout the entire period, he failed to visit even one of the affected areas.

14

The Accused (II):
The Prime Minister

Rajiv Gandhi was the eldest of Indira Gandhi's two sons. After attending the elite Doon School in Dehradun he went on to study engineering at Trinity College, Cambridge, and mechanical engineering at Imperial College London. However, he left both without completing his degrees and, after returning to India in 1966, he joined Air India as a commercial pilot. Unlike his younger brother, Sanjay, who was the political heir apparent of the Nehru-Gandhi dynasty, Rajiv showed no aspirations of following in the footsteps of his grandfather, Jawaharlal Nehru, and of his mother.

The catalyst to him becoming a reluctant prime minister was Sanjay's death in an airplane crash in 1980. Rajiv was persuaded to enter into the family business by his mother. He took up in earnest the political mantle thrust upon him in 1981 after winning the Amethi constituency in the northern state of Uttar Pradesh, the seat formerly held by his brother.

He viewed himself as a political moderniser who was determined to make India a player on the global stage. History, however, may well tell a different story. The genocidal massacres of November 1984 took place under his prime ministerial watch, and possibly with his actual or tacit approval or command. He prevaricated when others pleaded with him to call out the army to protect his

Sikh citizens, he attempted to justify and downplay the violence, and he shielded those who orchestrated it.

It is almost inconceivable to imagine that Rajiv Gandhi was unaware of the activities of the key members of his party for those four dark days. He had been general-secretary of the All-India Congress Committee (I) since 1982, had reorganised the party, presided over its training camps and was deeply involved in screening potential election candidates. He knew these cadres well enough; several were his own trained men – and it was no secret that they and some of the old guard (known as 'Sanjay's boys') had links with criminal gangs.

~

Some commentators have gone so far as asserting that Rajiv Gandhi may have encouraged the violence – one cited a conversation reported by a RAW intelligence operative on 31 October:

> Upon arrival at Palam airport in Delhi and hearing of his mother's assassination, Rajiv told those present, 'My mother has been shot dead. What are you doing here? Go, and take revenge. No turban should be seen'.

The prime minister was reported to have said other damning things at the airport. At a meeting of the National Executive of the Bharatiya Janata Party (BJP) during a review of reports from various states cataloguing the attacks against Sikhs, it came to light that Shyam Khosla, a senior journalist, and Krishan Lal Maini, former Punjab finance minister, had enquired from several unnamed senior government and military officials what had happened and why. They were told that at the airport, 'one of the senior officers had whispered something into his ears and Shri Rajiv Gandhi was heard saying "Yes, we must teach them a lesson"'.

While the anger at his mother's assassins was understandable, Rajiv Gandhi and those around him appeared to blame the entire Sikh community for the actions of two individuals. Shanti Bhushan, a former minister and senior advocate of the Supreme Court, was shocked when he tuned into Doordarshan to see the prime minister passively listening to the slogans calling for revenge.

Journalist Tavleen Singh had a similar reaction when she watched the broadcast of Rajiv Gandhi's first speech as prime minister:

> In a calm, emotionless voice, he said India had lost a great leader. Someone who was not just his mother but the mother of the country, or words to that effect. Then he stopped and stared sadly at the camera while Doordarshan showed shots of H. K. L. Bhagat and his supporters beating their breasts and shouting, '*Khoon ka badla khoon se lenge*.' Blood will be avenged with blood.

Pupul Jayakar, a cultural activist closely associated with Nehru-Gandhi family, immediately went to see Rajiv Gandhi to insist the army be deployed after a reporter informed her of the violence: 'Gurdwaras are being burnt down; crowds are dragging Sikhs by their hair out of their homes and making bonfires of them before our eyes'. Rajiv Gandhi asked Home Minister Rao as to what should be done but he remained silent. The prime minister then turned to Jayakar and asked her the same question. No stranger to speaking her mind, she reminded him that his mother would have called out the army by now and would not have allowed the butchery that was taking place. But no firm action was taken and the killings continued unabated and unchallenged for a further three days.

When *Observer* reporter Shyam Bhatia met Rajiv Gandhi at Teen Murti House on 2 November, he brazenly asked if the prime minister was aware that the attacks had resulted in the deaths of so many innocent Sikhs. His response was, 'What can I do? My mother's been killed'.

The president, Zail Singh, was unable to even get hold of the prime minister to raise his concerns. According to Zail Singh's press secretary, Tarlochan Singh, the prime minister did not respond to his telephone calls and 'neither the PM nor the Home Minister took any interest in defusing the situation or help[ing] the victims'.

As his citizens burned, it was become increasingly clear that Rajiv Gandhi was not fulfilling his constitutional or moral duties. Although he was understandably grieving, Nicholas Nugent, his biographer, would later write: 'Nobody, it seemed, had orders to seek out and try to prevent the holocaust that was taking place. Rajiv Gandhi seemed to be preoccupied with organising the funeral rites of his mother, and receiving the visiting dignitaries'.

~

By the second week of November, word began trickling out from victims, journalists and human rights activists of the very real possibility that members of his party – especially senior Congress figures in Delhi – had been deeply involved in the massacres. Several prominent party members, former ministers and army chiefs notified him of this in the hope that he would distance himself from the perpetrators.

Among those who attempted to communicate their concerns with the prime minister included a group of senior figures including the country's only marshal of the Indian Air Force, Arjan Singh, Lieutenant General Aurora, and I. K. Gujral. On 12 November, after waiting two hours to meet Rajiv Gandhi, they were informed by a messenger that the meeting could go ahead immediately if they wished to condole with him. When Aurora responded that they obviously wanted to express sympathy for the prime minister's loss but they also wished to tell him about the horrors endured by Sikhs and the need to punish the guilty, the meeting was abruptly cancelled.

The reason was apparent, as explained by Rajni Kothari, President of the People's Union of Civil Liberties at the time:

> The more one thinks about it, and examines the evidence, the more it becomes clear that Mr Rajiv Gandhi must also take the blame for the revenge following his mother's assassination. Gandhi not only knew of, allowed

and condoned the violence, he took advantage of it. He was advised that this was politics as usual, and he did not question this advice in any way.

During the 1984 election campaign, *The Indian Express* reporter Sanjay Suri probed the prime minister about the alleged involvement of Congress Party leaders. Gandhi's telling response was that evidence was found in one case and that individual had been punished.

The minister in question was Dharam Dass Shastri and his 'punishment' was not being allowed to run for re-election. Although the admission of a Congress leader having been involved was significant, Rajiv Gandhi had also sent a clear message - he was not prepared to take more than superficial action (Shastri was punished for 'political misdemeanour'). The encounter left Suri questioning why the prime minister had not taken further action; where was the legal inquiry into his own party members? He had squandered a precious opportunity to take a stand at that crucial moment in his career.

~

When the new Indian parliament opened in January 1985, the two houses adopted a common resolution expressing condolence for Indira Gandhi's death. No mention was made of the thousands of Sikhs who had been massacred in her name.

In his first interview as newly elected prime minister, Rajiv Gandhi told M. J. Akbar, founding editor of India's first weekly political news magazine, *Sunday*, that the killings were only extensive in those areas where the Sikhs were rumoured to have celebrated his mother's death by distributing sweets – in essence, they only had themselves to blame.

He also repeatedly dismissed calls for an inquiry stating that one would never be instituted as 'it would do more damage to the Sikhs, it would do more damage to the country by specifically opening this whole thing up again'. In April 1985, however, he grudgingly ordered a judicial inquiry into the violence as part of the Punjab Accord, driven not by the search for truth and justice but by political expediency to facilitate a settlement with the Akali Dal.

Those seeking the truth, like Lakhwinder Kaur, would just have to wait. When they came to kill her husband she was an eighteen-year-old mother of a five-month-old daughter and two months pregnant: 'It seemed easy for Rajiv Gandhi to say, "When a giant tree falls, the earth below shakes", she told a reporter twenty-five years later. 'Our trees were felled and we can still feel the tremors.'

15

The Accused (III):
The People

By overtly campaigning on an anti-corruption ticket in the December 1984 election, Rajiv Gandhi was implicitly admitting that his ruling Congress Party had a serious problem with fraud and arrogance.

It was known that he wanted to clean up his mother's party and rid it of 'hooligans' and *purana papi* – 'old sinners' in Hindi, which is shorthand for corrupt politicians. However, owing to his mother's centralised reign, and the subsequent atrophying of the party organisation, unsavoury characters who could help muster the vote and intimidate rival parties had still to be relied upon in the 1980s.

It has been asserted that the mobs who wrought destruction in November 1984 were mobilised by Congress-sponsored criminal gangs drawn in particular from Delhi's outer resettlement colonies where much of the most devastating violence occurred.

Some colonies like Trilokpuri had arisen during the Emergency when slum-dwellers – who had been evicted from the capital's *jhuggi-jhopri* (huts and shacks) clusters as part of a slum-clearance drive led by Sanjay Gandhi – were rehoused there.

In all, half a dozen slums were razed and their lower caste inhabitants – comprised primarily of 'untouchable' Hindu, but also some Muslim, factory labour, casual shop workers and the self-employed such as rickshaw pullers and hawkers – were forcibly re-located. Though these areas lacked water, electricity or proper drainage facilities, the provision of land and small concrete houses uplifted the perceived status and conditions of their new residents. This translated into a solid support base and vote bank for Indira Gandhi and the Congress Party.

In the case of their Sikh inhabitants, they had been already living on the sites of the resettlement colonies in what were effectively shanties. They predominantly hailed from the working-class Labana Sikh community whose Rajput ancestors were originally involved in salt trading, weaving string cots and transportation during the days of the British Raj. They had primarily migrated from Sindh to Rajasthan after Partition and, by the late 1960s they had begun resettling around Delhi in areas such as Trilokpuri, Nangloi, Sultanpuri, Geeta Colony, Patparganj and Mangolpuri. When the resettlement colonies were developed, the Sikhs found themselves living alongside the erstwhile slum-dwellers.

These areas were ripe for exploitation by Congress who financially supported the local underworld, mobilising them when needed particularly during elections. This toxic combination – Congress corruption, organised criminality and poor, illiterate potential mercenaries – helps explain the ease with which well-organised armed mobs were rallied so quickly. And it was clear that someone had mobilised them and given assurances that they would not face prosecution. How else could they have done what they did in daylight and so boldly in front of witnesses?

Some of those who participated were identified by survivors as hailing from the 'scheduled' castes – those 'untouchable' groups that have historically faced severe social and economic disadvantage – such as Chamars and Bhangis. Others, such as some of the local police, identified themselves with these communities, whilst a small number of poor Muslims were also known to have taken an active role in the atrocities.

The motivation for looting, raping and killing was driven in part by hatred of middle-class Sikhs in more affluent areas. Gujjar and Jat farmers, who had become prosperous overnight after having sold their land to the government to establish the resettlement colonies, now saw an opportunity to steal back their plots. For many, payment was forthcoming from gang masters and politicians, and there was always the opportunity for looting.

Yet they could not have acted without a degree of support – implicit and explicit – from members of the middle-classes, who either participated in, or ignored, the mass murders taking place under their noses. Some are even reported to have revelled in what they regarded as deserved punishment meted out to Sikhs.

Surviving film footage of the massacres, primarily shot by UK media organisations such ITN and BBC, lends credibility to this claim. From the recordings, thousands can be seem roaming the streets to hunt down Sikhs. Judging from their attire, they appear to come from all strata of Indian society. In the central and southern Delhi suburbs, members of the middle classes can be seen attacking Sikhs publicly on the streets. One commentator even recalled seeing an image of the owner of an elite boutique 'directing a gang of arsonists with his golf club'. Another accused middle-class Hindus of having 'nearly complete sympathy with the killing and lynching of Sikhs'.

~

While much of the violence in Delhi appears to have been conducted by villagers living on the capital's outskirts who had been transported into Sikh neighbourhoods by criminal gangs, the killers were not always strangers. Some victims have spoken of the deplorable complicity of some of their own neighbours.

Satpal Kaur of Nand Nagri in East Delhi witnessed the murders of both her parents and brother. Neighbours, who had assured the family that they would be protected, later arrived with a mob. They locked the family in their house, preventing their escape and, one by one, exterminated them all.

In some instances, neighbours permitted Sikh women to seek shelter but refused to allow any men. Somti Bai and her family hid in the house of a local politician in Trilokpuri. While he initially assured her that her sons were safe, he subsequently threw them out. All three sons were killed.

Other neighbours passive observed. An attack on an elderly man and his son in the middle-class colony of Shankar Garden in West Delhi was watched by swathes of neighbours from rooftops but no one was willing to intervene. After initially escaping the father took shelter in a neighbour's house, which then came under attack. On fleeing through a back exit he was caught by the mob who stoned him. His son was also caught and torched.

An anthropologist who worked with the widows of the massacres soon after the violence had abated found that in one housing block in Sultanpuri, communities protected one another, whereas in another block residents had turned on their Sikh neighbours. 'Neighbours did not help,' one survivor told her, 'since they were themselves the killers.'

Nanki Bai, a widow from Kalyanpuri, was adamant that all the attacks in her locality were committed by her neighbours.

> It's all lies that they were outsiders. No one was from outside. They were all from here. We went to the back lane to hide but nobody was willing to hide us. Now of course they're all saying that they helped a lot. The same people were killing and the same people were doing everything [else].

~

Justifications for the violence included the allegation that Sikhs had overtly celebrated Indira Gandhi's murder – specifically that they had distributed sweets and danced in jubilation. However, human rights activists who recorded interviews with survivors as well as other inhabitants of Delhi, has debunked these arguments. Of those questioned who purportedly 'knew' Sikhs had distributed sweets, not one person could give an actual instance of this having taken place. It transpired that on 31 October, some Sikhs were distributing sweets but had done so in anticipation of the coming birth anniversary of Guru Nanak, as was customary. They had stopped when they learnt of the assassination. That same day, Sikh students at Khalsa College in Delhi who had been practicing dance moves also stopped on hearing the news of Mrs Gandhi's death. Yet, there were no repercussions for a Hindu wedding procession that continued with typical pomp replete with a band that very same day.

Was there some confusion? Had an ITN news report on 31 October showing celebrations in Southall and Birmingham by some Sikhs, who were distributing sweets, setting off fireworks and drinking champagne, been attributed to those in Delhi? The Indian government was clearly aware of the broadcast as they had sent a message the next day to the British government expressing how they and the people of India were 'both indignant and distressed' by the scenes. Speaking to the press about these concerns before her departure to attend the funeral of Indira Gandhi, Margaret Thatcher condemned the 'outrageous behaviour of a tiny minority' of Sikhs in Britain who 'gloated' over her murder.

As commentators were quick to point out, nothing could justify the massacres – all Sikhs could not be held responsible for the actions of a few. In a television interview on 1 November, author Khushwant Singh, who had strong Congress leanings, had observed with trepidation how the tide had turned against Sikhs nationwide. The day before he had, on the advice of President Zail Singh, sought refuge to escape the mobs:

For the act of three Sikhs in killing Mrs Gandhi, it would seem that a community of over 13 million Sikhs are being held to ransom.

Rahul Roy, who had been a volunteer at the Farsh Bazar relief camp at Shahadra, the largest in Delhi, made a keen observation. Those who knew they were culpable 'escape the tag of being communal by putting the blame on the state. [The] state becomes some amorphous creature which can carry the blame and the people themselves stand exempted [of blame]'.

Indeed, by holding only government agencies to account, local residents who joined the ranks of the death squads could conveniently escape recognition, punishment and even their own sense of guilt.

Some Delhiites such as Shuddhabrata Sengupta, an artist and writer who witnessed Sikh men being burnt alive when he was sixteen, felt a deep sense of anger at what had taken place. He is not alone when he says he has 'never forgiven this city'.

Another was journalist Sanjay Suri. After Operation Blue Star and the November massacres, fears of a backlash against Hindus in Punjab were always raised but 'hardly a Hindu was attacked across Punjab. In 1984 I grew proud of Punjab, and ashamed of Delhi'.

16

Judicial Scandal (I): Misra

Communal violence has erupted on several occasions across independent India. From Malegaon (1967) in the west, to Jamshedpur (1979) and Nellie (1983) in the east, stretching north to Nonari and Sajni (1972), and southwards down to Hyderabad (1983), incidents largely relating to local political and economic issues between Hindu and Muslim communities have often led to bloodshed in the thousands. The worst cases occurred in Moradabad in Uttar Pradesh in 1980 and Nellie in Assam in 1983 in which approximately 2,000 were slaughtered in each incident. However, none were on a scale even remotely as large as 1984.

In the two decades preceding 1984, no fewer than ten judicial commissions had been appointed in the immediate aftermath of such incidents. The only exception was Malegaon, which experienced a delay of a month between the violence and the appointment of a commission following vociferous demands by certain human rights groups.

Nineteen-eighty four, however, sat in stark contrast, with the Congress government taking six months to appoint a commission. And when it eventually did, it was fraught with complications.

~

On securing victory in the December 1984 elections, Rajiv Gandhi came under pressure from a consortium of human rights organisations, Sikh associations and political parties including the Akali Dal Party, Citizens for Democracy, the People's Union for Democratic Rights (PUDR) and the People's Union for Civil Liberties (PUCL), to hold an official inquiry and to provide protection for survivors from harassment by the perpetrators.

These demands were encapsulated in a petition. The response from the commissioner of police, S. S. Jog, was to state that the Delhi police had already instituted an independent investigation, registered cases and made several arrests. When the matter was taken to court, Justice Dayal of the Delhi High Court dismissed the request and criticised those involved in the petition as merely seeking publicity and accused them of wasting the judiciary's time. The government also refused demands for an inquiry with the new prime minister stating that 'such an inquiry would not serve any purpose' and would 'do more damage to the Sikhs'.

Meanwhile in Punjab, tensions continued to simmer. The state had been under central government control, or president's rule, since October 1983. Settling this issue would be the first real test of Rajiv Gandhi's leadership skills. Political parties, including the Akali Dal, made it clear that an inquiry into the backlash after Indira Gandhi's death were 'a precondition for any attempt to diffuse the situation in Punjab'. Thus, any attempts by Rajiv Gandhi to resolve the Punjab crisis that had plagued his mother hinged on the appointment of an inquiry.

Arjun Singh, a former chief minister of the central state of Madhya Pradesh and confidante of the Gandhi family who was appointed governor of Punjab in March 1985, was tasked with solving these prickly issues. Gandhi also released several Akali Dal leaders from jail, including its president Harchand Singh Longowal, who had been incarcerated since the June 1984 attack on the Golden Temple complex. This conciliatory approach was a significant shift from the confrontationist methods employed up until then by the centre.

One of the least controversial parts of the resultant Punjab Accord was the agreement on 26 April 1985 that the central government would appoint a commission of inquiry with a twofold remit: to inquire into 'the allegations in regard to the incidents of organised violence' that took place in Delhi; and to recommend solutions to prevent such incidents recurring. Further pressure from the Akali Dal helped expand the inquiry's focus to include Kanpur in the northern state of Uttar Pradesh and Bokaro in the eastern state of Bihar (now in Jharkhand).

Rajiv Gandhi appointed Ranganath Misra, a sitting Supreme Court judge, as the inquiry's sole member. Justice Misra could boast of a long and distinguished legal career spanning over three decades before being appointed to the country's highest judicial forum in 1983.

On paper, therefore, all signs pointed towards the likelihood of a thorough and transparent investigation. The reality, though, would be quite different and far from satisfactory.

~

Serious shortcomings of the one-member Misra Commission of Inquiry became evident from the outset.

It was sluggish in gathering information whilst also facing a wall of non-compliance from those being investigated. On 5 November 1985, an entire year after the massacres had occurred, it had to order the Delhi Administration to co-operate so that the investigation could continue with its work.

It took ten more months before the report was submitted to government in August 1986. The government only placed the final report before parliament a further six months later in February 1987.

Critics regarded the inquiry as essentially nothing more than a cursory gesture by the government. Its strict terms of references meant that no individual could specifically be investigated. Out of 2,905 affidavits – sworn written testimonies made by survivors and witnesses – that were submitted, the Commission only selected 128, out of which only thirty – just one per cent of the total – were eventually used in the investigation. The PUDR argued that the basis for selection was never made clear, in particular why certain affidavits, which could have potentially contradicted the Commission's conclusions, were excluded.

Among the victim affidavits rejected outright, Misra refused to take testimony from journalists Rahul Kuldip Bedi and Joseph Maliakan of *The Indian Express*, who had been among the first outsiders to witness the aftermath in the killing lanes of Trilokpuri. Maliakan later revealed that he was called into the court chamber by an officer of the Commission in order to dissuade him from filing an affidavit as he 'had not suffered in the anti-Sikh pogrom'.

At times, relevant documents were either not produced or disallowed entirely. When they were brought out, they were not shown to the victims' representatives. And, in the cases of the deposition of officials, important questions were disallowed because they were deemed to be 'against the public interest' or 'irrelevant'. According to another human rights organisation, the Citizen's Justice Committee (CJC), among the questions that were deemed irrelevant 'were those concerning the details of firing on riotous mobs in Delhi between 31 October and 5 November!'

The CJC made requests to cross-examine nine key officials they regarded as having played significant roles during the massacres. These included Lieutenant Governor Gavai who was responsible for law and order in Delhi, his replacement and former home secretary, Mr Wali, and Police Commissioner Tandon. Misra refused these requests on the bewilderingly vague grounds that they were 'inexpedient' to the investigation without so much as a qualification as to why.

The inquiry also suffered from a serious lack of transparency. Proceedings were conducted in closed sessions with both the media and even victims' lawyers prevented from attending, precluding any possibility of the cross-examination of witnesses.

However, this did not prevent lawyers representing several anti-victim groups gaining access to sensitive information in advance, in particular prior to victim testimony hearings. Groups including the Citizens Forum for Truth, Citizens Committee for Peace and Harmony and the Nagrik Suraksha Samiti (Arya Samaj), had all argued that the massacres had not been organised but were a spontaneous reaction to both Mrs Gandhi's murder and earlier killings of Hindus in Punjab. The lawyer acting on behalf of the victims, H. S. Phoolka, characterised these groups as 'proxies for the culprits as they were using information to intimidate the victims just before their deposition'.

The primary representatives of the victims, the CJC, eventually walked out. With the blanket ban on press coverage in place, the public were left in the dark as to the dubious manner in which the inquiry was being conducted.

~

The Commission's final report was divided into two parts. The first provided an account of the events, an examination of affidavits, the role of the police and administration, and an analysis of *The Anti-Sikh Violence*. The second recommended more police resources and explored the role of voluntary social agencies and education, and the influence of mass media.

However, it lacked clarity including any clearly set-out methodology. The scant attention to facts or details, its repetitions and contradictions were only the beginning of its problems.

Basic errors were apparent throughout: there were six police districts split into two ranges in Delhi, not five of each; the position of deputy inspector general didn't exist because it had been abolished in 1978; and New Delhi became a police district in 1969, not in 1986.

Misra delved into irrelevancies, quoting writers and intellectuals such as Adam Smith, Karl Marx and Rabindranath Tagore in a bizarre attempt to offer lessons on morality and behaviour for Indians.

But most damning was Misra's sympathetic bias towards the official line – that what took place in November 1984 was more of an unavoidable backlash than organised mass murder. Of course, if the latter was in any way conceded it would have opened a Pandora's Box of questions as to who exactly was behind the genocidal massacre. It was clear that the main purpose of the inquiry was to shield the government from complicity and place blame in the direction of 'criminal elements'.

One young lawyer at the time later recalled how Judge Misra had responded to a grieving father, who had just described the brutal murder of his son, with a ridiculous and deeply insensitive analogy:

> Sir, your story is a bit like this one. Listen to me carefully. Imagine you and your son are going somewhere on a scooter. You stop at the railway crossing. Zillions of cars and scooters are waiting for the train to pass by. No one has any idea about a huge vulture flying high up in the skies, right above you. In the vulture's beak, there is a snake. Suddenly, it slithers and manages to free itself; the snake falls down, and finally lands on your son, sitting behind you on your scooter. The snake bites his neck. Your son dies that very instant. And that very instant, the vulture lands, collects the snake and flies away. See, it is no one's fault. Do you think it is somebody's fault? Not really. This is exactly what happened to your family. It is no one's fault.

Misra did offer some explanations for the violence, but these were as ludicrous and incoherent as some of his other statements. He blamed 'anti-social forces' and the great number of 'criminals' in Delhi, which in part was due to the rise in the city's population, without attempting to define who exactly he meant. Police culpability for the failure to stop the violence was placed squarely on the heads of local police stations and junior officers for failing to communicate with their senior officers, who were themselves absolved of any dereliction of duty. The issue of political pressure on the police was never properly addressed. According to Misra, the police had a tendency to always side with the government of the day, a hangover from the days of the British Raj.

The report contained numerous apologetic statements on behalf of the police, arguing that they were 'often accused of aggravating and inciting tension. These accusations are often untrue'. Misra did, however, concede that there were 'policemen in uniform [who] have participated in looting' and could have been co-operating with 'anti-social elements in their respective localities' but these were 'few in number'.

When examining the role of the Congress Party, the majority of its members under examination were found innocent of any involvement in the violence. Nineteen, however, were found guilty though their identities were not divulged except for six who had already been mentioned in the PUDR-PUCL's *Who are the Guilty* report published in November 1984. The list of the nineteen members had been submitted to the Commission by the Delhi Sikh Gurdwara Prabhandak Committee, which had managerial responsibilities for the capital's gurdwaras. They had also handed over a list naming thirteen Congress MPs and workers – including Bhagat, Kumar, Shastri and several Congress councillors – which tallied with the PUDR-PUCL list but provided additional details such as the names of witnesses and what they had seen. But Misra failed to take this information into account and withheld the names.

On the other hand, outrageously, the names and addresses of witnesses who testified against senior Congress leaders and police officers were shared with the anti-victim groups and lawyers despite warnings from human rights organisations. These disclosures led to victim intimidation and threats.

The Delhi Administration's written submission to the Commission was aimed at exonerating the police while heaping blame on Sikhs for the suffering they endured. They had, according to the administration, celebrated Mrs Gandhi's assassination, attacked first and some were of an 'anti-national character'. The administration also attempted to discount all affidavits filed by survivors and wrote off the human rights reports on the carnage of 1984 as 'politically motivated and irrelevant'.

Although most Congress leaders implicated in the attacks were either overlooked or absolved without investigation, particular attention was paid by the Commission to challenging the allegations levelled against H. K. L. Bhagat. Misra argued that, having examined the relevant affidavits, he found the accusations to be baseless, concluding that 'Mr. Bhagat, being a sitting MP and Minister, was not likely to misbehave in the manner alleged'. Misra never called Bhagat to be cross-examined.

By way of an epilogue to his report, Misra echoed Rajiv Gandhi's metaphor to explain away the massacres: 'As in nature, so in society nothing happens without a backdrop. In some instances, the background is in bold relief, perceptibly clear and prominent: in others it is withdrawn and insignificant. The November 1984 riots were no exception'.

Astonishingly, Misra rounded off his report with a request that people forget what had happened: 'Indians should join the national march ahead by forgetting the unpleasant episodes of the cloudy days and looking forward to bright sunshine ahead'. He then went on to extol the merits of education, the importance of good manners and the virtues of patriotism: 'Every Indian must feel proud to have been born in India'.

When the government tabled the report in February 1987, the presiding officers of the two houses of parliament appeared to have acted impartially by ruling out any debate on its findings. Thus, the parliament of the world's largest democracy abdicated its primary function to hold the government of the day to account.

According to a Human Rights Watch report on the Commission,

> it recommended no criminal prosecution of any individual, and it cleared all high-level officials of directing the pogroms. In its findings, the commission

did acknowledge that many of the victims testifying before it had received threats from local police. While the commission noted that there had been 'widespread lapses' on the part of the police, it concluded that 'the allegations before the commission about the conduct of the police are more of indifference and negligence during the riots than of any wrongful overt act'.

Misra went on to become the country's chief justice in 1990. Three years later, he was appointed the first chairman of the National Human Rights Commission of India. The mask finally slipped in 1998 when he took his place as a member of the Rajya Sabha, the upper house of the Indian parliament, as a Congress Party representative.

~

In the wake of the Misra Commission, six committees were appointed, three of which were recommended by Judge Misra. Unlike a wide-ranging commission that was government-appointed and bound to report to parliament, these committees were established by the government of the day to each investigate a single, well-defined issue and instruct the police to file criminal proceedings against the accused.

The three committees established on Misra's recommendation began their work on 23 February 1987 with remits to investigate specific aspects of the massacres. Notably, each would go on to contradict the findings of the Misra Commission, especially with regards to Congress complicity.

The first to report was the Jain-Bannerjee Committee, headed by Justice Jain, a former judge of the Delhi High Court, and Mr Bannerjee, a retired police officer. They were tasked with examining whether a large number of cases, particularly those that named political leaders or police officers, had been properly registered and investigated.

In August 1987, the committee recommended that a number of cases should be registered against former Congress minister Sajjan

Kumar for allegedly leading a mob that killed Navin Singh in Sultanpuri. However, in December 1987, one of his co-accused, Brahmanand Gupta, filed a petition in the Delhi High Court and obtained a stay against the Committee's recommendations, which the government did not oppose. Although the CJC filed an application opposing the stay, the High Court upheld Gupta's petition in October 1989. The presiding judge in the case, Yogeshwar Dayal, had in 1984 dismissed the original petition requesting the setting up of an independent inquiry into the massacres. This legal intervention meant that not only had key Congress party leaders been insulated from prosecution, but it effectively led to the abolishing of the Jain-Bannerjee Committee. None of its recommendations were implemented.

The Ahuja Committee was headed by Mr Ahuja, a secretary in the Ministry of Home Affairs, to determine the total number of killings in Delhi only. In its report submitted in August 1987, it found that the total number of deaths in the capital came to 2,733. This figure was in stark contrast to Home Minister Rao's figure of 800 a month after the violence and somewhat higher than the Misra Commission's 2,307. All fell well below the CJC's estimate of 3,949.

The third committee recommended by Misra was the Kapur-Mittal Committee headed by Justice Kapur and Mrs Mittal, the retired secretary of the state of Uttar Pradesh. Its task was to investigate the role of the police. The Marwah Commission had previously been established to inquire into police misconduct but had been forced to abort its investigation by the government in 1985. Most of its findings (excluding Marwah's written notes) were later made available to the Misra Commission. Following on from Marwah's work, the Committee submitted its final report in February 1990. It identified seventy-two police officers either for their connivance or gross negligence and recommended that thirty of them be immediately dismissed. The accused moved the High Court in the hope of quashing the Kapur-Mittal panel. This went to the Supreme Court, which issued a stay on the proceedings. Consequently, no action was taken against the thirty police officers.

~

Further enquiries ensued. In March 1990 the new prime minister, V. P. Singh of the Janata Dal Party, appointed a successor to the Jain-Bannerjee Committee. This fourth entity, the Poti-Rosha Committee, was headed by Justice Poti, a former chief justice of the Kerala and Gujarat High Courts, and Mr Rosha, a retired officer of the Indian Police Service. It was to examine and investigate the registration of cases, making recommendations based on affidavits. As before, they recommended that the Central Bureau of Investigation (CBI) register a case against Sajjan Kumar, this time for allegedly leading a mob that killed Anwar Kaur's husband. When a CBI team went to Kumar's home to file charges they were threatened and locked up by a mob of his supporters. The team made frantic calls of help but the Delhi police failed to intervene. Soon after, the perceived threat led Poti and Rosha to decline a renewal of their tenure.

In December 1990 the Jain-Aggarwal Committee was appointed as a successor to the Poti-Rosha Committee. Justice Jain returned to join Mr Aggarwal, a retired director general of police in Uttar Pradesh. Over the next three years, they recommended forty-eight cases to be registered, including against Congress politicians H. K. L. Bhagat, Sajjan Kumar, Dharam Dass Shastri and Jagdish Tytler. The CBI, which was still reeling from the Sajjan Kumar arrest fiasco, failed to register any of them.

The Delhi Administration ostensibly accepted all of the recommendations made by the Jain-Aggarwal Committee, which required all the affidavits filed by victims to be transcribed verbatim into First Information Reports (FIRs).

Sajjan Kumar's was the very first case to be registered in September 1990 based on the affidavit of Anwar Kaur. The CBI completed its inquiry and drafted the charge sheet in March 1992. The Home Minister even declared in parliament that the charge sheet against Kumar was ready. The CBI had only to file it in court so that the trial could begin but it departed from standard procedure and instead referred the case to the Home Ministry for approval.

By this time, however, a new Congress government was in power with Prime Minister P. V. Narasimha Rao, who had been the home minister in 1984, at the helm. The central government sat on the case for two years before it was decided in 1994 that it did not fall under its jurisdiction. The case was transferred to the Delhi Administration.

Similarly dark machinations would also reveal themselves in Bhagat's case, which the Jain-Aggarwal Committee had recommended be registered based on Harminder Kaur's affidavit. The Delhi Administration, headed by Lieutenant Governor Markandey Singh, accepted the recommendation and referred the matter to the CBI. However, Bhagat intervened to get the case thrown out, citing in letters to the administration his exoneration as per the Misra report.

As the case began to stall, the Jain-Aggarwal Committee opposed Bhagat's intervention by declaring that Harminder Kaur's affidavit had not been seen by Judge Misra. The CBI then stepped in, refused to deal with the affidavit and returned it, along with twenty other politically sensitive affidavits, stating that the Delhi police's special riot cell – one of the branches of police that had been implicated in the violence of 1984 – was now dealing with them.

Remarkably, even the head of this unit, Akhtar Ali Farooquee, admitted that they were not best placed to be involved in the investigation, questioning whether they could be considered an independent agency to investigate cases where they themselves were the accused party.

The resulting conflict of interest undoubtedly influenced the decision to proceed with only eight cases – these were regarded as the weakest, being most based on hearsay. Not one of them mentioned any direct evidence against the accused Congress leaders. Astonishingly, the solid testimonies, which named Bhagat and Kumar, were discarded outright.

~

In September 1993, *India Today* journalist, Manoj Mitta, exposed the delays that had thus far taken place: 'A closer scrutiny shows an elaborate cover-up operation'. It was clear to him that there were 'calculated moves made by three wings of the government – the Home Ministry, the Delhi Administration and the CBI – to shield Bhagat and Kumar'.

The sixth attempt to secure some form of justice came in December 1993 in the form of the Narula Committee. It was initiated by the chief minister of Delhi, Madan Lal Khurana of the BJP. Once again, recommendations were made to register cases against Bhagat and Kumar, and once again the cases were passed on to Rao's government, which delayed them for two years before deciding that the issue actually fell under the remit of the Delhi Administration.

The CBI finally filed the charge sheet against Kumar in December 1994. But it took them a further five years – a total of fifteen years after the massacres had occurred – to record the statements of witnesses. Two of the witnesses testified seeing Kumar addressing a meeting where he incited people to kill Sikhs but their testimony was recorded incorrectly in court. The session judge, Manju Goel, gave priority to Kumar's own witnesses who were two police officers, despite accusations that the police had falsified FIRs. In December 2002, the first case against Kumar was dismissed.

It was only when the Congress Party were voted out of power in 1996 that the police finally registered the case against Bhagat. The case against him was based on the affidavits of Darshan Kaur, a survivor of the Trilokpuri atrocities, and Harminder Kaur, whose son, son-in-law and husband, a Delhi police head constable, were allegedly killed by a mob instigated by Bhagat.

Bhagat was finally arrested on 25 January 1996. In a show of legal force, he entered court accompanied by a hundred lawyers. The defence was led by R. K. Anand, Chairman of the Delhi Bar Council, who would later become a Congress MP. As one of the witnesses had turned hostile to the prosecution's case and others were dropped, it was left to Darshan Kaur to testify despite threats to her life. In the end, the case against Bhagat collapsed as a conviction could not be secured on the testimony of one sole witness. The judge rejected the prosecution's request to call further witnesses.

Twenty years after the crimes has been committed, a petition to include further witnesses in Bhagat's case was finally approved. But by then, May 2004, the senior Congress politician's lawyers were arguing that, as he was suffering with dementia, no warrants could be issued.

17

Judicial Scandal (II): Nanavati

With the collapse of the case against H. K. L. Bhagat, the continuing state of impunity for others such as Sajjan Kumar and Jagdish Tytler, and a change in government, human rights lawyer H. S. Phoolka pushed for a fresh judicial inquiry in 1999.

The cause was taken up by the Akali Dal Party, which had become part of the ruling BJP-led coalition government, the National Democratic Alliance (NDA), with Atal Bihari Vajpayee as prime minister.

On 10 May 2000, the NDA appointed Justice G. T. Nanavati, a retired Supreme Court judge, as the sole member of an eponymous commission to investigate a broad range of issues, including the causes of the 'criminal violence and riots' that targeted members of the Sikh community, the sequence of events leading up to the 'violence and riots', and whether any authorities or individuals were responsible.

Nanavati was a controversial choice – less than two years earlier he was part of a two-member Supreme Court bench that had commuted the death sentence for 'the butcher of Trilokpuri', Kishori Lal, to life imprisonment. The judgement excused Lal's actions as having been committed under the influence of the 'collective fury' of the mob, which was not deemed to be working in an 'organised systematic' way. The absence of medical evidence (from the bodies having already been disposed of by the police) also went in Lal's favour, as did the 'redeeming feature' that the mob he was a part of had not killed women or children.

Nanavati was required to report his findings to government within six months but it took him five years to complete his work, the final report being submitted in February 2005. By this time Congress had returned to power with Sonia Gandhi, Rajiv Gandhi's widow, as the party's president and Dr Manmohan Singh as India's first Sikh prime minister (in 1984 he had been govenor of the Reserve Bank of India). The government sat on the report for a full six months before finally tabling it on 8 August 2005 – the last day it could be submitted by law for consideration by parliament.

When the report went public, there was widespread outrage at its findings. Veteran human rights activist Professor Uma Chakravarti summed it up as a 'damp squib, wishy-washy and reads like a whodunit without an ending'.

~

During his investigations, Nanavati found he had six thousand fresh affidavits to work with in response to public notices issued by the Commissions. These included those given by politicians, policemen, survivors and witnesses. A further eighty-nine individuals who had not previously filed affidavits, including police officials, politicians and army officers, were invited to be questioned by the Commission.

Once again, the final report contained a number of disconcerting, if not downright outrageous, errors, omissions and vagueness of language. In his opening remarks, Nanavati counted the death toll as being in the 'hundreds', while further on he stated merely that certain Congress leaders were 'probably' involved.

Nanavati also didn't take into account crucial evidence that may well have led to him to conclude that the violence was genocidal in nature – the use of housing and other lists to identify targets, the airing of hate slogans on state media, the incitement to violence by local Congress leaders at political meetings, the large number of attacks on gurdwaras, the shearing of male hair and the mass rapes.

However, in discussing the horrific nature of the attacks, including the act of 'necklacing' and use of kerosene, Nanavati concluded that 'what had initially started as an angry outburst became an organized carnage.' It then became 'systematic' in nature, and was conducted without 'fear of the police'. He highlighted how mobs 'were assured that they would not be harmed while committing those acts and even hereafter'.

None of this, concluded the judge, could have occurred without the 'help of influential and resourceful persons' who helped with 'the provisions of weapons and transportation of killers [which] required an organised effort'. But, he failed to identify who those 'influential and resourceful persons' were or establish their roles. He came close when he gave weight to the evidence of meetings being held on 31 October in which 'persons who could organize attacks... were given instructions to kill Sikhs and loot their houses and shops'. Ultimately, though, he didn't point the finger of blame, and so implicate senior politicians and confirm the conspiracy to commit genocidal massacres.

~

Since so many affidavits incriminated local Congress leaders and workers, Nanavati explored the possible involvement of each leader in turn.

On the evidence of several witnesses who testified that Jagdish Tytler led mobs and complained to them that fewer Sikhs had been killed in his constituency than elsewhere, the Commission found 'credible evidence against Shri Jagdish Tytler to the effect that very probably he had a hand in organising attacks on Sikhs'.

As a result of a protest movement initiated by widows and orphans (who had to endure police water cannons and baton-charges) and supported by several opposition parties, Tytler was forced to resign from his government post as minister for non-resident Indians affairs on 10 August 2005, two days after the report was made public. Prosecuting him, however, was another matter and proved elusive. A subsequent CBI investigation absolved him, claiming that witness statements were 'inconsistent, unreliable and unworthy of credit'.

The case against Sajjan Kumar was the strongest; the five testimonies against this one MP exceeded any of the other accused, particularly his involvement in the massacres at Mangolpuri and Sultanpuri. Nanavati took the view that there was 'credible material' against Kumar that showed he was 'probably involved as alleged by witnesses'. However, the Commission's recommendations to government to only pursue those cases in which charge sheets had not yet been filed meant that, where acquittals had previously taken place, as had happened to Kumar, those cases should not be reopened.

The day after Tytler resigned, Kumar followed suit. On the strength of Nanavati's comments and unrelenting protests, he was forced to relinquish the chairmanship of the Delhi Rural Development Board.

The fresh CBI investigation initiated against him rolled on for several years. When the case finally had its day in court in 2012, CBI prosecutor, R. S. Cheema, said the massacres were a result of a conspiracy of terrifying proportion with the complicity of police and patronage of local MP Sajjan Kumar. In spite of the evidence against him, and his five co-defendants being convicted, Kumar was acquitted, prompting another wave of protests.

Although Bhagat and other Congress leaders such as Rampal Saroj and Dr Ashok Gupta were found to be guilty for their role in the Trilokpuri massacres, the Commission failed to recommend further action against them, citing their acquittals in earlier criminal cases – even though these had been fraught with poor police investigations and witness intimidation. Bhagat by then was deemed unfit for trial as he was suffering from Alzheimer's.

He died in October 2005, having escaped justice for over twenty years.

In the case of Kamal Nath, only one witness, Mukhtiar Singh, testified to him having led an armed mob that attacked Sikhs at Gurdwara Rakab Ganj on the morning of 1 November, resulting in two being burnt to death. Others such as the journalist Sanjay Suri had seen Nath 'controlling' the crowd in the aftermath of the killings. Nath's defence was that he was merely visiting the gurdwara to investigate the agitation and to placate the mob.

The Commission found Nath's testimony to be 'vague' and 'not consistent with the evidence' – it also thought it 'a little strange' that he left without telling police officers, with whom he was seen standing with for some time. The contradictions were justified by the Commission on the grounds that the matters under discussion had occurred twenty years earlier, so 'he was not able to give more details'. Nanavati said that it would not be 'proper' to reach the conclusion that Nath had in any way 'instigated the mob'.

Others disagreed. Lawyer H. S. Phoolka, who had represented victims at every step, and campaigning journalist, Manoj Mitta, felt that there were enough grounds for further investigation:

> Having spent two hours with the mob in front of Rakab Ganj Gurdwara, having done nothing to help the two Sikhs lying in a critical condition, having allowed the mob and the police to carry on with their hostilities against the targeted community, Kamal Nath was clearly part of the problem, not the solution. The unanswered questions about his role in the Rakab Ganj Gurdwara episode might well hold the key to uncovering the high-level conspiracy behind the 1984 carnage.

In the case of Dharam Dass Shastri, Nanavati found there was evidence suggesting he 'was actively involved in the riots'. He had been identified by witnesses as having led a mob that looted and burned Sikh houses and was known to have later marched with local leaders and 3,000 people to Karol Bagh Police Station to demand the release of rioters for looting. He had threatened police officers 'with dire consequences if they took any action against those persons for being in possession of looted property'. Nanavati's recommendation that Shastri's role be further investigated came to nothing as he died before the CBI could file a case against him.

Several people testified to the inaction, indifference and ineffectiveness of the then home minister and former prime minister, P. V. Narasimha Rao. Sharad Yadav, a secretary of the Lok Dal Party, met him twice on 1 November and found him to be 'almost indifferent and he did not respond to any of the requests for taking prompt action'.

Former prime minister, I. K. Gujral, also appeared before the Commission and gave evidence. He testified that Rao did not appear to be in possession of all the facts about the violence, though he appeared to be deeply involved with the planning around the foreign VVIPs who would be attending Indira Gandhi's funeral. Rao admitted that 'he was aware that Police was not able to handle the situation and that he was taking steps to call the Army'. Rao's competency was also called into question by others who met him at the time, including the historian Patwant Singh, former Minister for Law and Justice, Shanti Bhushan, and Lieutenant General J. S. Aurora.

Nanavati, however, was quick to exonerate Rao, stating that in his opinion there was 'no delay or indifference at the level of the Home Minister'. Rao had passed away in December 2004, just over a month before Nanavati submitted his report to government, yet Mitta and Phoolka asserted that the judgement in his favour had been political – finding Rao, a former prime minister, to be at fault would have had serious ramifications for the ruling Congress Party under the stewardship of Sonia Gandhi.

Equally, Nanavati went to great lengths to absolve Rajiv Gandhi. He had been assassinated in 1991 by Tamil separatists while

Prime Ministers Indira Gandhi and Margaret Thatcher [1] in the former's Delhi office. The two shared a strong mutual admiration and were both known by the moniker of 'Iron Lady'. Questions have arisen in recent years as to Britain's role in the planning of Operation Blue Star, the military attack on the Golden Temple complex [2] that led to Mrs Gandhi's assassination.

On the evening of 31 October 1984 [3], Arun Nehru MP (left) and President Zail Singh (right) arrive at the All India Institute of Medical Sciences (AIIMS). Ominously, the president's cavalcade came under attack by a volatile crowd. The following day Mrs Gandhi's body lay in state at Teen Murti House, New Delhi [4], where her son and successor Rajiv Gandhi (in white, to the right) and nephew Arun Nehru MP (in white, left) were in attendance. The national media broadcast the fervent crowd shouting the chilling slogan 'blood for blood'. Already innocent Sikhs, their property and places of worship were coming under coordinated attack.

In discussion outside Teen Murti House on 1 November [5] are H. K. L. Bhagat MP (left) and the new prime minister, Rajiv Gandhi (right). Congress leaders had held clandestine meetings the day before to finalise plans to massacre Sikhs to 'teach them a lesson'.

That day, sustained and highly organised attacks began in earnest across Delhi and elsewhere [6]. Sikh homes were identified for destruction and their inhabitants set upon by death squads, which roamed with impunity in the streets and on public transport.

Heavy black smoke hung over large areas of Delhi as looting and arson [7] ensued from 1 to 5 November. One of the worst hit areas was the white-colonnaded Connaught Circus shopping district in central New Delhi where the Marina Hotel [8] burned out of control after an adjacent Sikh-owned shop was set ablaze.

9

Four Sikh brothers, the owners of the burning Sahni Paints [9], are roasted alive by a mob in Paharganj, New Delhi, on 2 November. The organised state-sponsored rampage continued unabated for four days, with businesses and homes devastated and livelihoods lost. Sikh-owned taxis [10] were burned at their stands.

Gangs, sometimes numbering in the thousands, roamed unchallenged by the authorities. As the onslaught continued, the streets and alleys of the capital and elsewhere began to fill with the corpses of the victims [11]. Often dismembered, scalped, and with horrific injuries still visible, the sometimes charred remains of innocent Sikhs were left where they had fallen, as passers-by gazed upon them [12].

Many were cut down on trains where officials were often complicit with the roaming killers in catching Sikhs for slaughter. Railway carriages, tracks and even platforms filled with their bodies [13].

14

Entire Sikh districts of Delhi and elsewhere were targeted in a systematic fashion. Written lists containing Sikh names and addresses were distributed, houses pre-marked by 'surveyors', gurdwaras destroyed and communities deliberately disarmed by police. Murderous gangs closed off areas such as the Trilokpuri colony [14], often with the connivance of the local police, and went about their sickening work of butchering, burning and raping.

Human remains littered what was left of Sikh neighbourhoods [15], which were often reduced to ashes [16]. Those who did survive, often women and children, were left in a hopeless condition [17], suffering post-traumatic stress and with little or no aid or comfort provided by their government.

15

16

18

19

20

In the aftermath of four days onslaught, Sikh survivors, mainly from lower caste backgrounds and concentrated particularly in East Delhi neighbourhoods, found themselves in a state of utter destitution. Mothers and wives of murdered Sikh males were left with tragic remnants – such as strands of hair [18] or a single finger [21] – of their loved ones, which included babies and children. Many victims had been killed by the barbaric practice of 'necklacing', being burnt alive with a kerosene-soaked, burning tyre strung over their bodies. The uncontrollable grief of survivors was all too evident [19, 20].

21

22

Born on October 1, 1984, Manjit Singh was just a month old when their house in Mangolpuri, his father, grandfather and three uncles were all burned, their bodies never found. Fate dealt other cruel blows: his mother died of a brain tumour. 'I stopped going to school when in Class 9, as someone had to run the house.' He took up work driving a school van and is now a driver with a family in New Delhi. 'Nothing can make me forget the fate of my family', he says. But he has learnt to move on. The community of 1984 victims is his one unfailing source of succour and comradeship. October 2009.

Excerpted from the 1984 notebooks by Gauri Gill.

23

Taranjeet Kaur's grandfather Jeevan Singh was killed on 1 November 1984. 'A mob of 400–500 people followed my husband and before he could reach a safe house in Pandav Nagar, they knifed him and left him to die on the rail tracks,' recounts Taranjeet's grandmother Surjit, crying uncontrollably. It hasn't been easy since. 'I have spent my life struggling, but I want my granddaughter to study hard,' she says. October 2009.

Excerpted from the 1984 notebooks by Gauri Gill.

24

Gopi Kaur testified against Sajjan Kumar whom she saw at the head of a crowd near her home in Sultanpuri, with police following behind him. 'As he passed in front of our house, we said, "Please save our people" but instead to our horror he told the crowd to kill us.' Her husband was killed. Their sons were hidden under the bed, after their hair was cut. Later, she says, 'I never knew how to take a bus, had never stepped out of the home. I was given work as a water woman in Kailash Nagar and would first be dropped by my brother, then my son. In the bus, I used to go crazy crying right until Daryaganj.' September 2014.

Excerpted from the 1984 notebooks by Gauri Gill.

Bhaggi Kaur at the Shaheedi Memorial Museum, Tilak Vihar. 53 year-old Bhaggi lost her husband in '84, while her son committed suicide by overdosing on painkillers three years ago. September 2014.

Excerpted from the 1984 notebooks by Gauri Gill.

26

Refugees in their own country: when relief did come for the victims it primarily came from other Sikhs and local human rights groups. Volunteers worked tirelessly to bring food and comfort to the stricken [26]. Government-created refugee camps in Delhi were late in being erected and dismantled with damnable haste.

Survivors, mainly women of all ages who had become victims of mass genocidal rape and their children [27], found some safety in the camps. Many families were resettled together in The Widow Colony in West Delhi where they tried to rebuild their lives. The mental scars and trauma would last a lifetime, as would their fight for justice against senior members of the Congress Party who had led the attacks.

27

campaigning in South India. At the time, he had been personally implicated in the Bofors scandal, involving bribery in connection with a high-profile arms deal, which had severely damaged his image as an honest politician and lost him the 1989 election. However, a Delhi High Court had posthumously cleared the ex-prime minister of any wrongdoing in February 2004. A year later, Nanavati would follow suit.

In fact, his report was somewhat gushing in its claims that Rajiv Gandhi had shown 'much concern' about what was happening in the capital. 'He had issued an appeal for remaining calm and maintaining communal harmony,' going so far as to visiting 'the affected areas' on the night of 1 November.

The testimony of journalist, historian and former vice-president of the BJP, K. R. Malkani – that he had been told by colleagues that 'Shri Rajiv Gandhi had whispered into the ears of that senior officer that "Yes, we must teach them a lesson"' – was deemed to have no substance behind it. Nanavati cast doubt on the context and found this piece of evidence 'vague' and 'not believable'.

In a strident vindication, Nanavati concluded that there was 'absolutely no evidence suggesting that Shri Rajiv Gandhi or any other high-ranking Congress (I) leader had suggested or organized attacks on Sikhs'. The implication that only local Congress leaders were involved overlooked in particular the role of Arun Nehru, who escaped all scrutiny.

Furthermore, all police officials in the worst affected areas of East and West Delhi were acquitted. Nanavati justification was that police departmental inquiries had already exonerated them. The records of the subsequently held disciplinary proceedings against the police officers were kept secret.

Crucial records relating to the deployment of the army were either not released or reported missing. These included the affidavits from the Misra Commission of the army's then chief of staff, A. S. Vaidya, and of Major Sandhu of the 15th Sikh Light Infantry

– whose troops were the first to patrol Delhi in serious numbers on the morning of 1 November but were ordered back to barracks just as the mass killings commenced.

There was also no examination of the reports of the violence that occurred on trains or the forty-six unauthorised stoppages that enabled the mobs to hunt down Sikh passengers. No investigation into these killings was ever carried out and not a single person was arrested by the Railway Police Force from 31 October to 4 November. Despite scores of affidavits and witness testimonies outlining the scale of the killings, Nanavati decided against pursuing the trail, stating that 'no one has made any grievance as regards the incidents which had happened at Railway Stations or in trains'.

~

During a parliamentary debate on the Nanavati report in August 2005, Prime Minister Manmohan Singh, a Sikh himself, apologised for what had happened:

> I have no hesitation in apologising not only to the Sikh community but the whole Indian nation because what took place in 1984 is the negation of the concept of nationhood and what is enshrined in our Constitution.

Citing Nanavati, he refused to accept that the upper echelons of a Congress government were in any way responsible for the events of November 1984: 'The Report is before us, and one thing it conclusively states is that there is no evidence, whatsoever, against the top leadership of the Congress Party'. He continued, referring to the massacres as 'riots', criticised the Akali Dal for their 'divisive rhetoric' and ended with hopes for a national reconciliation.

But for many, the Nanavati Commission had failed to secure the closure the country so desperately needed. As Siddharth Varadarajan, deputy editor of *The Hindu*, would so eloquently remark:

Modern states do not allow small men like Jagdish Tytler, Dharam Dass Shastri and Sajjan Kumar to unleash – as part of some sort of private initiative – murder on a genocidal scale. Modern states do not allow their police system to fall apart, except by design. Modern states do not allow Army commanders to say they do not have enough troops to do the job at hand. Littered through Mr Justice Nanavati's text are all the tell-tale dots of official guilt but these have been left unconnected, allowing the institutional rot to remain and infect our body politic once again.

The Indifference of the West

In April 2011, a WikiLeaks cable contained a startling revelation in the wake of the Nanavati Commission's findings.

On 12 August 2005, Robert O'Blake, Deputy Chief of Mission at the American Embassy in New Delhi, sent a cable that represents the first significant acknowledgement by a foreign government official of the Congress Party's responsibility for the violence of November 1984.

The American diplomat praised Prime Minister Manmohan Singh for apologising the previous day for 'one of the saddest and darkest moments in recent Indian history'. He went on to describe how this act of 'political courage' was 'something that no Indian leader in 20 years has been willing to do'. It stood in 'exquisite contrast to the opportunism and hatred directed by senior GOI [Government of India] officials against Sikhs in 1984'.

Other disclosures, particularly relating to the UK government, were to follow. In 2014, the thirtieth anniversary of the events of 1984, The National Archives in the UK made public government records under the '30 year rule' that revealed how Margaret Thatcher's government had secretly lent the assistance of an SAS officer to the Indian government to advise on plans to flush out Sikh dissidents from the Golden Temple complex.

The declassified records would also furnish evidence of the extent to which the Thatcher administration was prepared to go to ensure the stability of trading arrangements with India were not jeopardised by protests in the UK over the massacres.

In response to concerns raised by British Sikhs, Prime Minister David Cameron took the decision in January 2014 to instruct his cabinet secretary, Sir Jeremy Heywood, to conduct an urgent investigation into the matter.

~

As well as playing a major role in India's independence movement, Sikhs also bore a proud history of serving in Britain's Indian Army in the century leading up Partition. Their loyalty and valour had not gone unnoticed – General Sir Frank Messervy, who was stationed in India between 1913 and 1947, extolled the sacrifices made by Sikh soldiers in the two World Wars:

> They all died or were wounded for the freedom of Britain and the world, and during shell fire, with no other protection but the turban, the symbol of their faith.

In the 1970s, several retired British officers who had served alongside Sikhs supported the campaign to allow them to ride motorcycles without crash helmets as was then required by law. They argued that Sikhs should be granted an exemption in civilian life as military authorities during the World Wars had not forced combat helmets upon them in combat situations owing to religious sensitivities.

Another supporter who lent their voice to the debate was Winston Spencer-Churchill, a Conservative MP and grandson of former prime minister Sir Winston Churchill:

> For me it is sufficient that in our time of need twice this century, when we needed the Sikhs to stand by us they did so and, in the case of too many, died beside us in two world wars to enable us to live in the freedom which we today enjoy.

The significance of this contribution had also been recognised by Margaret Thatcher. In 1976, not long after becoming leader of the opposition, she was chairing a shadow cabinet meeting to discuss immigration policy when proceedings were interrupted by a bell. When she was told it was for a vote that was about to take place in the House of Commons on a motion to grant the exemption to turbanned Sikhs, she stopped the meeting. What happened next was described by Michael Portillo, then a young researcher who would later on become one of her junior ministers:

> 'I must go,' she said. 'I am pledged to support them.' One of the giants [from the Heath cabinet], Lord Carrington, muttered something she didn't catch. Like a schoolboy, he was made to repeat it. 'I said it was ironic that here we are devising how to keep people out of the country, while you are off to vote for the Sikhs.' Silence. 'It was a joke.' She looked at the former defence secretary as though he were a piece of dirt. 'Well, it wasn't very funny. These people fought for us in the war, Peter, fought for us in the war. Have you got it?' And off she flounced to record her vote.

Within a decade, Thatcher's perception of the Sikh community would shift dramatically owing not only to her relationship with India's female prime minister, but also to the pressure to secure trade deals with India in the face of a burgeoning Sikh separatist movement in the UK, which itself had gained ground as a result of the terrible events of 1984.

~

Although they operated at different ends of the political spectrum, Thatcher and Gandhi had found in each other a kindred spirit.

Both were alumni of Somerville College at Oxford, both performed household duties alongside shaping the course of nations, and both surprised their enemies with swift and aggressive military decisions. Charles Moore, Thatcher's biographer, noted that both PMs found common ground as working mothers, equally comfortable discussing their children as politics and global affairs.

When Thatcher escaped an attempt on her life by the Irish Republican Army on 12 October 1984, Gandhi had sent her a letter questioning how such a thing could happen in a democracy. Gandhi's death less than three weeks later caused Thatcher considerable consternation:

> Only a few days ago, Mrs. Gandhi sent me a message in which she said: 'All terrorism and violence are condemnable and contemptible'. The murder of a democratic leader is an attack on democracy itself. We utterly condemn this savage and treacherous crime. Let there be no doubt that acts of terrorism will only strengthen the resolve of free peoples that those who resort to violence shall not prevail.

But of course, when an important trading partner was the one inflicting the violence on its own people, high-minded objections such as those articulated by Mrs Thatcher were conveniently overlooked.

A year before the assassination, the 'Sikh' issue is believed to have emerged in discussions as bilateral trade talks got underway. In early 2014, Tom Watson MP (currently deputy leader of the Labour Party) was provided with a letter dated 9 November 1983 written by Margaret Thatcher's private secretary, David Barclay. It highlighted discussions that Britain was having with India concerning the sale of military equipment and mentioned a meeting between the prime minister and India's defence minister. Watson questioned: 'Could it be that Mrs Thatcher's eagerness to seal a defence equipment deal led to the decision to authorise SAS planning support for the military action in Amritsar?' He was of course referring to papers released to the public by The National Archives in early 2014 that described both backchannel and formal discussions concerning the British government's role in this controversial affair.

The Indian government had sought advice on 'the removal of dissident Sikhs from the Golden Temple' on 3 February 1984. Two weeks later in a letter from the Foreign and Commonwealth Office (FCO) to the private secretary of the home secretary, Leon Brittan, it was revealed that an SAS officer had visited India and drawn up a plan that could be implemented by Indian Counter Terrorist Team commanders. Consideration had also been given to the wider impact of such a plan in terms of the possibility of communal violence both in Punjab and the Indian community in the UK. The letter was only to be shown 'strictly to those who need to consider the possible domestic implications'.

In response to Operation Blue Star, the British government maintained a deafening silence. The only recorded discussion in parliament occurred on 30 July, when John Watts, Conservative MP for Slough asked the secretary of state for foreign and Commonwealth affairs 'what discussions Her Majesty's Government have had with the Government of India' about 'the storming of the Golden Temple in Amritsar'? The response was remarkably for brevity:

> As this is an internal Indian matter, we have not sought
> to discuss it with the Indian Government.

But that was not entirely true. Fearing aftershocks from the Sikh diaspora in the UK, Indira Gandhi had written at length to Margaret Thatcher more than a month earlier on 14 June, outlining her justification for the operation. 'We have a troubled situation in Punjab,' her remarkable letter began. 'Of all malefactors, those who wear the religious garb are the most dangerous.' What followed was a carefully crafted appeal aimed at securing the ongoing support and sympathy of an important ally.

The Indian prime minister set the scene by providing some background to the relationship between Congress and the Akali Dal in Punjab, who had 'raised a number of demands, hoping to regain their following among Sikhs' after their 1980 election loss but 'shifted their stand and in the end hardened their attitude considerably'.

As political talks continued, 'the terrorists were strengthening their position' with the help of unnamed 'hostile outside elements'. As their objective was 'secession and disrupting the unity of our country' and the country's paramilitary forces had been ineffectual in controlling 'growing terrorist activities...unleashed from the Temple complex', which had been 'converted by terrorists into a base of operations', the decision was made 'to send in the army'.

'We had no choice,' she claimed, 'but to send an army unit which exercised the utmost restraint, using a minimum of force.' As they had strict orders not to damage the Golden Temple, 'they suffered heavy casualties'. The other sacred shrine, the Akal Takht, 'which we had asked our forces to avoid' was the site of the fiercest fighting as it was 'used by the terrorists as their hide-out and was full of grenades and other weapons'. The severe damage to its façade 'was also largely due to explosions from within'.

Though her government was aware of an arsenal being built up in the complex, Mrs Gandhi claimed that the Indian government had only become aware of exactly how 'vast and sophisticated' the stash of weapons was after the military strike had ended. Besides many of the arms bearing 'foreign markings', they had also discovered 'some foreign nationals among the desperadoes'.

Having 'liquidated' the 'hard core of the terrorists within', a difficult period lay ahead for Mrs Gandhi. 'Many in the Sikh community have been shaken by this traumatic event,' she explained. 'The process of healing and conciliation will take time but we shall persevere.'

In her concluding remarks, she entreated Mrs Thatcher:

> I have written at some length because there are a large number of Sikhs in the United Kingdom and many of them, not owing loyalty to India, have been too ready to play into the hands of or even be the spokesmen of secessionists. Their propaganda, other activities and dire threats must have come to your notice.

Fearful of the 'international aspect' of the problem, Mrs Gandhi was confident she could depend on her British counterpart's understanding of the situation: 'We appreciate the precautions your Government has taken'.

~

The British government were forced to break their self-imposed silence following several vociferous statements made by Dr Jagjit Singh Chauhan, a UK-based Sikh activist who had briefly become finance minister of Punjab in the late 1960s.

His separatist bent came to the fore in 1966 with the break-up of Punjab state into a smaller Sikh-dominated Punjab and a Hindu-dominated Haryana. By the 1970s he was running a Khalistani 'government-in-exile' from London, making trips to the US, Canada and Pakistan to develop his support base. From India's perspective, an advertisement in *The New York Times* in 1971 proclaiming a separate Sikh state of Khalistan effectively made him an enemy of the state.

On 12 June, the president of the Khalistan National Organisation (KNO) gave what would become a notorious interview on BBC Radio 4's 'World at One' programme. After expressing his horror at the military action and the media blackout in Punjab, Chauhan predicted dire consequences for the Indian prime minster and her family:

> But within a few days you will have the news that Mrs Gandhi and his [*sic*] family has been beheaded. That is what Sikhs will do, I tell you. I am sorry to say that.

The following day he declared himself the president of the so-called Republic of Khalistan, a government-in-exile, and went on to appoint a cabinet, issue symbolic passports and print the Khalistan dollar. This self-styled Sikh leader was now also becoming a thorn in the side of the British.

The remainder of June saw the BBC rejecting a complaint made by the Indian government in respect of the Chauhan interview and

Sikhs organising protest marches against the Indian government across England. The FCO also refused to entertain petitions submitted by members of the Sikh community that objected to the storming of the Golden Temple complex and subsequent killings of innocent pilgrims on the grounds that it was a matter for the Indian authorities to deal with.

The chairman of the KNO, Mehtab Singh, also wrote to Mrs Thatcher condemning the violence and urging her to lodge a formal protest to the Indian government for the military operation on behalf of British Sikhs. Unsurprisingly this was ignored.

On 30 June, Margaret Thatcher responded to Mrs Gandhi's letter of the 14th to reassure her that she appreciated her concern about extremists and promised to prevent them from using violence for their own political ends. Her comments regarding how the media operated in the UK were noteworthy, especially considering the media blackout that was in place in Punjab at the time:

> As you know, the media are independent in Britain, as they are in India. This means that the government does not intervene in media decisions, however much we may personally regret them.

~

Before boarding her plane to join other world leaders at Indira Gandhi's funeral on 2 November, Margaret Thatcher publicly condemned those British Sikhs who had celebrated the death 'of a great personal friend'. Privately, Thatcher was also preoccupied with the state of trade relations with India.

Records at The National Archives show that on 1 November there was growing concern for a deal relating to Westland plc, a financially ailing British helicopter manufacturer that had received an order for twenty-seven W30 helicopters from India. The deal had had the backing of Mrs Gandhi and was due to be signed off on the day of the assassination but was now thrown into a state of uncertainty.

As defence sales to India had totalled £1.28 billion since 1975, Mrs Thatcher was keen to ensure this beneficial relationship continued in the wake of Mrs Gandhi's death. To facilitate matters, the British government had agreed that the purchase could be financed entirely from the aid programme at a cost of £65 million. Peter Warry, a special adviser to Thatcher, warned that unless there was continued support at the highest levels of the Indian government, the order could be lost to the French.

Fearful that a change in India's stance could scupper the deal, senior members of the Thatcher government did their utmost over the following six months to secure this significant sale.

On 4 November, Thatcher met with Sir Robert Wade-Gery, the high commissioner to India, and Swraj Paul, an Indian-born British-based magnate who was a close confidant of both Indira Gandhi and Thatcher. Paul's powerful connections – including with Arun Nehru – granted him the unofficial status of 'alternative Indian High Commissioner in London', making him a valuable intermediary in negotiations. During the meeting, he stressed how Indian politicians were unhappy with Dr Chauhan's statements and there had been talk of a trade boycott. Mrs Thatcher had a challenge on her hands.

Cabinet discussions during November 1984 touched several times upon how Sikh discontent in Britain posed a threat to Indo-British trade relations. On both 8 and 15 November, under pressure from the Indian High Commission, the government discussed banning a march in London to mark the birth anniversary of Guru Nanak. Ministers were worried that the occasion could turn into a protest against India. The march was banned but, on 22 November, the cabinet expressed concern over how the ongoing 'Sikh situation' could threaten export contracts worth £5 billion.

On 12 December 1984, Sir Geoffrey Howe sent a cable to Margaret Thatcher entitled 'Sikh Extremists: Damage to Indo-British Relations'. It quoted Wade-Gery in Delhi who conveyed how Rajiv Gandhi's 'entourage' were extremely angry towards the British government for the perceived lack of action against Chauhan and the Sikh threat to Rajiv Gandhi's life. As such, they had 'ordered all government departments to consult with them before undertaking any important contracts with us'. Further cause for concern were the postponement by the Indians of a state visit by Defence Minister Michael Heseltine and a threat to delay a planned visit to India by Norman Lamont, the trade and industry minister.

In an attempt engender some much-needed goodwill, the FCO moved to organise a state visit from Rajiv Gandhi. Legal options to nullify Chauhan – including prosecuting him for incitement for murder, conspiracy to murder, threatening behaviour, causing racial hatred and the possibility of deportation – were also explored but with little success, since 'Dr Chauhan and other Sikh extremists take very considerable care to ensure that their activities in this country remain within the law'. Chauhan was never prosecuted, although he was given an official warning over his behaviour.

~

The precariousness of the relationship with India was also causing concern and some dismay amongst MPs of all backgrounds as well as business leaders.

Soon after the events of November 1984, Indarjit Singh, editor of *The Sikh Messenger* magazine (and later Lord Singh of Wimbledon), met David Waddington MP, a minister of state at the Home Office to express concern over the UK government's silence regarding the fate of Sikhs in India. 'Indarjit,' he responded, 'we know what is going on; we're walking on a tightrope; we have already lost one important contract, what can we do?' According to Lord Singh, the contract in question was Westland.

The company's chairman, Lord Toby Aldington, had written to Thatcher on 4 January 1985 imploring her to help his company for a third time in respect of Indian contracts:

> It may appear ungrateful of me, but I must now ask
> for your further help in view of the decision taken by

the Prime Minister of India to stop all contractual negotiations with British firms. I understand this is due to the Indian resentment at statements made by a leading Sikh in Britain concerning the assassination of Mrs Gandhi – a resentment which in many ways I share.

Aldington signed off with a warning: 'The financial consequences to Westland of a delay in receipt of these orders – or even worse, of the denial of them – are I am sure quite clear to you'.

In her reply, Thatcher made it clear that other British companies had also raised concerns about their contract negotiations with India. She reassured that while her officials were monitoring the situation closely, there was no evidence to suggest that Rajiv Gandhi had himself decided to put a general stop on negotiations. The delay in 'resuming normal business' according to her understanding was the recent election and subsequent ministerial changes.

She went on to confirm that according to the UK's high commissioner in India, the delays 'were not related to Sikh extremists in this country nor meant as political pressure'. In fact, Rajiv Gandhi's private secretary had let it be known that there had been a misunderstanding and that 'negotiations on the contracts could resume in whatever way the negotiators wished'.

Mrs Thatcher and Rajiv Gandhi were finally able to sit down for the first time since Mrs Gandhi's funeral in March 1985 at the British Embassy in Moscow (they had just attended the funeral of the Soviet politician, Konstantin Chernenko). During the frank discussion, the Indian prime minister identified Sikhs as one of his major problems, and outlined the technical flaws with the Westland helicopter, stating that his 'technical chaps' preferred a French model. Once again, the deal was teetering dangerously close to the edge.

Wider trade issues were also at stake. On 13 May 1985, Sir Geoffrey Howe outlined the importance of avoiding a row with India as exports to it were now worth £600 million, of which over ten per cent were accounted for by defence sales. Future lucrative contracts were also at risk.

In October 1985, Rajiv Gandhi made his first visit to the UK as prime minister and was duly greeted by 2,000 Sikh protesters. In a poignant rephrasing of a famous teaching of Guru Nanak's concerning the need to live a truthful life, Indarjit Singh remarked how 'Truth is high, but higher still is trade'.

The Westland negotiations continued until a formal agreement for the acquisition of twenty-one W30 helicopters financed by £65 million from the British aid budget was finally signed in March 1986. Thatcher had warned Gandhi that future economic aid could become 'problematic' if this deal was declined.

~

While a vocal segment of British Sikhs thought they had been sacrificed at the altar of commercial self-interest, some MPs came forward to take up the Sikh cause. One of the more controversial figures was Terry Dicks, who was the MP for Hayes and Harlington between 1983 and 1997. A hard-line, right-wing Conservative, Dicks had attracted his fair share of controversy over the years.

In 1978, he had prevented an Asian family from Kenya from getting a council house. A few years later he described immigrants to Britain as 'flotsam' and 'jetsam'. He would later call Nelson Mandela a 'black terrorist' for refusing to meet Margaret Thatcher on a visit to the UK in 1990. In his maiden speech in parliament, John McDonnell, who succeeded Dicks as MP for Hayes and Harlington, described him as a 'stain on the character of this House'.

Nonetheless, Dicks embraced the fight with gusto. His first foray was during a House of Commons debate in December 1986 in which he brought up the issue of two Sikh constituents, Paul Bedi and his wife Kuldip Kaur. They had been imprisoned in India, Kaur solely for possessing a newspaper cutting with details of a Sikh extremist organisation.

After condemning the Indian government for their appalling behaviour and their failure to behave in a humane manner, Dicks demanded that Britain should stand up for its subjects, 'no matter where they are and where they are being abused,' even if it meant harming Anglo-Indian relations. In response, Lynda Chalker MP, representing the FCO, stated that Kaur's case had to be heard within the Indian legal system, although she would continue to get support as a British citizen. She was eventually released after eight months.

In October 1988, Dicks raised the issue of Sikh human rights in parliament. He asked the secretary of state for foreign and commonwealth affairs to discuss the alleged human rights violations against a delegation of British Sikhs in India. Timothy Eggar MP denied the request since India was a 'democratic country', a 'secular state' and its constitution prevented 'discrimination on grounds of religion'. Those who felt they had been mistreated could 'take advantage of the remedies available to them under India's independent legal system'. But Dicks was unrelenting.

A month later he made his most powerful and lengthy address to the House of Commons, criticising his own Conservative government and bringing up the plight of Sikhs in India who were embroiled in the separatist movement.

After condemning the British government for not granting Sikhs the respect they deserved for their significant contribution in two world wars, he took the gloves off when launching his attack on the Indian government:

> While Rajiv Gandhi, the so-called leader of the world's largest democracy, struts like a bloated peacock on the international stage, condemning South Africa for its alleged abuse of human rights, he has been responsible for the murder, torture and imprisonment without trial of thousands of his fellow countrymen and he has left a great many others fearing for their lives.

Dicks claimed the Indian prime minister was not only aware of the killings and torture, orchestrated by his own security forces and the police, but supported them. Atrocities were most widespread in Punjab, where security forces routinely tortured prisoners, including by hanging them from ceilings and giving them electric shocks. They also operated a shoot-on-sight policy, all the while enjoying immunity from prosecution.

The British government, Dicks continued, was turning a blind eye to Sikh concerns as well as to reports from human rights organisations such as Amnesty International, yet it had intervened in South Africa in the case of the Sharpeville Six.

The British government, it was claimed, had allowed the Indian security services to operate within the British-Indian community to discredit Sikhs who were hard-working people with high regard for Britain. Dicks questioned why their concerns were not being heard. The tepid response from William Waldegrave, the minister of state for foreign and commonwealth affairs, urged using democratic means to resolve the issues.

Dicks would bring up the issue again in the House of Commons on 29 November 1991. He discussed the moral responsibility of the British after assurances they gave Sikhs before Independence in 1947, and an Amnesty International report that stressed how no police officer had ever been convicted of human rights violations in Punjab. He urged the British government to uphold their proud record for human rights and to pressure the Indian government into action.

The reply from Tristan Garel-Jones, minister of state for the FCO, did not bode well:

> We must judge carefully just how much prominence to give to human rights issues in our relationships with other governments. Sometimes, with a friendly Government, that makes for hard choices. If we had dealings only with countries with impeccable human

rights records, our influence in the world would be significantly reduced and there would almost certainly be a consequent loss of jobs in this country.

Dicks was right regarding the British government's vociferous condemnations of other nations guilty of human rights abuses. For example, in 1989 following the Tiananmen Square massacre in Beijing, the Chinese authorities were widely censured. Mrs Thatcher said she was 'shocked and appalled', while her foreign secretary, Geoffrey Howe, stated that 'we and our European Community partners have firmly condemned the brutal actions of the Chinese Government'. Sanctions were quickly imposed by the west, including an arms embargo. But in the case of India, its democratic cloak and the overriding desire by some for profitable trade deals with it, effectively shielded it from undue scrutiny and criticism.

Dicks would retire from front-line politics in 1997, citing as a reason the unfriendliness of his local Conservative Party towards Sikhs.

~

Max Madden, the Labour MP for Bradford West, also embraced the Sikh issue after visiting India in 1990. His report to parliament detailed the scale of abuses against Sikhs in Punjab before describing his visit to Delhi, where he had visited 1,200 widows of the 1984 massacres.

He explained how they struggled to survive, living in pitiful conditions with no water or electricity and at risk of typhoid and cholera. One lady he met had lost eighteen members of her family:

> None of these people, the victims of murderous communalism, believe that what happened was spontaneous. The mobs were organised. They were led. The plan was to kill as many male Sikhs as possible, including boys and even babies.

Speaking on the government's behalf, Tim Sainsbury, the under-secretary of state for foreign and commonwealth affairs, responded in stock fashion – India was a 'democratic country' with 'an independent legal system' and a 'vibrantly free press in which injustices can be and are exposed'. Subsequent UK governments, Conservative, Labour and coalition (Conservative-Liberal Democrat), have not sought to challenge this stance.

~

Sir Jeremy Heywood's investigation into Britain's role in Operation Blue Star ran for a little over two weeks. Limiting his search to the events leading up to the attack, between December 1983 and June 1984, his team scoured 200 files containing in excess of 23,000 documents. The events of November 1984 and beyond were outside the scope of his remit.

In his report to Prime Minister David Cameron in February 2014 he stated that the Ministry of Defence had routinely destroyed several military files on various operations in November 2009, including one on 'the provision of military advice to the Indian authorities on their contingency plans for the temple complex'. However, copies of 'at least some of documents on the destroyed files' were found in other departmental files, which allowed him to form a 'consistent picture of what happened'.

His assessment of the available material led him to conclude that assistance had been 'advisory' and given several months before the attack took place. The Indian government had appealed to the British government for help to wrest control of the Golden Temple complex from Sikh militants. In February 1984, an unnamed British military adviser had been sent to India and recommended that an attack should be the last resort, only if all negotiations had failed. The adviser advocated using the element of surprise and helicopters – neither of which featured in the final operation. No equipment, tactical intelligence or training were offered.

The investigation was criticised by Sikh groups for its lack of transparency and narrow focus. Other files, including several that potentially reveal a far greater role played by the SAS in crushing Sikh dissent following Operation Blue Star, were withdrawn from The National Archives by the FCO in the summer of 2016. It remains to be seen if calls urging the government to set up a public inquiry and full disclosure of all files relating to Britain's involvement in 1984 ever amount to anything.

19

The Living Dead

In 2013, nearly three decades after the events of November 1984, a Congress government minister laid bare to India's parliament the tally of convictions secured in respect of the violence that occurred in Delhi.

Of the 3,163 people arrested in the capital, just *thirty* individuals in approximately as many years, mostly low-ranking Congress Party supporters, had been convicted for killing Sikhs. This represents less than one per cent of all those arrested.

In comparison with the estimated death toll racked up over those four terrifying days, the figure beggars belief: half of the 8,000 men, women and children who were butchered were killed in the capital.

Out of those arrested, a staggering 2,706 were subsequently acquitted. Convictions for riot-related offences amounted to 412. One hundred and forty-seven police officers were indicted for their role in the killings but not one officer has been prosecuted. Nobody has ever been prosecuted for rape.

These grim statistics embody the catastrophic plight of the survivors that continues to cast a long, dark shadow over their lives. The trauma and hardship endured by those families has conspired to keep them locked in a vicious cycle of inter-generational suffering for thirty-three years, and quite possibly for decades to come.

In contrast with the failure to prosecute those involved in the massacres, Mrs Gandhi's assassins were swiftly brought to justice. Beant Singh was killed at the scene while Satwant Singh was put on trial along with alleged co-conspirator Kehar Singh, despite his case only being based on circumstantial evidence. Both were hanged in January 1989.

~

The aftermath of the violence in Delhi saw tens of thousands of survivors seek sanctuary in hastily erected shelters in schools, gurdwaras and police stations. Close to 12,000 'internally displaced persons' sought refuge in Punjab, while others, who had the means, left India altogether, escaping to the US, Canada and the UK primarily through family connections.

The Sikh residents of hard-hit locations such as Sultanpuri, Nand Nagri, Shakarpur, Shahdara, Mangolpuri and Trilokpuri abandoned their devastated homes and resettled in areas such as Garhi and Bhogal in South Delhi, and Tilak Vihar in West Delhi. In the latter, approximately 1,932 families were either housed or awarded plots of land by the government. Over time their bleak settlement became known as The Widow Colony (Vidhva Colony).

Unsurprisingly health and social problems have plagued these survivors. The women, often the main breadwinners, suffered from bouts of depression, cardiovascular problems, hypertension and anxiety attacks. When Barbara Crossette of *The New York Times* visited The Widow Colony in 1989, she found broken families wavering 'between cold bitterness and emotional collapse'. Yet scant research has been conducted to establish the after-effects of the trauma on both the women and surviving children.

Some men, particularly those who had lost their fathers and were plagued with mental health issues, sought solace in alcohol and drugs, turning to crime to support their addictions. Allegations of a deliberate campaign by the authorities and police to spread drug addiction amongst survivors in The Widows Colony have been levelled by some. They point to the easy availability of smack (an adulterated form of heroin) and highly addictive painkillers, which are openly sold and on occasion even distributed freely in these neighbourhoods. It has been estimated that in this small area alone, two hundred youths have lost their lives to drugs.

The threat of further violence continued to hang over the survivors. Several violent incidents in which Hindus and Sikhs came to blows occurred in and around their neighbourhoods in 1986. In one instance in July, approximately 2,000 Hindus went on a rampage in retaliation for the killing of Hindus by Sikh extremists in Punjab. Sword-wielding Sikhs fought back but five people were killed (three having been shot by police) and a copy of the Guru Granth Sahib burnt following an attack on a gurdwara. In another incident in December, again following the killing of Hindus in Punjab, fierce encounters occurred at the historic Gurdwara Sis Ganj in Old Delhi and at another gurdwara in East Delhi. Police arrested 1,500 people as they struggled to control the 16,000-strong Hindu mob.

More recently, sporadic incidents have kept the fear of reprisals alive. A few years ago in Shakarpur in East Delhi, several drunken Dalit (untouchable) youths obstructed a religious procession that had set off from the local gurdwara. In the fracas that followed, the shrine was stoned and several Sikhs arrested for using caste slurs. One of these was Gurpal Singh, who as a five-year-old had witnessed his father being burnt alive. 'The drunken youth asked us not to show off our wealth,' he recalled, 'or they could repeat 1984'. As a father of a seven-year-old, he fears for his son: 'That's why I am ashamed to be a citizen of India'.

In another attack in 2013, it was reported that before committing a brutal attack on a Sikh family near Mangolpuri in October 2013, the assailant taunted them by saying '*1984 Bhool gaye? Sallo yaad karwata hoon*' ('Have you forgotten 1984? Let me remind you'). He then beat the turbaned father, dragging him by his beard and hair, and repeatedly punched the mother in her face, smashing several teeth. Their daughter was also assaulted.

Adding to the misery of the survivors was their fragile financial situation. The widows were in many cases not provided with jobs. Those fortunate enough to secure employment were offered low-paid work.

In the first two years, the government hurriedly announced a compensation package of a paltry 10,000 rupees – equivalent to £125 at a time when average annual income was approximately £210 – in respect of those killed. Although this was increased to 700,000 rupees – approximately £10,000 versus average income of around £400 – in 2005 following the release of the Nanavati Commission's report and the subsequent protests, widows had to prove their links with the victims or otherwise provide documentation. For several this requirement was difficult, if not impossible, to meet as they had lost their entire lives in the pogroms.

To add insult to injury, further financial stress was inflicted on some by the state government, which began to demand mortgage payments for the homes that they had been allocated. In 2000, Harpreet Singh, who had lost his father in 1984, was asked to pay 32,000 rupees (approximately £460 when average income was £291 per annum). Incremental interest lifted the debt to 250,000 rupees (approximately £3,000 versus an average annual income of £998) by 2013.

~

The lives of the survivors have also been tainted by political opportunism. Sunny Singh from The Widow Colony explained how 'every year, on the 1984 anniversary, people come here, feast on our lives, journalists get their stories, politicians their mileage, and then they just forget about us'. Author, activist and film-maker, Reema Anand, who worked with victims, noted how this extended to Sikhs from several gurdwara committees who sought to exploit the victims' suffering by holding rallies ostensibly in support of their plight, but in the final analysis taking very little concrete action to help solve their many problems.

Some widows have also felt let down by the wider Sikh community. Kamla Devi's husband was killed in 1984 but his body was never found, though she did manage to find his wristwatch, at Mangolpuri Police Station. 'Lots of people came to us and promised to help us,' she said in an interview in 2013, 'but no one comes back with any kind of help. Even our own community doesn't help us.'

As the journalist Sanjay Suri and others have suggested, this may, in part, have something to do with the backgrounds of the majority of the victims. They hailed from two traditionally poor, nomadic communities, the Labanas and Sikligars. Both groups trace their ancestry back to another clan of itinerant traders, the Banjaras. While Labanas occupied a variety of trades, the Sikligars were essentially blacksmiths who engaged in the manufacture of swords, knives and metal utensils.

Prior to the Partition in 1947, the Labana Sikhs and Sikligar Sikhs had been settled in areas that would be allocated to Pakistan. Before finally relocating to Delhi they had originally headed west to Rajasthan. Although it is hard to give a precise figure, it is thought that up to two-thirds of those killed in Delhi were from these backgrounds.

The other factor seems to be that the atrocities didn't occur within Punjab, the Akali Dal's power base. It's easy to speculate that had the victims been 3,000 Jat Sikhs – the majority agriculturalist Sikh community that forms the Akali Dal's core vote bank – the political outcomes would have been very different.

~

Sikh members of the Congress Party must also shoulder their share of the blame. Those who had the power to raise concerns over the events of 1984 and the injustices that followed were too loyal to the party to ever step out of line.

The most high profile was President Zail Singh, the head of state in 1984, who point-blank refused to take responsibility. His press secretary at the time, Tarlochan Singh, believed that Zail Singh knew of his colleagues' plan to exact revenge on the Sikhs on 31 October. When the author Patwant Singh asked him the following morning to take steps to curb the violence, he responded glibly: 'I have no right to intervene'.

Shyam Bhatia of the *Observer* met the president a few days after making the shocking discovery of over a hundred burnt corpses at a makeshift mortuary in Subzi Mandi. As he described that and other scenes of Delhi under siege that he had witnessed, the president wept and kept repeating, 'What have they done?'

When confronted with the opportunity to take a stand, Zail Singh chose instead to serve party interests. One can only imagine how the victims felt when the Sikh president of India later personally awarded bravery medals to police officers who had been implicated in the violence.

Other loyal Sikh members of the Congress Party demonstrated similar behaviour – some going as far as bestowing Sikh ceremonial honours on Tytler and Bhagat, whilst others have been exposed via a sting operation at attempting to bribe and apply pressure on prosecution witnesses in the case against Kumar.

Punjab's current chief minister, Captain Amarinder Singh, who hails from the erstwhile royal family of Patiala, had been a friend of Rajiv Gandhi's since their days at the Doon School in the 1950s. He won his first election for Congress in 1980 but resigned both his membership of the Congress Party and parliamentary seat in protest against Operation Blue Star. He would later rejoin its ranks in the late 1990s after Sonia Gandhi had taken over the party's reins.

In April 2014, he went on record asserting that Tytler had not been involved in the massacres. He did however concede the involvement of other Congress figures such as Bhagat, Kumar and Maken.

Prime Minister Manmohan Singh's apologetic address to parliament following the release of the Nanavati Commission's report in 2005 touched upon the need to address the needs of the survivors of the tragedy:

> Mr. Speaker, Sir, the most important issue is the need to rehabilitate the families of those affected by that national tragedy. Twenty years after the event, it may be considered late in the day to be saying this. However, if there have been any shortcomings in this regard, it is our solemn assurance that we will make sincere efforts to redress these shortcomings. We will try to ensure that widows and children of those who suffered in this tragedy are enabled to lead a life of dignity and self-respect. It will be our honest attempt to wipe away the tears from every suffering eye.

In stark contrast to these commendable words of comfort, however, were his comments regarding the exoneration of senior Congress figures:

> We had no hands in the choice of who will be heading this Commission of Inquiry and the very fact that this Commission has unambiguously, categorically stated against all the whispering campaign that has been going on for the last 21 years against the top leadership of the Congress Party. They have finally nailed the lie and they have shown that all these canards which have been spread about the involvement of the top leadership of the Congress Party in those dastardly acts were totally untrue.

~

More recently, political debate around 1984 has continually failed to penetrate beyond the lies and inaccuracies. When discussed, it has inevitably been within the framework of the limiting misnomer of 'anti-Sikh riots', curtailing any serious understanding of the nature of the killings.

The events of 1984, like those of the anti-Muslim pogroms of 2002 in the state of Gujarat, have become political footballs, kicked about by the Congress Party and BJP in dismal attempts to score cheap political goals against one another. One example saw Rahul Gandhi, Rajiv Gandhi's son and the then vice-president of the Congress Party, deliver an impassioned election speech in October 2013 in Alwar in the state of Rajasthan. He spoke of his 'anger' at his grandmother's assassination and how he had twice been a victim of terrorism. A few days later, the BJP's Narendra Modi, now prime minister but himself accused of complicity in the 2002 massacres, seized on the comments, asking if it was true that

> your party men in that anger had burnt thousands of Sikhs alive and not a single person has been punished?

In January 2014, Rahul Gandhi spoke about 1984 in an interview with the editor of *Times Now*, Arnab Goswami. Gandhi admitted that some Congressmen were 'probably involved' and they had been punished. He said the government had done 'everything it could to stop the riots'. Goswami was quick to challenge this version of events:

> If the government in Delhi and in the centre was trying to stop the riots in 1984, then tell me, how is it possible that Sajjan Kumar was named in First Information Reports on the grounds of inciting violence in outer Delhi leading to the murder of Sikhs? The status of the case is known. How is Jagdish Tytler accused of inciting the mob in Pulbangash leading to murder and rioting in the area? How is the late H. K. L. Bhagat accused of inciting violence? And you know that a plea in the Delhi Court was closed after his death. How did these Congress leaders do what they did allegedly, if the government was so strongly and proactively acting against the riots?

Caught in the lights, Rahul Gandhi skirted the points raised by saying: 'There is a process. See there is a legal process. And that process is on. Okay?'

Despite admitting that 'some Congressmen were probably involved', Rahul Gandhi appeared to have overcome any lingering reticence with regards to Kumar and Tytler when he allowed both to sit on a panel tasked with overseeing his party's campaign for the Delhi Assembly in late 2014. More recently, however, he has expressed his support for the quest for justice.

~

In the wake of the massacres, as survivors languished with the threat of further attacks looming over them, several of the accused enjoyed successful political careers, albeit under the fear of assassination.

Having been named in the PUDR-PUCL's *Who are the Guilty* report, which was published in November 1984, several Congressmen found themselves on the hit lists of Sikh militant groups. The first to be targeted was Lalit Maken. On 25 July 1985, the day after the signing of the Punjab Accord, his police guard was removed. Just a few days later, he and his wife were gunned down outside their home in New Delhi by three men. The two shooters, Sukhdev Singh and Harjinder Singh Jinda, were members of an armed Sikh group, the Khalistan Commando Force.

The killing triggered a dramatic security response by government in which just over a hundred people in the capital – including the prime minister, his cabinet colleagues, a few secretaries to the government, several MPs, Congress leaders and businessmen – would be guarded by 2,000 armed personnel drawn from various police and intelligence agencies to avert the threat to their lives.

Among these was Arun Nehru. After winning the Rae Bareli constituency vote in December 1984 he joined Rajiv Gandhi's cabinet as union minister of energy. The following year, he took over the portfolio of minister of state for internal security and promptly oversaw the implementation of draconian laws in Punjab.

However, he left Congress to start a new political party after Rajiv Gandhi became embroiled in a corruption scandal in the late 1980s. Nehru died in July 2013 having evaded judicial scrutiny for his role in 1984.

Another target was H. K. L. Bhagat, who was the minister of information and broadcasting in Rajiv Gandhi's cabinet in 1984. In the 1984 parliamentary elections, Bhagat secured the second highest number of votes in the country for his East Delhi constituency. In the 1990s he held several ministerial posts and became president of the New Delhi chapter of the Congress Party. He was arrested in 1996 but exonerated when only one witness testified against him. He escaped a subsequent court appearance that would have seen prosecution witnesses testify when his lawyers argued in 2004 that the onset of dementia precluded the issuing of a warrant for his arrest. Bhagat died in October 2005 shortly after the publication of the Nanavati Commission's report, which indicted him for his alleged role in the Trilokpuri massacre. The Congress Party wasted no time in elevating him for the final time, furnishing his legacy with tributes from the highest levels of government.

In many ways, Sajjan Kumar fared worse politically than his co-accused, being dropped from the general elections of 1984 and 1989 due to the taint of the allegations against him. He did, however, return to the party fold in 1991, and remained the MP for Outer Delhi until 1996. He made a dramatic comeback in 2004, winning the seat with 55% of the vote, one of the largest wins in the country. That year he also became chairman of the Delhi Rural Development Board but was forced to resign just the following year following the release of Nanavati's report. He remained an MP until 2009 when his constituency was abolished following a reorganisation of parliamentary areas. In 2013, Kumar was acquitted of murdering five Sikhs in 1984, a decision that met with strident protests, which included the hurling of a shoe at the judge by Karnail Singh, president of the All India Sikh Students Federation. Kumar's son was shortly after fielded as a Congress hopeful in a South Delhi constituency in 2013 but failed to get elected. Kumar has continued to take active part in Congress politics and as recently as August 2017 campaigned in assembly elections in the town of Bawana in Haryana, a state ravaged by the anti-Sikh violence in 1984. An appeal against the 2013 acquittal is currently underway.

In December 1984, Jagdish Tytler became the MP for Delhi Sadar, after which he took up significant ministerial posts in the civil aviation and surface transport departments. He narrowly lost his seat in the 1996 elections and, although denied a party ticket in 1998, he won in 2004 and was appointed minister of state for non-resident Indians affairs. In 2005, the Nanavati Commission found 'credible evidence' against him but he was twice absolved by the CBI, first in 2007 and then in 2009. In an internal CBI report leaked in 2009, a CBI joint director and deputy inspector general recommended that there was a strong case against Tytler for 'a string of charges including murder, rioting and damage to property'. However, the agency's director, Ashwini Kumar, decided to give Tytler a 'clean chit'. In 2013, Kumar became the first head of the CBI to be appointed as a governor.

The CBI was ordered to reopen the case in April 2013 by a Delhi court. A former joint director of the CBI, Mr M. Narayanan, who was involved in the investigations but retired soon after they had been closed, claimed there was 'sufficient evidence' to continue the probe. He insinuated that the CBI had come under pressure not to indict Tytler after he personally presented investigating officers with a copy of the Doordarshan television footage purportedly showing him at Teen Murti House at the time of the attacks. But Narayanan stressed that these were 'not credible reasons to close the case, since Mr Tytler could have slipped out of Teen Murti at any time, unnoticed by the TV cameras'. Tytler's presence there has also been questioned by Bollywood actor, Amitabh Bachchan, who said in a statement that he had 'no recollection of Mr Tytler being at Teen Murti Bhavan that day'. Bachchan, who had been close to Rajiv Gandhi and had become a Congress MP in 1985, was himself accused of inciting violence, which he 'vehemently' denied in 2011.

A further twist in the case against Tytler came in 2013 when an Indian arms dealer, Abishek Verma, deposed before the CBI that Tytler had in 2008 'boasted of having met the Prime Minister [Manmohan Singh] who in turn would ask Director/CBI to get the investigating conducted in his favour'. He also stated that Tytler had paid hefty sums to one of the key prosecution witnesses and facilitated his son's resettlement abroad. Tytler had been referred to by Manmohan Singh in his 2005 apology as a 'valued colleague'. The investigation is still pending.

Kamal Nath retained his Chhindwara constituency in the central state of Madhya Pradesh in 1985, 1989 and 1991 before holding a number of ministerial roles. He was acquitted in the Nanavati Commission, although his evidence was found to be 'vague'. In 2011 he attended the World Economic Forum at Davos as India's minister of urban development. He is currently the Protem Speaker of the 16th Lok Sabha, India's parliament, and in June 2016 took up a new role of general-secretary of the All India Congress Committee in-charge of Punjab and Haryana. He was, however, forced to resign this last position amid protests that highlighted his alleged complicity in the siege of Delhi's Gurdwara Rakab Ganj in 1984. Nath remains a senior figure in the Congress Party.

When Dharam Dass Shastri was prevented from standing for election in the December 1984 election as punishment for attempting to ensure the release of looters at Karol Bagh Police Station, he is said to have disclosed the fact that 'Congress leaders had planned the riots'. The Nanavati Commission found credible evidence against him but he died before any prosecutions could be pursued.

The Nanavati Commission went out of its way to exonerate Home Minister Narasimha Rao, despite there being evidence of his negligence. He went on to become prime minister in 1991, heralding the era of India's economic liberalisation. The quelling of militancy in Punjab and its reduction in Kashmir were attributed to him, though at the cost of human rights violations. Rao's premiership also witnessed the pogroms in Ayodhya in 1992 following the demolition of a mosque by Hindutva militants, and in Bombay in 1993 after a series of bomb attacks. The stench of corruption was also never far away. A 'cash-for-votes' scandal ahead of a knife-edge no-confidence vote in 1993 saw Rao sentenced to three years imprisonment in 2000. This was the first time an Indian prime minister has been found guilty in a criminal case. His sentence was later reduced to a fine before he was finally acquitted in 2003. He died the following year.

~

Lalit Maken's daughter, Avantika, was only six years old when her parents were killed. In 2008, after meeting with the surviving member of the three-man team responsible for the hit (the other two were hanged in 1992 for the murder of the general who had planned Operation Blue Star), she forgave the murderers in an attempt to bring closure to this painful period in her life.

The anguish of loss and suffering, however, remains for so many others. Gurcharan Singh Gill lost not only his father but also ten members of his family in 1984. One of those was his grandfather, Mangal Singh, who had retired from the army and worked as a social worker. In articulating his dilemma, he speaks for many of the survivor families:

> If the 1984 victims had received justice, then people would not have dared to do the same in Gujarat in 2002. My grandfather, uncles, all served the nation, but what did they get in return? Now, we are 100 years behind. If our fathers and other family members were alive then we would have been educated and would have had respectable jobs. The government hasn't done anything to make our lives better.

20

Truth, Justice & Reconciliation

Superficially, the nation state of India appears to have worked well since Partition.

Sixteen national elections and the peaceful transference of power (barring Indira Gandhi's experiment with autocracy in 1975), the non-interference of the army in politics (even if it has itself been used as an agent of the state against its own people), a move away from single-party dominance towards a greater multi-party system, a growing political assertion of regional identities (albeit sometimes accompanied with strong communal overtones) plus a largely free media, all support the notion of India as a diverse, functioning democracy.

However, as Human Rights Watch noted in their 2016 country report, a number of issues and rising intolerance offer cause for concern. Attacks on religious minorities – often perpetrated or instigated by right-wing Hindu groups intent on pushing a virulent Hindutva ideology (the establishment of the hegemony of Hindus and Hinduism within India) – continue to blight the world's largest democracy. Caste-based prejudice and violence also continue to stain India's record, seemingly indelibly. And the government has yet to repeal laws that grant public officials and security forces effective immunity from prosecution.

Indeed, security forces, including both the police and the army, are rarely held accountable for abuses they commit, which at times are all too prevalent. Parts of the country have remained in a state of permanent conflict, often with armed secessionist forces calling for independence from the furthest regions of the north-east, to the Naxalite movement across southern and eastern regions of the country, to Kashmir – a particularly vicious and somewhat intractable situation with global significance, in which tens of thousands have lost their lives since 1947. In such circumstances the normal rules of security and policing are often circumvented and human rights abuses become rife, as they were in Punjab during the 1980s and 1990s.

Freedom of speech has at times been severely curtailed with the government using defamation laws to prosecute those who criticise it. The country with the freest press on the subcontinent still manages to rank as the 13th most dangerous country in the world for journalists, with some such as Gauri Lankesh, a prominent journalist critical of Hindu nationalist politics, paying the ultimate price as recently as August 2017.

Human rights defenders and organisations also face inordinate difficulties and often violent opposition from state authorities and others. As Human Rights Watch notes:

> The Indian government has escalated pressure on civil society groups critical of its policies, using harassment, intimidation, and restrictions on foreign funding. Free speech has come under attack from both the state and interest groups, and critics of the government often face charges of sedition and criminal defamation, and are labelled 'anti-national'.

Some, as in the case of Punjab's Jaswant Singh Khalra, have faced an even worse fate.

Khalra was a human rights activist who exposed how the Punjab police were involved in the extra-judicial killings and mass cremations of thousands of people during the 1980s and early 1990s. Armed police commandoes abducted Khalra in September 1995. Tortured and shot dead, his dismembered body was thrown into a river.

The lack of women's rights also continues to cast a long shadow. During 2016, a spate of disturbing stories of sexual assault, acid attacks and murder hit the headlines, highlighting to the wider world India's dangerously endemic, misogynistic cultural attitudes. In 2012, India was ranked the worst G20 country in which to be a woman.

India's often corrupt legal system appears to offer little hope of delivering justice to its 1.3 billion citizens, especially the 680 million or more who lack the means to meet their basic needs. At present, over 22 million cases languish, waiting for a hearing in district courts whilst the quality and number of judges is lamentable. Such factors exacerbate an already intolerable state of affairs. Justice delayed, or otherwise perverted, is justice denied.

These, and other issues, are not problems confined solely to India. But they are significant and telling. Although undoubtedly the world's largest democracy, it is hard to describe India as a liberal one. A dangerously corrupt and criminal political class has often aided, abetted and profited from the country's anomalies, adding to the sense that India is failing its own people.

~

Within this wider context, 1984 has great importance in and of itself but also in the role it and its perpetrators have served in the watering down of India's democratic credentials.

Nineteen eighty-four set a terrible precedent of how those with power can and have sought to violently suppress minorities with impunity. The killings of Gujarati Muslims in 2002, and the subsequent electoral gains by those who organised them, and numerous incidents since, have been made that much more possible by the outrageous genocidal massacres of 1984, which have served as a sickening blood-stained blueprint for state-directed mass killings.

So what can and should be done? There is an urgent need to address the shocking truth behind the 1984 pogroms and bring about long awaited justice for the victims as well as punishment for the perpetrators. This can only be achieved if there is an acknowledgment at the state, civic and international level of the reprehensible events, their significance, and the importance of finally and fully closing this dreadful chapter of independent India's story.

As long as the guilty, particularly those in power or public office, continue to evade the rule of law, India's democracy will continue to be one where justice is hoped and fought for rather than expected.

The burden of responsibility also lies overseas. Western governments need to re-examine their often hypocritical role – evangelically preaching democracy whilst turning a blind eye to human rights abuses. Are trade deals more important than crimes against humanity? The UK, in particular, has a history of imposing sanctions against for example Myanmar (Burma), China and North Korea for human rights abuses whilst a period of divestment was introduced against South Africa, which hastened the dismantling of the Apartheid regime. Greater pressure from key western powers could have resulted in swifter justice and could yet prove decisive.

TRUTH, JUSTICE, RECONCILIATION

A number of states, including South Africa, Chile, Rwanda and Bosnia, have held independent truth and reconciliation commissions in order to uncover crimes – committed either by past governments or others – in the hope of resolving continuing conflict or injustices.

Priscilla Hayner, a transitional justice expert, has offered a widely drawn upon definition of a truth commission. For her, they are temporary bodies authorised by the state to investigate human rights abuses by the military or other government forces. There is however no one model of a commission; their focus and purpose vary according to the cultural, historical and social contexts of the crimes involved. This is certainly evident in how different governments have tried to move a nation forward through reconciliation. Whilst justice has been a necessary goal for some, whether it should take a restorative or retributive form has been a matter of debate. Although such commissions do not have the powers to prosecute perpetrators, some have recommended that prosecutions take place, sharing their information with relevant authorities, such as the Truth and Reconciliation Commission in Peru, whilst others have openly named culprits of crimes, such as the Commission for Truth and Reconciliation in South Africa.

Previous calls to introduce such a commission in India, whether domestic or international, have been met with resistance. For example, in 2004 the UK's Green Party MEPs, Caroline Lucas and Jean Lambert tabled a declaration in the European Parliament for India to set-up a truth commission to investigate 1984. The proposal was supported by the UK-based NGO, the 1984 Genocide Coalition. India's National Security Adviser J. N. Dixit responded angrily:

> They will first have to seek our permission if the Commission wants to carry out any investigations. We will never allow such a thing. It is motivated mischief by some people and should be nipped in the bud.

Yet, a thorough and in-depth independent commission is still required, especially considering the failings of past investigations. This is the only way to ensure that lessons are learnt and implemented, a semblance of justice for the victims is secured and closure achieved to allow the healing process for Indian society as a whole to truly begin.

Any commission's scope should include:

• The precise nature of the conspiracy to murder Sikhs *en masse*. When were plans first mooted, hatched and subsequently brought forward? Who was involved, when and why?

- The role played by Rajiv Gandhi, senior Congress leaders such as Arun Nehru, the police, the military and any other state bodies in the planning, execution and subsequent cover-up of the genocidal massacres.

- The role played by Sikh members of the Congress Party in the cover-up.

- The role of the Akali Dal Party and their relative inaction in the pursuit of justice.

- The on-the-ground organisation and implementation of the pogroms. Specifically, who led the mobs and who provided them with electoral lists, transport, weapons, and the tyres, phosphorous and kerosene used to 'necklace' and incinerate victims?

- The role of hospitals that refused to treat the injured victims and who instructed them.

- The rushed disposal and cremation of corpses on the outskirts of Delhi and in mortuaries, including the means of transportation.

- The role of the media and state apparatus in propagating lies to support the notion that Sikhs were a threat to the public.

- The delay in deploying the army, and the lack of effective policing or humanitarian aid.

- The effect on the survivors, their offspring and communities then and since.

- The pursuit for justice by human rights activists and survivors and what outcomes they would like to see such as jobs, counselling and any further reparations.

~

As well as within the scope of any commission, there needs to be a broader, fundamental change in the way that such crimes are perceived in India.

Issues surrounding the (mis)use of language, legal redress, women's rights and impunity for the powerful or those protected by them all need addressing. India cannot act alone. It needs international support and oversight, as part of the body of nations, in order to affect these changes and ensure it upholds human rights, protects the vulnerable and ensures justice is done and seen to be done, at long, long last.

A Shift in Language

There needs to be a shift in the language used to describe the events of 1984. The continued use of the phrase 'anti-Sikh riots' downplays the magnitude of what occurred, doing an injustice to the victims whilst concealing the true nature and extent of what took place.

The double-speak continues today even in Britain. When a BBC radio programme in 2013 was confronted with its repeated use of the word 'riot' to describe 1984, they responded by saying that they saw it as a 'neutral' term.

The current narrative, in both academic and in common parlance, continues to downplay the massacres and their ongoing consequences. This trivialisation has unfortunately passed on to the new generation. Journalist Hartosh Singh Bal notes that the new generation of liberals have

> refused to engage with the reality of what happened in 1984. This particular form of blindness leads them to believe that the Congress could not have orchestrated such terrible events, because it does not stand for such atrocities.

This denial also persists in current western narratives of 1984 as displayed by the distinguished American philosopher of law and ethics at the University of Chicago, Professor Martha C. Nussbaum, when she made the erroneous claim in 2007 that 'rape and killing-by-incineration were not central elements of the violence'.

The continued use of specious terminology by human rights activists, journalists, politicians and academics offers succour to the guilty and continues to cause distress to, and belittles the impact on, the victims. By continuing to refer to the events as 'riots', there can be no proper recognition of the nature of the crime and the need to deal appropriately with its perpetrators and survivors.

The anti-Jewish pogroms of 1938 were also described as such by the Nazis. The victims were blamed for 'provoking' the violence after a German diplomat was assassinated. Then, as now, the violence was portrayed as a 'spontaneous' outburst, whereas the reality was a series of vicious, premeditated, organised attacks by Hitler's thugs. A 'lesson' was taught to a 'troublesome' community. Following 1938, many world leaders sent telegraphs to Hitler to express their outrage. In 1984, there was no such outcry.

Lack of Legal Redress

What is unique in the case of 1984 is the continued lack of recognition and acceptance, including internationally, of the leading role of the Congress Party's leaders in the conspiracy.

It is this cancer of unaccountability that sets 1984 apart from previous genocidal episodes that came before. Amongst those international bodies entrusted to recognise, investigate and prosecute genocidal crimes, such as the United Nations and the International Criminal Court, 1984 has never figured, although two victims did manage to testify before the United Nations High Commissioner for Human Rights in 2014.

In the subsequent thirty years, there have been a number of genocidal massacres in India including at Hashimpura (1987), Bhagalpur (1989), Mumbai (1992), Sopore (1993), Hyderabad (1990), Coimbatore (1998), Gujarat (2002), Kokrajhar (2012) and

Muzaffarnagar (2013). Part of the problem lies in the Indian Penal Code. Although India remains a signatory to the 1951 Geneva Convention on Genocide, and is legally obliged to implement a specific law on all forms of genocide ensuring perpetrators are punished, this is something that does not feature in India's main criminal code. As Professor Abraham Joseph of Ansal University, Gurgaon recently stated: 'In the absence of such a legislative framework, it is hard not to conclude that India is in breach of its legal obligations'.

In April 2017, Canada's Ontario government passed a motion describing 1984 as a genocide. In response, Indian external affairs ministry spokesperson, Gopal Baglay, described it as 'misguided' and the defence minister, Arun Jaitley, said the language used in the motion was 'unreal and exaggerated'. And yet in December 2014, India's interior minister Rajnath Singh acknowledged the events of 1984 as a genocide:

> India's denial of the 1984 pogrom as genocide is problematic...given the non-existence of prescribed domestic standards to test such a claim. Claims of the 1984 pogrom being a genocide on certain occasions and a denial of the characterisation on certain other occasions reflect the casual and non-serious approach of the Indian political class to the human tragedy accompanying mass crimes in India. This problem is aggravated by the absence of a law laying down the contours of the offence like its essential elements, requirements and punishments.

Thus, the introduction of a proper legal framework and laws on genocide are clearly necessary and desperately required. Without them, the search for justice is severely hampered.

SEXUAL VIOLENCE

The horrific gang rape and murder of Jyoti Singh, a twenty-three-year-old woman in Delhi in 2012, stirred national and international outrage, resulting in mass protests across India and debate around the prevalence of sexual violence against women.

In response, the Indian government passed an amendment to rape laws in 2013, redefining consent and what constitutes rape, placing greater emphasis on removing stigma for victims and increasing punishments for perpetrators. However, human rights organisations continue to report that violent crimes against women and girls to be on the rise. Much more still is required to shift cultural and social norms.

The open discussion of the sexual violence of 1984 may be part of the process and is necessary in any case. Bringing these memories to the fore with professional support may offer a path to healing for the victims, as well as to their families, including children, who witnessed the rape of their mothers and sisters.

The cases of mass rape, and in many cases genocidal rape, has often been absent or downplayed in both official and unofficial narratives of 1984 with the exception of a handful of studies. An atmosphere should be created where victims of rape feel comfortable coming forward, without fear of intimidation or stigma.

The prosecution of those who instigated rape as a weapon must be made a priority. All victims of rape and sexual violence, child witnesses and the current generation who have had to deal with the after-effects, should be offered professional counselling as well as educational or employment opportunities, which they were denied due to decades of trauma.

India could do well to heed what was said by the United Nation's special representative of the secretary-general on sexual violence in conflict in 2014. Although her intervention was part of the debate on the genocides that had taken place in countries like Rwanda it set the tone in dealing with these crimes, irrespective of country:

> For the perpetrators, there can be no hiding place; no amnesty; no safe harbour. They will be pursued by any

and all means at our collective disposal. In the process we will begin to transfer the stigma of this crime from the victims, to the perpetrators.

AN END TO IMPUNITY

In a nation where the rich and powerful have the means to pervert and evade justice, there can be no closure for the victims. Enough evidence exists to prosecute the perpetrators despite the corruption and dysfunction that have blighted the commissions, committees and inquiries.

Judge Dhingra, who oversaw one of the cases in court (State v. Ram Pal Saroj), commented on the failure to deliver justice:

> A system which permits the legitimised violence and criminals through the instrumentalities of the state to stifle the investigation cannot be relied upon to dispense basic justice uniformly to the people.

Those who have insisted that India is a democracy, and thereby responsible for its own legal processes, including both Indian commentators and those in the West, should feel apprehensive. The legal processes in India cannot be trusted, even after thirty-plus years, to act in a fair and just manner without international pressure. Civil rights activists and legal reformers within India require global support.

BRITISH GOVERNMENT'S RESPONSIBILITY

The events of 1984 caused reverberations in the West, particularly in the UK with its long tradition of campaigning and free media and strong civic society.

However, when evidence of the mass murders came to light, as did evidence of state collusion in the killings and rapes later on, there was only silence from government quarters. As in other cases, such as the often quoted human rights abuses of Saudi Arabia, the British government seems to weigh up the value of trade deals versus human dignity and invariably comes down on the side of trade as shown again by the strength of recent arms sales to Saudi Arabia.

Further, in the case of 1984 questions have been raised by the release of government papers showing that the Indian authorities sought advice from British intelligence in the run up to the attack on the Golden Temple complex as part of Operation Blue Star. To rid itself of ongoing suspicion the British government needs to answer the following questions:

- When will they release all documents relating to 1984 and its aftermath?

- How much did British officials know about the November pogroms and when?

- Will it now work actively and openly to support human rights in India regardless of trade concerns?

When it comes to genocide there are never two equal sides, so one cannot adopt a position of neutrality. In the words of Auschwitz survivor and Nobel Laureate Elie Wiesel:

> We must always take sides. Neutrality helps the oppressor, never the victim. Silence encourages the tormentor, never the tormented. To remain silent and indifferent is the greatest sin of all.

~

In July 2015, world leaders came to the Bosnian town of Srebrenica to recognise the genocide, twenty years on, of 8,000 Muslims by Bosnian-Serb forces. In 1984, thousands had been killed, raped, traumatised and displaced from their homes. The lives of the survivors, their children and of the generations to come have been irrevocably impacted.

It is time for India and the world to take a similar stand. To this day more than ninety-nine per cent of the killers remain free and the Congress leaders who instigated the genocidal massacre remain mostly unpunished. We look forward to the day *Churasee* ('1984' in Punjabi) is acknowledged by that same world community and India demonstrates the courage to uphold the rights and dignities of its own people above those of its leaders and their henchmen.

Notes

Text extracts are listed in abbreviated form as per the page nos
on which they appear, followed by relevant source citation

PREFACE

ix 'Sikh houses and shops': Khushwant
Singh, *My Bleeding Punjab*, 1992, p 93

xx 'Nowhere else': 'The Ghosts of Mrs
Gandhi' by Amitav Ghosh. Copyright
© Amitav Ghosh, originally
published in the New Yorker, July
1985, used by permission of The Wylie
Agency (UK) Limited

xxii 'years have passed': 'PM's intervention
during the debate in Lok Sabha on
motion for adjournment on need to
take action against persons indicated
by *Nanavati Commission*', Lok Sabha,
*Press Information Bureau, Government
of India*, 11 August 2005

xxiv police had begun: Nikita Lamba,
'Have 1984 Anti-Sikh Riots
Evidences Been Destroyed?', *Tehelka*,
13 April 2015

INTRODUCTION: A DEADLY SPARK

2 up to twelve million: 'The End of the
British Empire in India', in Claude
Markovits (ed), *A History of Modern
India: 1480-1950*, 2002, pp 468–91;
Sugata Bose & Ayesha Jalal, *Modern
South Asia: History, Culture, and
Political Economy*, 2004, pp 135–66

2 kidnapped and raped: Harsh Dobhal
(ed), *Writings on Human Rights,
Law and Society in India: A Combat
Law Anthology, Human Rights Law
Network*, 2001, p 598

2 exceeded a million: Urvashi Butalia,
*The Other Side of Silence: Voices From the
Partition of India*, 2000, p 45

2 approximately 25,000: Vazira
Fazila-Yacoobali Zamindar, *The Long
Partition and the Making of Modern
South Asia: Refugees, Boundaries,
Histories*, 2010, p 21

2 pummel the mob: Nisid Hajari,
*Midnight's Furies: The Deadly Legacy of
India's Partition*, 2015, p 154

3 often intimate relationship: Charles
Moore, *Margaret Thatcher: The
Authorized Biography, Volume Two:
Everything She Wants*, 2015, Chapter
10: Irish Agreement, Brighton Bomb

3   beard-wearing Sikh: 'When NaMo, Swamy played hide and Sikh', *The Times of India*, 27 June 2015

3   dictator of India: Emma Tarlo, *Unsettling Memories: Narratives of the Emergency in Delhi*, 2003, p 34

3   'Campaign to Save Democracy': Harjinder Singh, *Reflection on 1984*, 2014, p 28

4   30 percent of the total: ibid

4   'Everything was ready': 'British actor Peter Ustinov said on French television Wednesday', *UPI*, 31 October 1984

4   dismissed as firecrackers: Sheamus Smith, *Off Screen: A Memoir*, 2007, p 189

5   warning or evacuation: Amiya Rao et al, *Report to the Nation: Oppression in Punjab*, p 60

5   foreign journalists: Michael Hamlyn, 'Journalists removed from Amritsar: army prepares to enter Sikh shrine, *The Times*, 6 June 1984

5   abuses inevitably followed: Sunny Hundal, 'Operation Blue Star: 25 years on', *The Guardian*, 3 June 2009

5   as they saw fit: Deep Basu, 'Beant Singh: The Man Who Killed Indira Gandhi!', *India Opines*

5   'No society, least of all a society like ours': Patwant Singh, 'Affidavit of Prominent Persons', *Justice Nanavati Commission of Inquiry*, 2005, at *Carnage '84*

6   organising committee: '1982: high on drama', *India Today*, 2 July 2007

6   'People spoke in hushed whispers': Professor Swaran Preet Singh, 'The assassination of Indira Gandhi: I was there', *The University of Warwick*, 2014

PART I – THE CRIME

1. INSTIGATION & PREPARATION

11   a transistor radio: William K. Stevens, 'Gandhi, slain, is succeeded by son', *The New York Times*, 1 November 1984

11   'What is the point': Amiya Rao et al, *Truth about Delhi Violence: Report to the Nation*, 1985, at *Carnage '84*

12   a local metropolitan councillor: 'We will not forget you,' *My Malice and Bias*, October 25, 2016

12   the attacks on Sikhs: *Justice Nanavati Commission of Inquiry*, 2005, at *Carnage '84*, pp 74–5

12   a Sikh man was brutally battered: Devika Chhibber, 'Rediscovering the phantoms of 1984', *Zee News*, 7 November 2009

12   'Blood for blood': C. G. Manoj, 'Rajiv Gandhi didn't take calls from President after 1984 riots broke out', *The Indian Express*, 30 January 2014

13   'two police officers, from my local police station': Professor Swaran Preet Singh, 'The assassination of Indira Gandhi: I was there', *The University of Warwick*, 2014

13   'Your water supply has been poisoned': Poonam Muttreja, Munirka Enclave, 'Affidavit', *Misra Commission*, 1987, at *Carnage '84*

13   'The killings started late that evening': Professor Swaran Preet Singh, 'The assassination of Indira Gandhi: I was there', *The University of Warwick*, 2014

13   'had to be burned': Dr Rajni Kothari, 'Genocide - 1984: The how and why of it all', *Angelfire*, 1994

14   330 Sikh places of worship: Sakshi

Arora, 'Gurdwaras became the first target, the last refuge', *The Times of India*, 2004

14 'his deep hurt': Uma Chakravarti and Nandita Haksar, *The 1984 Archive*

14 'where they burn books': Heinrich Heine, Almansor: *A Tragedy (1821)*, quoted in Thomas Pfau, *Romantic Moods: Paranoia, Trauma, and Melancholy*, 1790–1840, 2005, p 439

14 'the hair of both': Inder Singh, Farash Bazar Camp, 'Affidavit', *Misra Commission*, 1987, at *Carnage '84*

15 overflowing with the bodies of dead Sikhs: *Who are the Guilty?*, 1984

2. EXECUTION & DIRECTION

17 Sacks of white phosphorous powder: Jaspreet Singh, 'Carbon', *Open*, 9 November 2013

18 ration lists and electoral rolls: Amiya Rao et al, *Truth about Delhi Violence: Report to the Nation*, 1985, at *Carnage '84*

18 'They were carrying a list': Dara Singh, Patiala, 'Affidavit', *Justice Nanavati Commission of Inquiry*, 2005, at *Carnage '84*

18 'from door to door of Sikh houses': Amiya Rao et al, *Truth about Delhi Violence: Report to the Nation*, 1985, at *Carnage '84*

18 'like a battlefield': 'The Violent Aftermath', *India Today*, 30 November 1984

19 'The streets were empty': Aseem Shrivastava, 'The Winter in Delhi', *Counterpunch*, 10 December 2005

19 'Look, his name has not been struck off': Amar Singh, Yamna Vihar,

'Affidavit', *Justice Nanavati Commission of Inquiry*, 2005, at *Carnage '84*

19 'Kerosene was sprinkled on him': FIR no. 416 of Baljeet Kaur, Police Station Delhi Cantt., quoted in written arguments on behalf of Delhi Sikh Gurdwara Management Committee, to *Misra Commission*, 1987, at *Carnage '84*

3. BUTCHERING & BURNING

21 'While their hair was cut': Amiya Rao et al, *Truth about Delhi Violence: Report to the Nation*, 1985, at *Carnage '84*

22 'dragged her husband': Pranay Gupte, *Mother India: A Political Biography of Indira Gandhi*, 2009, p 76

22 'castrated and their genitals': ibid

22 she saw the heads of her two dead nephews: Smt Balwant Kaur, West Sagarpur, 'Affidavit', *Misra Commission*, 1987, at *Carnage '84*

22 stench reminiscent of the Blitz: 'British actor Peter Ustinov said on French television Wednesday', *UPI*, 31 October 1984

22 stabbing and burning alive: John Fear, *Exclusive Pedigree: My life in and out of the Brethren*, 2016, Chapter 37: Indian Experiences

23 In his opinion: ibid

23 'Once they shouted': William Dalrymple, *City of Djinns*, 2005, p 33

24 setting them alight: Rahul Kuldip Bedi, 'Politics of a Pogrom', in *The Assassination and After*, eds Arun Shourie et al, 1985, p 51; Rahul Kuldip Bedi, 'Affidavit', *Misra Commission*, 1987, at *Carnage '84*

24 '30 long and uninterrupted hours': 'Rahul

Kuldip Bedi, 'Politics of a Pogrom', in *The Assassination and After*, eds Arun Shourie et al, 1985, p 54

24 'Two lanes': ibid, p 54

24 one littered with the bloated bodies: Rahul Bedi, 'Indira Gandhi's death remembered', *BBC*, 1 November 2009

24 'laughed out of the control room': Ajaz Ashraf, 'Lest we forget: what five eminent Sikhs and a former prime minister witnessed during the 1984 riots', *Scroll*, 31 October 2016

25 still burning like wood: Andrew North, 'Delhi 1984: India's Congress party still struggling to escape the past', *BBC*, 18 February 2014

25 burning of garbage: Devika Chhibber, 'Rediscovering the phantoms of 1984', *Zee News*, 7 November 2009

25 'As we turned': Ram Jethmalani, New Delhi, 'Witness statement', *Justice Nanavati Commission of Inquiry*, 2005, at *Carnage '84*

25 tossed onto makeshift bonfires: Pranay Gupte, *Mother India: A Political Biography of Indira Gandhi*, 2009, p 92

25 Men were dragged to the rooftops: Jarnail Singh, *I Accuse... The Anti-Sikh Violence of 1984*, 2011, p 23

25 Children were lynched: Madhu Kishwar, 'Gangster Rule: Massacre of the Sikhs in 1984', *Manushi*, 1985

25 Holy sites were burnt to the ground: Delhi Sikh Gurdwara Management Committee, written arguments to *Misra Commission*, 1987, at *Carnage '84*

25 set ablaze with his children inside: Madhu Kishwar, 'Gangster Rule', *Manushi*, 1985

25 were roasted alive: Delhi Sikh Gurdwara Management Committee, written arguments to *Misra Commission*, 1987, at *Carnage '84*

25 'The nights are ours': Amiya Rao et al, *Truth about Delhi Violence: Report to the Nation*, 1985, at *Carnage '84*

26 'One woman later described: Madhu Kishwar, 'Gangster Rule', *Manushi*, 1985

26 'Immediately when we came out': Narinder Singh, Gammon Colony, 'Affidavit', *Misra Commission*, 1987, at *Carnage '84*

26 'We saw a child': Uma Chakravarti and Nandita Haksar, *The 1984 Archive*

27 Six hundred Sikhs: *Who are the Guilty?*, 1984

27 sheltered by Hindus: ibid

27 Sikh-owned businesses: Madhu Kishwar, 'Gangster Rule', *Manushi*, 1985

27 a burning taxi: 'Was it a Communal Riot?,' *Outlook*, 11 August 2005

27 In Sadiq Nagar: ibid

27 Hindus were protecting her: ibid

27 A Hindu family in Shakurpur: Madhu Kishwar, 'In the name of secularism and national unity - how Congress engineered the 1984 pogroms', *Manushi*

27 later attend a ceremony: Madhu Kishwar, 'Affidavit of Prominent Persons', *Justice Nanavati Commission of Inquiry*, 2005, at *Carnage '84*

28 were hit hard by attacks: Delhi Sikh Gurdwara Management Committee, written arguments to *Misra Commission*, 1987, at *Carnage '84*

28 In the Govindpuri area: Jasneet Aulakh, 'Sikh and Hindu Resistance in the 1984 Anti-Sikh Pogrom', *USC*, 2012

28   Elsewhere voluntary groups: 'Was it a Communal Riot?', *Outlook*, 11 August 2005

28   who came to loot and kill: *Who are the Guilty?*, 1984

28   A Muslim risked his life: 'Was it a Communal Riot?', *Outlook*, 11 August 2005

28   a Sikh lady and her children: Madhu Kishwar, 'In the name of secularism and national unity - how Congress engineered the 1984 pogroms', *Manushi*

28   they would have been butchered: *Who are the Guilty?*, 1984

28   far superior in numbers: Amiya Rao et al, *Truth about Delhi Violence: Report to the Nation*, 1985, at *Carnage '84*

28   They volunteered in the refugee camps: 'Was it a Communal Riot?', *Outlook*, 11 August 2005

4. TERROR SPREADS

29   The attacks started at 7am: Devika Chhibber, 'Rediscovering the phantoms of 1984', *Zee News*, 7 November 2009

29   The rapes and killings began: ibid

29   finally imposed a curfew: ibid

29   indiscriminate in their decimation: 'Chapter 12: Bokaro & Chas', *Misra Commission Report*, 1987, at *Witness '84*

29   their trademark white Ambassador cars: ibid

30   She watched helplessly: Miss Jasbir Kaur, Gammon Colony, 'Affidavit', *Misra Commission*, 1987, at *Carnage '84*

30   'Were we all responsible?': Avalok Langer, 'Riots in Pataudi. Not a whisper escaped', *Tehelka*, 13 March 2011

30   'I want my children': ibid

31   'Sikhs are traitors': Ramaninder Bhatial, 'Killers motive was revenge at Hondh Chillar, mentions FIR', *The Times of India*, 24 February 2011

31   torched alive in their homes: Sakshi Dayal, '1984 anti-Sikh riots, 32 years later: 'They called my family out, burnt them alive', *The Indian Express*, 30 June 2016

31   they denied their decision: I. P. Singh, 'Man who exposed Hondh Chillar loses job', *The Times of India*, 13 March 2011

31   'In this house lived a scooter driver': 'Eastern Eye report on the violence', *ITV*, January 1985

32   first two days of November: Railway Protection Force, 'Annexure on Unauthorized Stoppages', quoted in Jaskaran Kaur, *Twenty Years of Impunity: The November 1984 Pogroms of Sikhs in India*, 2006, p 59

32   two young Sikhs: John Fear, *Exclusive Pedigree: My life in and out of the Brethren*, 2016, Chapter 37: Indian Experiences

32   The mobs boasted: ibid

32   'No Sikh': Professor Madhu Dandavate, New Delhi, 'Affidavit', *Misra Commission*, 1987, at *Carnage '84*

32   Three more dead Sikhs: ibid

32   'They searched the entire train': Rameshwar Dayal, Booking Clerk, Railway Station, Tughlakabad, 'F.I.R. No. 355/84', 1 November 1984, at *Carnage '84*

33   'please arrange to remove twelve dead bodies': Delhi Sikh Gurdwara Management Committee, written

arguments to *Misra Commission*, 1987, at *Carnage '84*

33　'Delhi is burning': Ajaz Ashraf, 'Lest we forget: what five eminent Sikhs and a former prime minister witnessed during the 1984 riots', *Scroll*, 31 October 2016

33　died the next day: Jaskaran Kaur, *Twenty Years of Impunity*, 2006, p 39

33　paralysed from the waist down: Affidavit of Amarjit Kaur, Kanpur, cited in Jaskaran Kaur, *Twenty Years of Impunity*, 2006, p 39

33　investigation into his death: Affidavit of Balwinder Singh, Sarai Rohilla, cited in ibid, p 40

33　leaving eight murdered: Government of India, *Kusum Lata Mittal Committee report*, 1990

34　mobs waiting outside: Jarnail Singh, *I Accuse… The Anti-Sikh Violence of 1984*, 2011, p 13

34　refused to admit them: Ram Jethmalani, New Delhi, 'Witness statement', *Justice Nanavati Commission of Inquiry*, 2005, at *Carnage '84*

34　Daltonganj Hospital in Bihar: Jaskaran Kaur, *Twenty Years of Impunity*, 2006, p 39

34　leave the hospital: ibid

34　following the massacres: Professor Swaran Preet Singh, interview with author, 21 February 2015

34　attended the funeral: William Claiborne and Lena Sun, 'Indira Gandhi Cremated in Hindu Ritual', *The Washington Post*, 4 November 1984

34　hear the sound of violence: Andy Hynes, 'Everett Rovers 3 St Albans 2', *Everett Rovers FC*, 20 November 2016

5. Mass Rape

35　In 2006, filmmaker Reema Anand: Gurcharan Singh, 'Scorched White Lilies of '84', review in *Institute of Sikh Studies*, January 2011

36　murdered family members: Madhu Kishwar, 'Gangster Rule', *Manushi*, 1985

36　being forced to watch: ibid

36　That morning the family: ibid

37　Also, in Trilokpuri; Another woman who tried: ibid

37　they were either killed: Manoj Mitta and Harvinder Phoolka, *When a Tree Shook Delhi*, 2007, p 68

37　identify the leader: *Sikri Report*, 1984, at *Carnage '84*

37　The women were horded together: ibid

38　She was abducted: Padmi Kaur, Sultanpuri, 'Affidavit', *Misra Commission*, 1987, at *Carnage '84*

38　girls as young as nine to ten: Madhu Kishwar, 'Gangster Rule', *Manushi*, 1985

38　on the orders of the local Congress leader: Jaskaran Kaur, *Twenty Years of Impunity*, 2006, p 38

38　their assailants poured acid: Affidavit of Sarabjeet Singh, cited in ibid

38　Elderly women: Madhu Kishwar, 'Gangster Rule', *Manushi*, 1985

38　destroy the victims' morale: ibid

38　cinders of their homes: *Who are the Guilty?*, 1984

6. The Body Count

39　'total death toll': 'The Ghosts of Mrs Gandhi' by Amitav Ghosh.

Copyright © Amitav Ghosh, originally published in the New Yorker, July 1985, used by permission of The Wylie Agency (UK) Limited

39 the corpses of 400 Sikhs: Joseph Maliakan, '1984 riots in Trilokpuri: bodies of hundreds of Sikhs were scattered, some showed signs of life', *The Indian Express*, 3 November 2014

39 'things are under control': *Who are the Guilty?*, 1984

40 'exaggerated accounts': Romesh Thapar, *These Troubled Times*, 1986, p 64

40 the official number: Amiya Rao et al, *Truth about Delhi Violence: Report to the Nation*, 1985, at *Carnage '84*

40 thousands were murdered: Pranay Gupte, *Mother India: A Political Biography of Indira Gandhi*, 2009, p 77

40 doused in oil and set ablaze: Moti Singh's testimony, Delhi Sikh Gurdwara Management Committee, written arguments to *Misra Commission*, 1987, at *Carnage '84*

40 half-burnt corpses: Dhoban Kaur's testimony, ibid

40 street sweepers removed the dead: Lakhbir Singh's testimony, ibid

40 "bodies piled up: Salawati Kaur's testimony, ibid

40 'half-burnt': Sanjay Suri, 1984: *The Anti-Sikh Violence and After*, 2015, p 110

41 'the stench refused to leave': Shyam Bhatia, *Bullets and Bylines: From the Frontlines of Kabul, Delhi, Damascus and Beyond*, 2016, p 41; Robin Lustig, *Is Anything Happening?: My Life as a Newsman*, 2017, Chapter 9: The Observer

41 transport bodies in trucks and vans:

'Babbar on 84', *Youtube*, posted by 'Sikh Channel Delhi Unit', 13 February 2014

41 'piled them [the bodies]': ibid

41 3,870 in Delhi alone: *Citizens Justice Committee*, quoted in the *Ahooja Committee Report*, 1986

41 exceeding 3,000: *Who are the Guilty?*, 1984

41 double this figure: Pranay Gupte, *Mother India: A Political Biography of Indira Gandhi*, 2009, p 77

41 half in the capital: 'Narendra Modi: a man of some of the people', *The Economist*, 18 December 2013

42 a staggering 35,000 claims: 'Report on 1984 Sikh Genocide', *Sikhs for Justice*, submitted to UN Secretary General, November 2013

42 The widow of Sanjay Gandhi; She went on; She went further: Dean Brelis, 'After Indira's death, her daughter-in-law Maneka hungers to head the Gandhi dynasty', *People*, 26 November 1984

7. THE AFTERMATH

43 up to 50,000: Lional Baixas, 'The Anti-Sikh Pogrom of October 31 to November 4, 1984', *SciencePro*, 9 June 2009

44 eighteen relief camps: *Who are the Guilty?*, 1984

44 around 18,000 internal refugees: ibid

44 unofficial relief centres: ibid

44 'There were all these grieving people': Manraj Grewal, *Dreams after Darkness, a search for a life ordinary under the shadow of 1984*, 2004, p 43

45 Both were later removed by the
    police: Ivan Fera, 'The Enemy
    Within', *Illustrated Weekly*, 23
    December 1985, p 17

45 proved futile: *Who are the Guilty?*,
    1984

45 survivors were herded: ibid

45 able to record and preserve: Uma
    Chakravarti and Nandita Haksar, *The
    Delhi Riots: Three Days in the Life of a
    Nation*, 1987 p 7

46 'She was taken to the hospital':
    Professor Swaran Preet Singh, interview
    with author, 21 February 2015

46 'The widows': Bobby Friction,
    'Assassination: when Delhi burned',
    BBC Radio 4, 31 October 2014

46 screaming in desperation: ibid

47 While initially calling for calm:
    Meenakshi Ahluwalia, *Assassination
    of Rajiv Gandhi*, 1991, pp 94–5

47 immediate parliamentary elections:
    'Gandhi, seeking sympathy vote,
    calls early election', *Los Angeles Times*,
    14 November 1984

47 shockingly overt: Hartosh Singh Bal,
    'Sins of commission', *The Caravan*,
    1 October 2014

47 Huge billboards went up: Khushwant
    Singh, *My Bleeding Punjab*, 1992, p 101

47 two Sikhs in uniform: ibid

47 'Will the country's border': ibid

48 the insinuation was abundantly
    clear: Pranay Gupte, *Mother India:
    A Political Biography of Indira Gandhi*,
    2009, p 98

48 'These people': Jaskaran Kaur, *Twenty
    Years of Impunity*, 2006, p 79

48 'urinated over it': Uma Chakravarti and
    Nandita Haksar, *The Delhi Riots: Three
    Days in the Life of a Nation*, 1987, p 90

48 'The other day I was in a bus': Uma
    Chakravarti and Nandita Haksar,
    The 1984 Archive

48 'What is a burnt Sikh?': ibid

PART II – THE COVER-UP

8. THE PLANNING

53 rogue Hutu elements: Gerald Caplan,
    'Who killed the president of Rwanda?',
    Pambazuka, 21 January 2010

53 'final solution': Gérard Prunier, *The
    Rwanda Crisis: History of a Genocide*,
    1999, p 200

53 thousands of machetes: 'The
    Machete', *Imaging Genocide*, 2017

53 anti-Tutsi propaganda: Gérard
    Prunier, *The Rwanda Crisis: History of
    a Genocide*, 1999, p 189

54 Prime Minister Rajiv Gandhi: 'Rajiv
    Gandhi exposed by Advo. H S Phoolka:
    Video of Boat Club Speech (Nov. 19,
    1984) released', *Youtube*, posted by
    'SikhSiyasat', 20 November 2015

54 'What happened here': 'India enters
    new political territory', *Lubbock
    Avalanche-Journal*, 12 June 2004

54 the murders and acts of looting: Amit
    Agnihotri, 'Sanjay Gandhi was much
    misunderstood, says President Pranab
    Mukherjee in memoir', *India Today*,
    30 January 2016

54 'People in Shivaji Park': Amiya Rao,
    'When Delhi Burnt', *Economic and
    Political Weekly*, 8 December 1984, p 2066

55 'The plan and its methodology' : Ram
    Narayan Kumar, *Terror in Punjab:
    Narratives, Knowledge and Truth*,

2008, p 129

55 'to take advantage': Cynthia Keppley Mahmood, *Fighting for Faith and Nation*, 1996, p 139

55 'the plan was': Puneet Bedi, *1984 Living History*, 4 June 2014

55 'informed by a Congress friend': Ranjit Singh Narula, 'Affidavit of Prominent Persons', *Justice Nanavati Commission of Inquiry*, 2005, at *Carnage '84*

55 'blood for blood': C. G. Manoj, 'Rajiv Gandhi didn't take calls from President after 1984 riots broke out', *The Indian Express*, 30 January 2014

56 'down the line': Manoj Mitta and Harvinder Phoolka, *When a Tree Shook Delhi*, 2007, p 115

56 'the entire Sikh community': Jarnail Singh, *I Accuse... The Anti-Sikh Violence of 1984*, 2011, p 26

56 These poisoned sentiments: Dr Rajni Kothari, 'Genocide - 1984: the how and why of it all', *Angelfire*, 1994

57 'unwilling to negotiate a settlement': *White Paper on the Punjab Agitation*, 10 July 1984

57 'took an intransigent stand': Kuldip Nayar and Khushwant Singh, *Tragedy of Punjab*, 1984, p 81

59 cash payments to the killers: ibid

59 evidence obliterated: Delhi Sikh Gurdwara Management Committee, written arguments to *Misra Commission*, 1987, at *Carnage '84*

9. THE MOTIVES

61 'small lesson': Aseem Shrivastava, 'The Winter in Delhi', *Counterpunch*,

10 December 2005

61 the 'aggressive' Sikh community: Madhu Kishwar, 'Gangster Rule', *Manushi*, 1985

62 the majority of victims: Aseem Shrivastava, 'The Winter in Delhi', *Counterpunch*, 10 December 2005

62 staunch supporters: Lional Baixas, 'The Anti-Sikh Pogrom of October 31 to November 4, 1984', *SciencePro*, 9 June 2009

63 They also made up: Patwant Singh, *The Sikhs*, 2008, p 253

63 strategically indefensible: Swaminathan Aiyar, 'Financial story of our independence', *The Times of India*, 17 August 2003

63 'Sikhistan' and 'Khalistan': Khushwant Singh, *The History of the Sikhs vol 2*, 1977, p 259

64 'The brave Sikhs': Jawahar Lal Nehru, 'Lahore Bulletin,' 9 January 1930, quoted in Giorgio Shani, *Sikh Nationalism and Identity in a Global Age*, 2008, p 163

64 comprising autonomous units: Gopal Singh, *South Asia: democracy, discontent and societal conflicts*, 1998, p 278

64 Millions of Sikhs: Khushwant Singh, *The History of the Sikhs vol 2*, p 282

64 exceeded a million: Urvashi Butalia, *The Other Side of Silence: Voices From the Partition of India*, 2000, p 45

64 kidnapped and raped: Harsh Dobhal (ed), *Writings on Human Rights, Law and Society in India: A Combat Law Anthology*, 2011, p 598

64 defining religious freedoms: Central Government Act, 'Article 25(2)', *The Constitution Of India*, 1949

64 feared the loss of identity: Nazer
Singh, *Guru Granth Sahib Over to the
West: Idea of Sikh scriptures translations
1810-1909*, 2005, p 21

64 a threat to the secular fabric: Karl J.
Schmidt, *An atlas and survey of South
Asian history*, 1999, p 88

65 Sikhs' support: Khushwant Singh,
The History of the Sikhs vol 2, p 308

65 to identify with Hindi: Patwant
Singh, *The Sikhs*, p 222; Khushwant
Singh, *The History of the Sikhs vol 2*,
pp 305–06

65 distribution of Punjab's river waters:
Kuldip Nayar and Khushwant Singh,
Tragedy of Punjab, 1984, pp 156–57

65 the green revolution: Mary Anne
Weaver, 'Sikhs and Hindus in Punjab
show rare unity in protest over
wheat', *The Christian Science Monitor*,
30 May 1984; Pritam Singh, *Political
economy of the Punjab: an insider's
account*, 1997, p 38

65 classified as a union territory:
Khushwant Singh, *The History of the
Sikhs vol 2*, p 307

66 given little consideration: Lional
Baixas, 'The Anti-Sikh Pogrom of
October 31 to November 4, 1984',
SciencePro, 9 June 2009

66 offered a sustained resistance:
Hartosh Singh Bal, 'The shattered
dome', *The Caravan*, 1 May 2014

66 Anandpur Sahib Resolution: Kuldip
Nayar and Khushwant Singh, *Tragedy
of Punjab*, 1984, p 61

66 never forgave the Sikhs: Patwant
Singh, *The Sikhs*, p 230

66 discredit and disrupt: John Keay,
*Midnight's Descendants: South Asia
from Partition to the Present Day*,
2014, p 225

67 blighted the Sikh peasantry:
Khushwant Singh, *The History of the
Sikhs vol 2*, p 329

67 with Zail Singh: ibid, p 332

67 according to some commentators:
Patwant Singh, *The Sikhs*, p 232

67 against the Akali Dal: John Keay,
Midnight's Descendants, 2014, p 226

67 'seemed too uneducated': Mary Anne
Weaver, 'India's warring 'ayatollah'
faced commando siege', *The Sunday
Times*, 4 March 1984

67 so too did the violence: John Keay,
Midnight's Descendants, 2014, p 226;
Khushwant Singh, *The History of the
Sikhs vol 2*, p 337

67 in connection with the murder:
Hartosh Singh Bal, 'The shattered
dome', *The Caravan*, May 1, 2014 67

that Bhindranwale chose when and
how: ibid

67 without the intervention: Khushwant
Singh, *The History of the Sikhs vol 2*, p 335

67 living within the sanctuary: Hartosh
Singh Bal, 'The shattered dome', *The
Caravan*, May 1, 2014

67 Punjab was engulfed in violence:
Khushwant Singh, *The History of the
Sikhs vol 2*, p 338

68 Bhindranwale's former advocate:
John Keay, *Midnight's Descendants*,
2014, p 228

68 violence was only set to escalate: ibid

68 Indian Army commandos were poised:
Mary Anne Weaver, 'India's warring
'ayatollah' faced commando siege', *The
Sunday Times*, 4 March 1984

68 shot dead on the spot: Kuldip Nayar
and Khushwant Singh, *Tragedy of
Punjab*, 1984, p 76

68 little media attention: ibid, p 77

68 a justifiable response: Madhu Kishwar, 'Gangster Rule', *Manushi*, 1985

68 to capture the votes: Indarjit Singh, 'Faith and reason: how to turn religious beliefs into a nuclear explosion', *The Independent*, 22 May 1998

68 placed atop a mosque: Thomas Blom Hansen, *Wages of Violence: Naming and Identity in Postcolonial Bombay*, 2001, p 77

68 looting, violence and killings: ibid

68 nearly 300 killed: ibid

69 'Majorities too have their rights': Indarjit Singh, 'Faith and reason: how to turn religious beliefs into a nuclear explosion', *The Independent*, 22 May 1998

69 Akali Dal called for a boycott: Kuldip Nayar and Khushwant Singh, *Tragedy of Punjab*, 1984, p 90

69 Bhindranwale's occupation: Joyce Pettigrew, *The Sikhs of the Punjab: Unheard Voices of State and Guerrilla Violence*, 1995, pp 34–5

69 a replica Golden Temple: Khushwant Singh, *The History of the Sikhs vol 2*, p 358

69 asked the British government: 'Golden Temple attack: UK advised India but impact 'limited'', *BBC*, 7 June 2014

70 'not to eliminate': Joyce Pettigrew, *The Sikhs of the Punjab: Unheard Voices of State and Guerrilla Violence*, 1995, pp 34–5

70 the casualties were believed: 'Golden Temple attack: UK advised India but impact 'limited'', *BBC*, 7 June 2014

70 At least 4,000 Sikh soldiers: Kuldip Nayar and Khushwant Singh, *Tragedy of Punjab*, 1984, p 107

10. KILLERS IN UNIFORM

71 capital's police stations: 'Chapter 84: Introduction', *Youtube*, posted by 'Cobra Post', 21 April 2014

71 'teach the Sikhs a lesson': 'Chapter 84: An investigation into the anti-Sikh riots in Delhi', *Cobrapost*, 1 July 2016

71 acted on orders from above: ibid

71 flooded with messages: 'Delhi cops, govt 'colluded' during 1984 anti-Sikh riots: Sting operation', *The Times of India*, 22 April 2014

72 removal of mutilated Sikh corpses: 'Chapter 84: An investigation into the anti-Sikh riots in Delhi', *Cobrapost*, 1 July 2016

72 every opportunity to deploy their resources: Sanjay Suri, 'In Kamal Nath, Congress finds a dubious general for Punjab', *CNN-News18*, 14 June 2016

72 to muster just three policemen: 'Annexure II, Eye-witness account – Rahul Kuldip Bedi and Joseph Maliakan', *Who are the Guilty?*, 1984

72 the majority felt: Amiya Rao et al, *Truth about Delhi Violence: Report to the Nation*, 1985, at *Carnage '84*

72 they were acting: 'Delhi Police kept eyes 'closed' during 1984 anti-Sikh riots: CBI', *India Today*, 31 March 2012

72 the would-be killers: Vidya Kaur, 'Affidavit', *The Tarkunde Report: Police Lawlessness*

73 'We are your husbands': ibid

73 mobs alleged to have: Manoj Mitta and Harvinder Phoolka, *When a Tree Shook Delhi*, 2007, p 25

73 Twenty-five Sikhs were arrested: ibid, p 27

73 fires continued to rage across the capital: Delhi Sikh Gurdwara Management Committee, written arguments to *Misra Commission*, 1987, at *Carnage '84*

73 only able to extinguish fires at four: ibid

73 the police simply waited: Amiya Rao et al, *Truth about Delhi Violence: Report to the Nation*, 1985, at *Carnage '84*

73 twenty policemen watched: ibid

73 encouraged to continue: ibid

74 a Sikh taxi driver was burnt: ibid

74 'Hindus are just burning garbage': Devika Chhibber, 'Rediscovering the phantoms of 1984', *Zee News*, 7 November 2009

74 'the police are with us': Amiya Rao et al, *Truth about Delhi Violence: Report to the Nation*, 1985, at *Carnage '84*

74 two other constables: ibid

74 roaming death squads: ibid

74 only applied to the Sikhs: Jaskaran Kaur, *Twenty Years of Impunity*, 2006, p 50

74 'Don't worry': Jarnail Singh, *I Accuse... The Anti-Sikh Violence of 1984*, 2011, p 26

74 recovered an identity card: Kuldip Singh Bhogal, Hari Nagar Ashram, 'Affidavit', *Nanavati Commission*, 2005, at Carnage '84

75 Dutch bounty hunters: 'Dutch bounty hunters preyed on Jews during Holocaust, study shows', *The Times of Israel*, 19 April 2013

75. 'otherwise apprehending and killing Sikhs': Manoj Mitta and Harvinder Phoolka, *When a Tree Shook Delhi*, 2007, p 77

75 'putting them to a loss': ibid, p 76; converted to pound sterling using historic rates (see FXTop.com and XE.com)

75 'You have thirty-six hours': Amiya Rao et al, *Truth about Delhi Violence: Report to the Nation*, 1985, at *Carnage '84*

75 burnt down the local gurdwara: ibid

75 'had the rest of the evening': ibid

75 death squads unleashed: ibid

75 'completed the job': ibid

75 'lay down their arms': Sanjay Suri, *1984: The Anti-Sikh Violence and After*, 2015, p 127

76 disturbances were taking place: ibid, p 97

76 their 'pin-drop silence' troubled him: ibid, pp 100–07

76 Next to no Sikh shops were attacked: ibid, p 131

77 a case of criminal negligence: Manoj Mitta and Harvinder Phoolka, *When a Tree Shook Delhi*, 2007, p 120

77 acted in accordance: ibid, p 39

77 placing the police: Tusha Mittal, 'A pack of wolves in khaki clothing', *Tehelka*, 25 April 2009

77 alleged perpetrators: *Twenty Years of Impunity*, p 53

77 'vague and generally worded omnibus': ibid, p 52; Tusha Mittal, 'A pack of wolves in khaki clothing', *Tehelka*, 25 April 2009

77 culprits were purportedly 'untraceable": Tusha Mittal, 'A pack of wolves in khaki clothing', *Tehelka*, 25 April 2009

77 registered them against Sikhs: ibid

77 wrote false affidavits: ibid

77 'absolutely casual, perfunctory and faulty': G. T. Nanavati, *Justice Nanavati Commission of Inquiry 1984 (Anti-Sikh Riots)*, Volume One, 2005, p 5

78 It is clear that: 'India: no justice for 1984 anti-Sikh bloodshed', Human Rights Watch, 29 October 2014

78 collaborated in the concealment: Tusha Mittal, 'A pack of wolves in khaki clothing', *Tehelka*, 25 April 2009

78 ashes were merely swept away: *Who are the Guilty?*, 1984

78 minimal numbers of deaths: 'Delhi cops, govt 'colluded' during 1984 anti-Sikh riots: Sting operation', *The Times of India*, 22 April 2014

78 attempts were made to halt: Sanjay Suri, 1984: *The Anti-Sikh Violence and After*, 2015, p 69

78 They failed to stop him: Aniruddha Ghosal, 'Often in records, no entries about police movements', *The Indian Express*, 3 November 2014

78 documents were gathered: ibid

79 police being culpable: Neeraj Chauhan, 'Police had shielded 1984 rioters', *The Times of India*, 31 January 2014

79 government has failed to defend: Sanjay Suri, 1984: *The Anti-Sikh Violence and After*, 2015, p 77

79 the mobs went on the attack: Tusha Mittal, 'A pack of wolves in khaki clothing', *Tehelka*, 25 April 2009

79 refusing to act: 'Chapter 84: An Investigation into the Anti-Sikh Riots in Delhi', *Cobrapost*, 1 July 2016

80 'questionable, partisan and

inexcusable': Kusam Lata Mittal, *Kusum Lata Mittal Commission of Inquiry*, 1990

80 remain as additional commissioner: H. S. Phoolka, '30 yrs of commissions & omissions', *The Tribune*, 2 November 2014

11. WHERE WAS THE ARMY?

81 fourth largest army in the world: Vernon Marston Hewitt, *The International Politics of South Asia*, 1992, p 17

81 'shoot-to-kill': S. Gopal (ed), *Selected works of Jawaharlal Nehru, Volume 4*, 1987, p 318

81 threat to the cohesion: ibid, p 494

82 calls for the army came: *Who are the Guilty?*, 1984

82 'a meeting had already taken place': Ajaz Ashraf, 'Narasimha Rao's role in anti-Sikh riots: evidence his supporters missed', *Outlook*, 28 October 2016

82 appeared 'indifferent': Ram Jethmalani, New Delhi, 'Witness statement', *Justice Nanavati Commission of Inquiry*, 2005, at *Carnage '84*

82 'looking into this matter': Ms Kamini Jaiswal, Saket, New Delhi, 'Affidavit', *Justice Nanavati Commission of Inquiry*, 2005, at *Carnage '84*

82 a curfew was to be imposed: *Who are the Guilty?*, 1984

82 just over 6,000 soldiers: Hartosh Singh Bal, 'Sins of commission', *The Caravan*, 1 October 2014

83 central and southern districts:

Patwant Singh, *The Sikhs*, 2008, p 237

83 to patrol them on 3 November: G.T. Nanavati, *Justice Nanavati Commission of Inquiry 1984 (Anti-Sikh Riots)*, Volume One, 2005, p 170; Manoj Mitta, 'Rao told me to protect friends', *The Indian Express*, 9 August 2005

83 no authority to intervene: Patwant Singh, *The Sikhs*, pp 237–38

83 the identity of the intelligence officer: ibid, p 239

83 to set up a joint control room: Brig. A.S. Brar, 'Witness statement', *Justice Nanavati Commission of Inquiry*, 2005, at *Carnage '84*; *Who are the Guilty?*, p 9

83 not enough army personnel available: Hartosh Singh Bal, 'Sins of commission', *The Caravan*, 1 October 2014

84 'clearly reflected his connivance': Lt. Gen. (Retd) J.S. Aurora. 'Affidavit of Prominent Persons', *Justice Nanavati Commission of Inquiry*, 2005, at *Carnage '84*

84 soldiers complained: *Who are the Guilty?*, 1984, p 9

84 horrific acts of violence: ibid, p 10

84 'biggest crime': '84 riots was state-sponsored terrorism, says Retd Brigadier', *Outlook*, 11 December 2001, quoted in Jaskaran Kaur, *Twenty Years of Impunity*, 2006, p 68

84 shoot-at-sight policy: 'Shoot-at-sight orders in Delhi, other cities', *The Indian Express*, 2 November 1984

84 the mob temporarily retreated: *Who are the Guilty?*, p 10

84 limited to patrolling the streets: ibid, p 11

85 'pointed warily at passers-by': Pranay Gupte, 'At Sikh shrine, worried and deep anger', *The New York Times*,

5 November 1984

85 'made a scapegoat': Manoj Mitta, 'Rao told me to protect friends', *The Indian Express*, 9 August 2005

85 a mob stormed the train: Bhupinder Malhi, 'What a young army officer saw in '84 riots', *NDTV*, 3 February 2014

85 pulverising another: ibid

85 shearing his hair: ibid

85 'serving Sikh defence personnel': 'High ranking Sikh army officers were killed in 1984 Sikh genocide', *Panthic*, 20 December 2012

86 second highest award: 'Service record of Wing Commander Manmohan Bir Singh Talwar', *Bharat Rakshak*, *IAF*

87 attempted to throw fireballs: Group Captain Manmohan Bir Singh Talwar, 'Affidavit of Prominent Persons', *Misra Commission* of Inquiry, 1987, at *Carnage '84*

87 While incarcerated: Manoj Mitta and Harvinder Phoolka, *When a Tree Shook Delhi*, 2007, p 45

87 thirty-four Sikh soldiers: 'Army admits 34 soldiers killed in '84 anti-Sikh riots', *Discrimination & National Security Initiative Blog*, 24 October 2008

87 dishonoured those unaccounted: 'Soldiers killed in 1984 riots: ex-servicemen to approach court', *The Indian Express*, 2 November 2008

12. THE BIG LIE

89 Some riots took place: 'Rajiv Gandhi exposed by Advo. H S Phoolka: Video of Boat Club Speech (Nov. 19, 1984) released', *Youtube*, posted by 'SikhSiyasat', 20 November 2015

90 investigate the crimes: Schona Jolly, 'Thirty Years on, Still No Justice for India's Sikhs', *The Huffington Post*, 31 December 2014

90 the only TV channel: 'History of Indian Television', India Netzone, 10 January 2015

90 police officials looked on: Manoj Mitta and Harvinder Phoolka, *When a Tree Shook Delhi*, 2007, p 13

90 repeated eighteen times: Justice Ranganath Misra Commission of Inquiry, *Misra Commission Report*,1987, at *Carnage '84*, p 43

90 well within earshot: Shanti Bhushan, 'Affidavit', *Justice Nanavati Commission of Inquiry*, 2005, at *Carnage '84*

90 aired throughout the day: Ranjit Singh Narula, Defence Colony, 'Affidavit of Prominent Persons', *Justice Nanavati Commission of Inquiry*, 2005, at *Carnage '84*

91 If someone had relied: Aseem Shrivastava, 'The Winter in Delhi', *Counterpunch*, 10 December 2005

91 the state-owned All India Radio: 'Sequence of events', at *Carnage '84*

91 exchange of fire': *Sikri Report*, 1984 at *Carnage '84*

91 Audiences nationally: Keval J. Kumar, *Mass Communication in India*, 2010, Chapter 5: Radio

91 a tool of propaganda: Maya Ranganathan and Usha M. Rodrigues, *Indian Media in a Globalised World*, 2010, p 189

91 press heavily censored: Coomi Kapoor, 'How Indira Gandhi gagged the media during Emergency', *Daily O*, 14 June 2015

91 severe restrictions were imposed: ibid

91 barrage of propaganda: Rueda Soriano, 'Manipulation of language as a weapon of mind control and abuse of power in 1984', *Rocio's Blog*, 28 October 2010; Saifuddin Ahmed, 'The Role of the Media during Communal Riots in India: A Study of the 1984 Sikh Riots and the 2002 Gujarat Riots', *Media Asia*, 37, 2, January 2010, p 105

92 A media blackout: Sanjoy Hazarika, 'News from Punjab: how New Delhi curbs what is reported', *The New York Times*, 13 June 1984

92 other 'anti-social' elements: '*White Paper on the Punjab Agitation*', Annexure H, reproduced in Kuldip Nayar and Khushwant Singh, *Tragedy of Punjab*, 198, p 171

92 self-censored their stories: Saifuddin Ahmed, 'The Role of the Media during Communal Riots in India: A Study of the 1984 Sikh Riots and the 2002 Gujarat Riots', *Media Asia*, 37, 2, January 2010, p 105

92 several of its employees: Devika Chhibber, 'Rediscovering the phantoms of 1984', *Zee News*, 7 November 2009

93 editorial pages blank: Amrith Lal, '40 years on, those 21 months of Emergency', *The Indian Express*, 20 July 2015

93 twenty-seven registered censorship violations: Gobind Thukral, 'The press and stress', *India Today*, 15 July 1984

93 It was first alerted: Sanjay Suri, 1984: *The Anti-Sikh Violence and After*, 2015, p 54 [hereafter referred to as '*The Anti-Sikh Violence*']

93 the horrific killings: ibid

93 only two people: William K. Stevens,

'Indian army goes into 9 cities as anti-Sikh battling flares; throngs file by Gandhi's bier', *The New York Times*, 2 November 1984

93 he revised the number of deaths: Mary Anne Weaver, 'Sikh-Hindu clash tests Mr. Gandhi; violent backlash could build pressure for independent Sikh nation', The Christian Science Monitor, 5 November 1984

93 '"200 bodies lying': 'Annexure – III', *Who are the Guilty?*, 1984

93 at least 3,000: *The Anti-Sikh Violence*, p 195

94 as 'opposition' propaganda: *Who are the Guilty?*, 1984

94 'utterly malicious': ibid

94 the government banned: James M. Markham, 'Rajiv Gandhi and Sikhs meet and he offers reassurances', *The New York Times*, 7 November 1984

94 despite journalists: *The Anti-Sikh Violence*, p 201

94 an already tense situation: ibid, pp 201–02

94 'inflammable material': James M. Markham, 'Rajiv Gandhi and Sikhs meet and he offers reassurances', *The New York Times*, 7 November 1984

94 'You have your right': ibid

94 'butchered in mob attacks': Michael Hamlyn, 'Sikhs butchered in mob attacks on trains to Delhi', *The Times*, 3 November 1984

94 'Congress Party for violence': Michael Hamlyn, 'Opposition leaders blame Congress Party for violence against Sikhs', *The Times*, 8 November 1984

94 'the senseless, cowardly assassination': 'Foreign Affairs and Overseas

Development', *Hansard*, HC, vol 67, c 324, 9 November 1984

95 'a ghastly series of riots and murders': ibid

95 The term 'riot': William K. Stevens, 'Indian army goes into 9 Cities as anti-Sikh battling flares', *The New York Times*, 2 November 1984; *Who are the Guilty?*, 1984

95 almost exclusively by: 'A searing look into the 1984 anti-Sikh riots', *The Hindu*, 19 June 2017

95 only Sikhs were looted and murdered: Amiya Rao et al, *Truth about Delhi Violence: Report to the Nation*, 1985, at *Carnage '84*

95 were only targeted: Pramod Nayar, *Writing Wrongs: The Cultural Construction of Human Rights in India*, 2012, p 69

95 Both the explicit targeting: Cynthia Keppley Mahmood, *Fighting for Faith and Nation*, 1996, p 138

96 defined as genocidal massacres: Leo Kuper, *Genocide: Its Political Use in the Twentieth Century*, 1981, p 10

96 devastating weapons: Ben Kiernan, *Blood and Soil: A World History of Genocide and Extermination from Spartan to Darfur*, 2007, p 13

96 an anti-Sikh genocidal massacre: For further discussions on pogroms and genocidal massacres, see: Paul R. Brass, *A New Cambridge History of India*, 1990, p 354; Paul Mojzes, *Balkan Genocides: Holocaust and Ethnic Cleansing in the Twentieth Century*, 2015, p 5; Leo Kuper, *Genocide: Its Political Use in the Twentieth Century*, 1981, p 10

96 helped positively re-brand: 'Model, Gandhi bahu, Modi's minister: Maneka's fight against dynasty',

Firstpost, 27 May 2014

96 ordered the removal of all copies: Jaskaran Kaur, *Twenty Years of Impunity*, 2006, p 72

96 ban all periodicals: James M. Markham, 'Rajiv Gandhi, in speech to nation, pledges a continuity of policies', *The New York Times*, 13 November 1984

96 he was arrested: 'A Canadian reporter is arrested in Amritsar', *The New York Times*, 12 November 1984

97 'waging war against the nation': Amaninder Pal Sharmal, '30 years on, book on 1984 victims still banned', *The Times of India*, 3 February 2014

97 a banned publication: ibid

97 worked in relief camps: Sumit Bhattacharya, 'If Fahrenheit 9/11 can, so can Amu', *Rediff*, 10 January 2005

97 the actor Anupam Kher: Latha Venkatraman, "A' for Amu, *The Hindu Business Line*, 6 January 2005; Someswar Bhowmik, 'Film censorship in India: Deconstructing an incongruity', in *Indian popular cinema: a narrative of cultural change*, eds K. Moti Gokulsing and Wimal Dissanayakepp, 2004, p 309

97 'young people do not need to know': Someswar Bhowmik, 'Film censorship in India: Deconstructing an incongruity', in Indian popular cinema: a narrative of cultural change, eds K. Moti Gokulsing and Wimal Dissanayakepp, 2004, p 309

97 'had it coming to them': Khushwant Singh, 'Oh, that other Hindu riot of passage', *Outlook*, 15 November 2004

97 '*The Hindu* cup of patience': ibid

97 Jain was well-known: Kuldip

Singh, 'Obituary: Girilal Jain', *The Independent*, 20 July 1993

98 resulting in over 200 deaths: Ramachandra Guha, *India After Gandhi*, 2007, pp 582–98

98 'anti-Muslim, anti-Christian': Khushwant Singh, 'Biased view', *India Today*, 31 August 1994

98 'The people know the truth': ibid

98 'victims of the communal holocaust': Girilal Jain, 'Editorial: Identify and Punish', *Girilal Jain Archive*, 7 November 1984

98 'lumpens who recognise no moral law': ibid

98 'allow gangsters to seek asylum': ibid

99 'the entire Sikh community': Salman Rushdie, *Joseph Anton*, 2012, p 83

99 'even more powerful': ibid, p 84

99 attempted to prevent the broadcast: ibid

99 'most moving moment': James Endrst, 'A look at the mystery of India's independence: Rushdie's 'riddle' unfolds in documentary,' *Los Angeles Times*, 7 July 1989

100 'What kind of justice is it': Salman Rushdie, *The Riddle of Midnight*, produced by Antelope South for Channel 4, 1988

100 'it was astonishing that': Salman Rushdie, *Joseph Anton*, 2012, p 84

13. THE ACCUSED (I): ALL THE PRIME MINISTER'S MEN

101 blame on Congress Party: Barbara Crossette, 'Mob's wrath brings death to Sikh area', *The New York Times*, 4 November 1984

101 'incited people': Michael Hamlyn, 'Opposition leaders blame Congress Party for violence against Sikhs', *The Times*, 8 November 1984

101 'certain Congress (I) leaders': *Who are the Guilty?*, 1984

102 named sixteen politicians: ibid

102 'not an ordinary holocaust': 'Civil rights group says ruling Congress Party was behind anti-Sikh riots', *The Guardian*, 30 January 1985

102 'with meticulous care': Amiya Rao et al, *Truth about Delhi Violence: Report to the Nation*, 1985, at *Carnage '84*

102 Arun Nehru: Kumar Anshuman, 'Arun Nehru: a business honcho who rose and fell due to his astuteness', *India Today*, 26 July 2013

102 Rae Bareli constituency: 'Rae Bareli Lok Sabha Elections and Results 2014', *Elections.in*

102 Operation Blue Star: Hartosh Singh Bal, 'The shattered dome', *The Caravan*, 1 May 2014; Hartosh Singh Bal, 'Sins of commission', *The Caravan*, 1 October 2014

102 Nehru's key role: Hartosh Singh Bal, 'Sins of commission', *The Caravan*, 1 October 2014

102 'frighteningly casual': Ashok Jaitly, 'Their demeanour was frighteningly casual', *Outlook*, 19 October 2009

103 Delhi police: Sangat Singh, *The Sikhs in History*, 2010, pp 395–96

103 'Clearance has been given': Hartosh Singh Bal, 'Sins of commission', *The Caravan*, 1 October 2014

103 'The strategy is to catch Sikh youth': ibid

103 'They have been provided this list': ibid

103 Nehru had overseen: ibid

103 possible repercussions of a military assault: ibid

103 Another senior Congress politician: Kuldip Nayar, *Beyond the Lines: An Autobiography*, 2012, Chapter 13: Operation Bluestar, Punjab in Flames

104 minister of Information and Broadcasting: ''Old fox' Bhagat passes away', *Rediff*, 29 October 2005

104 seeing him over the four days: Sukhan Singh Saina, Shakarpur, 'Affidavit', *Misra Commission*, 1987, at *Carnage '84*; Ajmer Singh and Etmad A. Khan, 'HKL Bhagat: a witness won over', *Tehelka*, 8 October 2005

104 'keep these two thousand rupees': Sukhan Singh Saina, Shakarpur, 'Affidavit', *Misra Commission*, 1987, at *Carnage '84*

104 'You need not worry': ibid

104 saw Sikhs being beaten: ibid

104 'not interfere for three days': Manoj Mitta and Harvinder Phoolka, *When a Tree Shook Delhi*, 2007, p 179

105 'given instructions in the meeting': Wazir Singh, Tilak Vihar, 'Affidavit', *Justice Nanavati Commission of Inquiry*, 2005, at *Carnage '84*

105 took part in the massacre: 'A method in the madness', *Outlook*, 11 August 2005

105 Having incited the murderers: Gurmeet Singh, Mohali, 'Affidavit', *Justice Nanavati Commission of Inquiry*, 2005, at *Carnage '84*

105 'He is the child of a snake': Satu Singh, Rana Pratap Bagh, 'Affidavit', ibid

105 Guru Gobind Singh: ibid

106 no Congress workers were involved: Inder Singh, Trilokpuri, 'Affidavit', *Misra Commission*, 1987, at *Carnage '84*

106 withdrew their allegations: Manoj Mitta and Harvinder Phoolka, *When a Tree Shook Delhi*, 2007, p 183

106 'Whatever you need': Tusha Mittal, 'Bhagat's men offered me Rs 25 lakh', *Tehelka*, 25 April 2009

106 'No one should be spared': ibid

106 She has been physically attacked: ibid

106 the evidence against Bhagat: Manoj Mitta and Harvinder Phoolka, *When a Tree Shook Delhi*, 2007, p 178

106 three other people: '3 convicted for lynching family in 1984 anti-Sikh riots', *Rediff*, 26 March 2007

107 to have been handpicked: Prabhu Chawla, 'New entrants: the Sanjay men', *India Today*, 31 January 1980

107 were burnt down: Balwant Kaur, West Sagarpur, 'Affidavit', *Misra Commission*, 1987, at *Carnage '84*

107 'Sikhs had killed Mrs Gandhi': Cham Kaur, Sultanpuri, 'Affidavit', ibid

107 'Sajjan was laughing': Sreenivasan Jain, 'Truth vs hype: 1984 Riots - political complicity, aborted justice', *NDTV*, February 8, 2014

107 as she begged him: Jaskaran Kaur, *Twenty Years of Impunity*, 2006, p 63

107 who were burnt: Bhagwani Bai, Sultanpuri, 'Affidavit', *Justice Nanavati Commission of Inquiry*, 2005, at *Carnage '84*

107 About ten police officials: Gurbachan Singh, Nangoi, 'Affidavit', *Misra Commission*, 1987, at *Carnage '84*

108 'made to fill out': Sreenivasan Jain,

'Truth vs hype: 1984 Riots - political complicity, aborted justice', *NDTV*, February 8, 2014

108 'No Sikh should live': Shobhita Naithani, 'I don't think justice will come', *Tehelka*, 25 April 2009

108 'to kill more Sikhs': Sreenivasan Jain, 'Truth vs hype: 1984 Riots - political complicity, aborted justice', *NDTV*, February 8, 2014

108 'end of the day': ibid

108 an active member: Prabhu Chawla, 'New entrants: The Sanjay men', *India Today*, 31 January 1980

108 'played a particularly grotesque role': Delhi Diary, 'Credible evidence that he played a role in organizing the communal attacks', *WikiLeaks*, 14 March 2014

108 'nominal killing of Sikhs': Sunetra Choudhury, Sidharth Pandey (ed Abhinav Bhatt), '1984 anti-Sikh riots case reopened against Jagdish Tytler', *NDTV*, 11 April 2013

108 Because of you: 'Exclusive Interview with Jasbir Singh', *NRI Internet*, 20 December 2007

109 He incited the mob: Surinder Singh, New Delhi, *Justice Nanavati Commission of Inquiry*, 2005, at *Carnage '84*

109 left the commissioner speechless: 'Leading police official replaced in New Delhi', *The New York Times*, 11 November 1984

110 the 'Eton of India': Will Brown, 'It's a Spartan life at 'the Eton of India', *The Spectator*, 18 March 2017

110 commemorates the spot: Manoj Mitta and HS Phoolka, 'The case against Kamal Nath', *Outlook*, 8 April 2010

110 the shrine being surrounded: Mukhtiar Singh, Rakab Ganj Sahib, *Justice Nanavati Commission of Inquiry*, 2005, at *Carnage '84*

111 the police fired several rounds: ibid

111 repeatedly surging forward: Sanjay Suri, 'In Kamal Nath, Congress Finds a dubious general for Punjab', *CNN-News18*, 14 June 2016; Monish Sanjay Suri, New Delhi, 'Witness statement', *Justice Nanavati Commission of Inquiry*, 2005, at *Carnage '84*

111 accepted him as their leader: Sanjay Suri, 'In Kamal Nath, Congress Finds a Dubious General for Punjab', *CNN-News18*, 14 June 2016

111 reportedly seen giving instructions: 'Annexure IV', *Who are the Guilty?*, 1984

111 'I saw it happen': James M. Markham, 'Anti-Sikh whirlwind: where did it come from?', *The New York Times*, 16 November 1984

112 provoking a mob: Davinder Singh, New Delhi, 'Affidavit', *Justice Nanavati Commission of Inquiry*, 2005, at *Carnage '84*

112 on copies of the Sikhs' holy scripture: Amrik Singh, West Patel Nager, 'Affidavit', *Misra Commission*, 1987, at *Carnage '84*

112 police had been instructed by Shastri: Chuni Lal, Karol Bagh, 'Affidavit', ibid

112 secure the release: 'Annexure IV', *Who are the Guilty?*, 1984

112 'only tried to gain the release': James M. Markham, 'Anti-Sikh whirlwind: where did it come from?', *The New York Times*, 16 November 1984

112 to personally urge him: Tavleen Singh, *Durbar*, 2017, Chapter 12: Rajiv

112 shocked a delegation of several notable citizens: Ajaz Ashraf, 'Lest we forget: what five eminent Sikhs and a former prime minister witnessed during the 1984 riots', *Scroll*, 31 October 2016

112 nearly 200 houses in Block 32: ibid

113 'vilest hour': Ajaz Ashraf, 'Narasimha Rao's role In anti-Sikh riots: evidence his supporters missed', *Outlook*, 28 October 2016

113 'hid like a rat': Renu Agal, 'Justice delayed, justice denied', *BBC*, 11 August 2005

14. THE ACCUSED (II): THE PRIME MINISTER

115 without completing his degrees: Shyam Bhatia, 'Rahul first in three generations with a world university degree', *The Tribune*, 18 February 2014

115 showed no aspirations: Meena Agarwal, *Rajiv Gandhi*, 2004, p 18

115 a political moderniser: Bhabani Sen Gupta, 'Rajiv Gandhi: Image building', *India Today*, 30 April 1985; Yoginder K. Alah, 'Rajiv Gandhi and the story of Indian Modernization', *Livemint*, 19 May 2013

115 to call out the army: Pranay Gupte, *Mother India: A Political Biography of Indira Gandhi*, 2009, p 92

116 links with criminal gangs: *Who are the Guilty?*, 1984, p 13; James M. Markham, 'Anti-Sikh whirlwind: where did it come from?', *The New York Times*, 16 November 1984

116 Upon arrival at Palam airport: Sangat Singh, *The Sikhs in History*, 2002, p 395

116 'Yes, we must teach them a lesson':

K.R. Malkani, 'Witness statement', *Justice Nanavati Commission of Inquiry*, 2005, at *Carnage '84*

117 the prime minister passively listening: Shanti Bhushan, 'Affidavit of Prominent Persons', ibid

117 'In a calm, emotionless voice': Tavleen Singh, *Durbar*, 2012, Chapter 12: Rajiv

117 'Gurdwaras are being burnt down': Pranay Gupte, *Mother India: A Political Biography of Indira Gandhi*, 2009, p 92

117 she reminded him: ibid, p 79

117 'What can I do?': Shyam Bhatia, *Bullets and Bylines*, 2016, p 43

117 'neither the PM nor the Home Minister': C. G. Manoj, 'Rajiv Gandhi didn't take calls from President after 1984 riots broke out', *The Indian Express*, 30 January 2014

118 'Nobody, it seemed': Nicholas Nugent, *Rajiv Gandhi – Son of a Dynasty*, 1990, p 26

118 notified him of this: *Who are the Guilty?*, 1984, p 12

118 the meeting was abruptly cancelled: Ajaz Ashraf, 'Lest we forget: what five eminent Sikhs and a former prime minister witnessed during the 1984 riots', *Scroll*, 31 October 2016

118 The more one thinks about it: Dr Rajni Kothari, 'Genocide - 1984: The How and Why of it All', *Angelfire*, 1994

119 Gandhi's telling response: Sanjay Suri, *1984: The Anti-Sikh Violence and After*, 2015, p 22

119 'political misdemeanour': ibid p 23

119 where was the legal inquiry: ibid

119 squandered a precious opportunity: ibid, p 26

119 they only had themselves to blame: 'Rajiv Gandhi', *Sunday Magazine* interview by M. J. Akbar, March 1985, quoted in Siddharth Varadarajan, 'Moral indifference as the form of modern evil', *The Hindu*, 12 August 2005

119 'it would do more damage to the Sikhs': 'The day India killed its own', *The Indian Express*, 31 October 2004

120 'It seemed easy for Rajiv Gandhi': Shobhita Naithani, 'I lived as a queen. Now, I'm a servant', *Tehelka*, 25 April 2009

15. THE ACCUSED (III): THE PEOPLE

121 had a serious problem: '1984: Rajiv Gandhi wins landslide election victory', On This Day, *BBC*

121 clean up his mother's party: James M. Markham, 'Anti-Sikh whirlwind: where did it come from?', *The New York Times*, 16 November 1984

121 unsavoury characters: ibid

121 Congress-sponsored criminal gangs: *Who are the Guilty?*, 1984, p 3

121 who had been evicted: Shalini Narayan, 'Trilokpuri: once upon a riot', *The Indian Express*, 2 November 2014

122 land and small concrete houses: Shashi Tharoor, *India from Midnight to the Millenium*, 2012, p 250

122 a solid support base: Madhu Kishwar, 'Gangster Rule: Massacre of the Sikhs in 1984', *Manushi*, 1985

122 the erstwhile slum-dwellers: Shalini Narayan, 'Trilokpuri: once upon a

riot', *The Indian Express*, 2 November 2014

122 ripe for exploitation: Madhu Kishwar, 'Gangster Rule', *Manushi*, 1985

122 well-organised armed mobs: ibid

122 How else could they have done what they did: Sanjay Suri, 1984: *The Anti-Sikh Violence and After*, 2015, p 75

122 a small number of poor Muslims: *Who are the Guilty?*, 1984; Madhu Kishwar, 'Gangster Rule', *Manushi*, 1985

123 hatred of middle-class Sikhs: Lional Baixas, 'The Anti-Sikh Pogrom of October 31 to November 4, 1984', *SciencePro*, 9 June 2009

123 saw an opportunity: Stanley J. Tambiah, 'Reflections on Communal Violence in South Asia', in Kamala Visweswaran (ed), *Perspectives on Modern South Asia: A Reader in Culture, History, and Representation*, 2011, p 181; *Who are the Guilty?*, 1984, p 3

123 as deserved punishment: Dr Rajni Kothari, 'Genocide - 1984: the how and why of it all', *Angelfire*, 1994

123 attacking Sikhs publicly: *BBC & ITN News* footage of the mobs, 1–3 November 1984

123 'directing a gang of arsonists': Ashis Nandy, 'The Politics of Secularism', in Veena Das (ed), *Mirrors of Violence*, 1990, p 89, quoted in Cynthia Keppley Mahmood, *Fighting for Faith and Nation*, 1996, p 143

123 'nearly complete sympathy': Ashish Banerjee, 'Comparative Curfew: Changing Dimensions of Communal Politics in India', quoted in Cynthia Keppley Mahmood, *Fighting for Faith and Nation*, 1996, p 141

123 deplorable complicity: Madhu Kishwar, 'Gangster Rule', *Manushi*, 1985

123 exterminated them all: Jarnail Singh, *I Accuse... The Anti-Sikh Violence of 1984*, 2011, p 102

124 permitted Sikh women: Madhu Kishwar, 'Gangster Rule', *Manushi*, 1985

124 All three sons were killed: ibid

124 His son was also caught and torched: ibid

124 'Neighbours did not help': Veena Das, Life and Words: *Violence and the Descent into the Ordinary*, 2007, p 157

124 'It's all lies that they were outsiders': Uma Chakravarti and Nandita Haksar, *The 1984 Archive*

124 had distributed sweets and danced: Cynthia Keppley Mahmood, *Fighting for Faith and Nation*, 1996, p 141

125 continued with typical pomp: Madhu Kishwar, 'Gangster Rule', *Manushi*, 1985

125 both indignant and distressed: 'Margaret Thatcher's disgust at Sikhs-1984, funeral of Indira Gandhi', *Youtube*, posted by 'Sikh2Inspire', 3 February 2014

125 'outrageous behaviour of a tiny minority': ibid

125 all Sikhs could not be held responsible: Dharma Kumar, *The Times of India*, 15 November 1984, cited from Pranay Gupte, *Mother India: A Political Biography of Indira Gandhi*, 2009, p 94

125 'For the act of three Sikhs': '1984 Anti Sikh Pogrom', *Youtube*, posted by 'Pav Singh', 27 July 2013

125 'escape the tag': Anshu Saluja, 'Shadows of 1984: Exploring the Communal Question', *Social Action*, 65, 2, 2015

126 'never forgiven this city': Harsh

Mander, 'Delhi's indifference to 1984 riots led to other massacres', *Hindustan Times*, 13 December 2014

126 'hardly a Hindu was attacked': Sanjay Suri, 1984: *The Anti-Sikh Violence and After*, 2015, p 185

16. Judicial Scandal (I): Misra

127 Hindu and Muslim communities: B. Rajeshwari, *Communal Riots in India: A Chronology (1947–2003)*, March 2004, pp 1–2

127 approximately 2,000 were slaughtered: ibid, p 9

127 ten judicial commissions: *Justice Denied: A Critique of the Misra Commission Report on the Riots in November 1984*, April 1987, p 2

127 following vociferous demands: ibid

128 "instituted an independent investigation: Delhi Sikh Gurdwara Management Committee, written arguments to *Misra Commission*, 1987, at *Carnage '84*

128 dismissed the request: *1984 Carnage in Delhi: A Report on the Aftermath*, November 1992, p 1

128 'such an inquiry': *Justice Denied*, p 2; 'The day India killed its own', *The Indian Express*, 31 October 2004

128 'a precondition for any attempt': *Justice Denied*, p 2

128 Harchand Singh Longowal: Pritam Singh, *Federalism, Nationalism and Development: India and the Punjab Economy*, 2008, p 46

128 the confrontationist methods: ibid

129 'the allegations in regard to': 'Delhi Massacres', *Misra Commission Report*, at *Witness '84*

129 a sitting Supreme Court judge: Lional Baixas, 'The Anti-Sikh Pogrom of October 31 to November 4, 1984', *SciencePro*, 9 June 2009

129 long and distinguished legal career: Priya Ranjan Sahu, 'Former chief justice Ranganath Mishra passes away', *Hindustan Times*, 14 September 2012

129 order the Delhi Administration to co-operate: *Justice Denied*, p 3

130 potentially contradicted the Commission's conclusions: ibid, p 4

130 Among the victim affidavits: 'had not suffered': Joseph Maliakan, '1984 riots in Trilokpuri: 'Bodies of hundreds of Sikhs were scattered', *The Indian Express*, 3 November 2014

130 'against the public interest': *Justice Denied*, p 5

130 'were those concerning the details': ibid

130 'inexpedient' to the investigation': 'A brief', *Misra Commission Report*, at *Witness '84*

130 prevented from attending: 'India: No justice for 1984 anti-Sikh bloodshed', *Human Rights Watch*, 29 October 2014

131 were a spontaneous reaction: Manoj Mitta and Harvinder Phoolka, *When a Tree Shook Delhi*, 2007, p 124

131 'proxies for the culprits': ibid, p 125

131 primary representatives of the victims: Inderjit Badhwar, 'Serious setbacks', *India Today*, 30 April 1986

131. recommended more police resources: 'A brief', *Misra Commission Report*, at *Witness '84*

131 Basic errors were apparent throughout: ibid

131 Misra delved into irrelevancies: ibid

132 place blame in the direction of 'criminal elements': ibid

132 'Sir, your story is a bit like this one': Judge Misra's statement from *Misra Commission* of Inquiry, 1987, quoted in J Singh, 'Sifting through the ashes of a charred history', *Open*, 9 November 2013

133 the police had a tendency: *Misra Commission Report*, 1987, at *Carnage '84*

133 'often accused of aggravating': ibid

133 'policemen in uniform': ibid

133 'anti-social elements': ibid

133 'few in number': ibid

133. failed to take this information: *Justice Denied*, p 9

133 victim intimidation and threats: ibid, p 16

133 'anti-national character': 'Written Arguments on Behalf of the Delhi Administration', quoted in Jaskaran Kaur, *Twenty Years of Impunity*, 2006, p 84

134 'politically motivated and irrelevant': ibid, p 88

134 Mr. Bhagat': *Misra Commission Report*, 1987, at *Carnage '84*

134 'As in nature': ibid

134 'Indians should join': ibid

134 'Every Indian': ibid

134 'it recommended no criminal prosecution': Patricia Gossman, *Punjab in Crisis: Asia Watch Report*, 1991, p 24

135 took his place as a member: '1st top

judge with Z-category cover', *The Times of India*, 29 August 2017

135 investigate a single, well-defined issue: 'Parliamentary Committees', at *Indian Parliament*

135 contradict the findings: *Jain Aggarwal report*, at *Carnage '84*

135 a large number of cases: ibid

136 led to the abolishing: Manoj Mitta and Harvinder Phoolka, *When a Tree Shook Delhi*, 2007, p 149

136 None of its recommendations: *Jain Aggarwal report*, at *Carnage '84*

136 below the CJC's estimate: *Ahooja Committe report*, at *Carnage '84*

136 identified seventy-two police officers: *Kusum Lata Mittal report*, at *Carnage '84*

137 allegedly leading a mob: Manoj Mitta and Harvinder Phoolka, *When a Tree Shook Delhi*, 2007, p 158

137 decline a renewal of their tenure: ibid, p 159

137 failed to register any of them: ibid, p 163

138 case was transferred: Manoj Mitta, 'Shielding the politicians', *India Today*, 15 September 1993

138 refused to deal with the affidavit: Manoj Mitta and Harvinder Phoolka, *When a Tree Shook Delhi*, 2007, p 172

138 admitted that they were not best placed: Manoj Mitta, 'Shielding the politicians', *India Today*, 15 September 1993

138 the solid testimonies: ibid

139 'A closer scrutiny': ibid

139 'calculated moves': ibid

139 the first case against Kumar: Jaskaran

Kaur, *Twenty Years of Impunity*, 2006, p 99

139 allegedly killed by a mob: Manoj Mitta and Harvinder Phoolka, *When a Tree Shook Delhi*, 2007, p 177

139. accompanied by a hundred lawyers: ibid, p 181

140 as a conviction could not be secured: ibid, p 186

140 suffering with dementia: ibid, p 187

17. JUDICIAL SCANDAL (II): NANAVATI

141 pushed for a fresh judicial inquiry: Manoj Mitta and Harvinder Phoolka, *When a Tree Shook Delhi*, 2007, p 190

141 The cause was taken up: 'FAQs', at *Carnage '84*

141 'criminal violence and riots': G. T. Nanavati, *Justice Nanavati Commission of Inquiry 1984 (Anti-Sikh Riots)*, Volume One, 2005

142 'redeeming feature': 'Kishori vs State Of Delhi', *Supreme Court of India*, 1 December 1998

142 'damp squib, wishy-washy': Uma Chakravarti, 'Long Road to Nowhere: Justice Nanavati', *Economic & Political Weekly*, 27 August 2005, p 3790

142 These statements included: Manoj Mitta and Harvinder Phoolka, *When a Tree Shook Delhi*, 2007, p 191

142 A further eighty-nine individuals: G. T. Nanavati, *Justice Nanavati Commission of Inquiry 1984 (Anti-Sikh Riots)*, Volume One, 2005

142 being in the 'hundreds': ibid, p 1

142 certain Congress leaders were 'probably' involved: ibid, p 153

143 'what had initially started': ibid, p 180

143 became 'systematic' in nature: ibid

143 'help of influential and resourceful persons': ibid

143 'persons who could organize attacks': ibid

143 'credible evidence against': ibid, p 153

144 'inconsistent, unreliable and unworthy of credit': '1984 riots: Tytler gets clean chit from CBI', *Rediff*, 2 April 2009

144 'credible material' against Kumar: G. T. Nanavati, *Justice Nanavati Commission of Inquiry 1984 (Anti-Sikh Riots)*, Volume One, 2005, p 162

144 Kumar was forced to follow: 'Sajjan Kumar resigns from Delhi govt post', *Outlook*, 11 August 2005

144 'a conspiracy of terrifying proportion': 'India Congress leader 'incited' 1984 anti-Sikh riots', *BBC*, 23 April 2012

144 Kumar was acquitted: '1984 anti-Sikh riots case: Sajjan Kumar acquitted in one case', *The Times of India*, 30 April 2013

144 Bhagat and other Congress leaders: G. T. Nanavati, *Justice Nanavati Commission of Inquiry 1984 (Anti-Sikh Riots)*, Volume One, 2005, p 166

145 only one witness: Mukhtiar Singh, Rakab Ganj Sahib, 'Affidavit', *Justice Nanavati Commission of Inquiry*, 2005, at *Carnage '84*

145 saw Nath 'controlling' the crowd: Sheela Bhatt, 'The trial of Kamal Nath', *Rediff*, 9 August 2005; Monish Sanjay Suri, New Delhi, 'Witness statement', *Justice Nanavati Commission of Inquiry*, 2005, at

Carnage '84

145 to investigate the agitation: Sheela Bhatt, 'The trial of Kamal Nath', *Rediff*, 9 August 2005

145 found Nath's testimony to be 'vague': G. T. Nanavati, *Justice Nanavati Commission of Inquiry 1984 (Anti-Sikh Riots)*, Volume One, 2005, p 141

145 'he was not able': ibid

145 'instigated the mob': ibid

145 'Having spent two hours': Manoj Mitta and Harvinder Singh Phoolka, 'The Case against Kamal Nath', *Outlook*, 8 April 2010

145 'was actively involved in the riots': G. T. Nanavati, *Justice Nanavati Commission of Inquiry 1984 (Anti-Sikh Riots)*, Volume One, 2005, p 145

146 'with dire consequences': ibid, p 146

146 'almost indifferent': ibid, p 133

146 'he was aware that Police': ibid, p 134

146 Rao's competency was also called into question: Patwant Singh/Shanti Bhushan, New Delhi/Lt. Gen. (Retd.) J. S. Aurora, New Delhi, 'Affidavit of Prominent Persons', *Justice Nanavati Commission of Inquiry*, 2005, at *Carnage '84*

146 'no delay or indifference': G. T. Nanavati, *Justice Nanavati Commission of Inquiry 1984 (Anti-Sikh Riots)*, Volume One, 2005, p 178

146 would have had serious ramifications: Manoj Mitta and Harvinder Phoolka, *When a Tree Shook Delhi*, 2007, p 57

147 posthumously cleared the ex-prime minister: 'Rajiv Gandhi cleared over bribery', *BBC*, 4 February 2004

147 'He had issued an appeal': G. T.

Nanavati, *Justice Nanavati Commission of Inquiry 1984 (Anti-Sikh Riots)*, Volume One, 2005, p 182

147 'Yes, we must teach them a lesson': ibid, p 135

147 'vague' and 'not believable': ibid, p 182

147 'absolutely no evidence': ibid

147 records of the disciplinary proceedings: Manoj Mitta and Harvinder Phoolka, *When a Tree Shook Delhi*, 2007, p 191

148 were ordered back to barracks: Jaskaran Kaur, *Twenty Years of Impunity*, 2006, p 95

148 the violence that occurred on trains: Railway Protection Force, 'Annexure on Unauthorized Stoppages', quoted in ibid, p 59

148 'no one has made any grievance': G. T. Nanavati, *Justice Nanavati Commission of Inquiry 1984 (Anti-Sikh Riots)*, Volume One, 2005, p 14

148 I have no hesitation: 'PM's intervention during the debate in Lok Sabha on motion for adjournment on need to take action against persons indicated by *Nanavati Commission*', Lok Sabha, *Press Information Bureau, Government of India*, 11 August 2005

148 'The Report is before us': ibid

148 referring to the massacres as 'riots': ibid

149 'Modern states do not allow': Siddharth Varadarajan, 'Moral Indifference as the Form of Modern Evil', *The Hindu*, 12 August 2005

18. THE INDIFFERENCE OF THE WEST

151 'one of the saddest and darkest moments': 'Manmohan Singh a True

Statesman in Reacting to Sikh Riot Report', *WikiLeaks*, 12 August 2005

151 'something that no Indian leader': ibid

151 'exquisite contrast to the opportunism': ibid

151 revealed how Margaret Thatcher: Phil Miller, 'Revealed: SAS advised 1984 Amritsar raid', *Stop Deportations*, 13 January 2014

152 Prime Minister David Cameron: Nicholas Watt, Jason Burke and Jason Deans, 'Cameron orders inquiry into claims of British role in 1984 Amritsar attack', *The Guardian*, 14 January 2014

152 They all died or were wounded: General Sir Frank Messervy, quoted in Colonel F. T. Birdwood, forward to *The Sikh Regiment in The Second World War*, 1953, p 41

152 Sikhs should be granted an exemption: 'Motor-cycle crash-helmets (religious exemption) bill', *Hansard*, HL, vol 374, cc 1055–69, 4 October 1976

152 'For me it is sufficient': Winston Spencer Churchill, 'Amendment of Road Traffic Act, Committee Stage, 23 June 1976, *House of Commons*, quoted in Sydney Bidwell 'The Turban Victory', 1987

153 'I must go,' she said': Michael Portillo, 'Britain had to change, Margaret Thatcher had the courage to make it happen', *The Guardian*, 14 April 2013

153 both PMs found common ground: Charles Moore, *Margaret Thatcher: The Authorized Biography, Volume Two: Everything She Wants*, 2015, Chapter 10: Irish Agreement, Brighton Bomb

154 Gandhi had sent her a letter: ibid

154 'Only a few days ago': 'Mrs. Indira Gandhi', *Hansard*, HC, vol 65, c 1297, 31 October 1984

154 'Could it be that': Tom Watson, 'Blog: Margaret Thatcher's interest in aiding Operation Bluestar,' *NDTV*, 15 January 2014

155 'the removal of dissident Sikhs': 10 Downing Street, 'Letter concerning attack on Golden Temple', found on Sikh Council UK website, 6 & 23 February 1984

155 an SAS officer had visited India: Jeremy Heywood, 'Allegations of UK involvement in the Indian operation at Sri Harmandir Sahib, Amritsar 1984', *Cabinet Office*, 4 February 2014

155 'strictly to those': 10 Downing Street, 'Letter concerning attack on Golden Temple', found on Sikh Council UK website, 6 & 23 February 1984

155 'As this is an internal Indian matter': 'Golden Temple, Amritsar', *Hansard*, HC, vol 65, c 111, 30 July 1984

155 'We have a troubled situation': Letter from Indira Gandhi to Margaret Thatcher, dated 14 June 1984, *The National Archives*

156 'I have written at some length': ibid

157 'We appreciate the precautions': ibid

157 proclaiming a separate Sikh state of Khalistan: Randeep Ramesh, 'Jagjit Singh Chauhan', *The Guardian*, 10 April 2007

157 'But within a few days': Dr Jagjit Singh Chauhan, interview on 'World at One', *BBC Radio 4*, 12 June 1984

157 Republic of Khalistan: Haresh Pandya, 'Jagjit Singh Chauhan, Sikh militant leader in India, dies at 80',

The New York Times, 11 April 2007

157 issue symbolic passports: ibid

157 *BBC* rejecting a complaint: letter
from Stuart Young, Chairmen of
the *BBC*, to Pushkar Johari, Acting
Indian High Commissioner in the
UK, dated 14 June 1984, *The National
Archives*

158 Sikhs organising protest marches:
'Sikh Demonstration (London)',
Hansard, HC, vol 61 c 602, 15
June 1984; 'Sikh Demonstrations',
Hansard, HC, vol 62, cc 296–97, 22
June 1984

158 The FCO also refused: 'Golden
Temple, Amritsar', *Hansard*, HC, vol
65, c 111, 30 July 1984

158 lodge a formal protest: letter from
Mehtab Singh, Chairman of KNO
to Margaret Thatcher, dated 18 June
1984, *The National Archives*

158 'As you know': telegram from Sir
Geoffrey Howe to Indira Gandhi
conveying Margaret Thatcher's
words, dated 30 June 1984, *The
National Archives*

158 'of a great personal friend': 'Press
Conference leaving for India
(Mrs Gandhi's funeral)', *Margaret
Thatcher Foundation*, 2 November
1984; 'Margaret Thatcher's disgust
at Sikhs-1984, funeral of Indira
Gandhi', *Youtube*, posted by
'Sikh2Inspire', 3 February 2014

159 the highest levels of the Indian
government: 'Westland chopper
deal Achilles heel in UK-India ties',
Business Standard, 18 July 2015

159 an Indian-born British-based
magnate: 'Indira Gandhi's 'confidant'
Lord Swraj Paul was reliable source
of information to Margaret Thatcher',
News World India, 19 July 2015

159 'alternative Indian High
Commissioner in London': ibid

159 Indian politicians were unhappy:
note of a meeting between Margaret
Thatcher, Sir Robert Wade-Gery
and Lord Swraj Paul in New Delhi,
dated 4 November 1984, *The National
Archives*

159 turn into a protest against India:
'Conclusions of a meeting of the
Cabinet at 10 Downing Street',
8 November 1984, *The National
Archives*; 'Conclusions of a meeting of
the Cabinet at 10 Downing Street',
15 November 1984, *The National
Archives*

159 the ongoing 'Sikh situation':
'Conclusions of a meeting of the
Cabinet at 10 Downing Street',
22 November 1984, *The National
Archives*

160 'ordered all government departments':
cable from Sir Geoffrey Howe to
Margaret Thatcher entitled 'Sikh
Extremists: Damage to Indo-British
Relations', dated 12 December 1984,
The National Archives

160 postponement of a state visit: ibid

160 to organise a state visit: ibid

160 incitement for murder: ibid

160 'Dr Chauhan and other Sikh
extremists': ibid

160 'Indarjit,' he responded, 'we know';
According to Lord Singh: Lord
(Indarjit) Singh, 'Religion and religious
freedom in international diplomacy',
Network of Sikh Organisations, 19
October 2016; David Waddington
identified by Lord Singh in an email to
the author dated 7 April 2017

160 'It may appear ungrateful of me':
Letter from Lord Aldington to
Margaret Thatcher, dated 4 January

1985, *The National Archives*

161 'The financial consequences': ibid

161 'resuming normal business': ibid

161 'were not related to Sikh extremists': ibid

161 'negotiations on the contracts': ibid

161 his 'technical chaps': note of a meeting between Margaret Thatcher and Rajiv Gandhi, dated 13 March 1985, *The National Archives*

162 Future lucrative contracts: 'Conclusions of a meeting of the Cabinet held at 10 Downing Street', 22 November 1984, *The National Archives*

162 'Truth is high': 'UK Government involvement in the attack on the Golden Temple and its failure to respect the human rights of Sikh in Genocide of 1984, *Network of Sikh Organisations*, 9 February 2014

162 future economic aid could become 'problematic': 'Helicopter deal: India's jinxed Westland saga', *Rediff*, 20 February 2013

162 prevented an Asian family: 'Terry Dicks - an 80s Tory Politician', *The Thatcher Crisis Years*, 29 December 2012

162 'flotsam' and 'jetsam': 'Tories split over immigration', *Gadsden Times*, 13 October 1983

162 'black terrorist': Anthony Bevins, 'Nelson Mandela: from 'terrorist' to tea with the Queen', *The Independent*, 8 July 1996

162 'stain on the character of this House': 'John McDonnell maiden speech to Parliament', *Hansard*, HC, c 733, 6 June 1997

163 'no matter where they are': 'Mrs Kuldip Kaur', *Hansard*, HC, vol 107

cc 1504–15, 19 December 1986

163 'take advantage of the remedies': 'India', *Hansard*, HC, vol 139, c 484, 31 October 1988

163 bringing up the plight of Sikhs: 'India (Sikh Community)', *Hansard*, HC, vol 140, cc 718–26, 11 November 1988

163 'While Rajiv Gandhi': ibid

164 Atrocities were most widespread in Punjab: ibid

164 yet it had intervened in South Africa: ibid

164 The tepid response: ibid

164 Dicks would bring up the issue: 'Sikhs in India (Human Rights)', *Hansard*, HC, vol 199, cc 1241–48, 29 November 1991

164 to uphold their proud record: ibid

164 'We must judge carefully': ibid

165 'shocked and appalled': 'China', *Hansard*, HC, vol 156, c 965–67, 12 July 1989

165 the unfriendliness of his local Conservative Party: Stephen Goodwin, 'Tory MP says party biased against Asians', *The Independent*, 28 October 1995

165 'None of these people': 'India', *Hansard*, HC, vol 169, c 1333–40, 22 March 1990

166 'democratic country': ibid

166 Subsequent UK governments: David Miliband MP, 'Reply to Jeremy Dear', General Secretary National Union of Journalists, 8 January 2010; Hugh Swire MP, 'Reply to Michelle Stanistreet', General Secretary National Union of Journalists, 20 July 2014

166 his team scoured through 200 files:
Jeremy Heywood, 'Allegations of UK
involvement in the Indian operation at
Sri Harmandir Sahib, Amritsar 1984',
Cabinet Office, 4 February 2014

166 'the provision of military advice': ibid

166 'at least some of documents': ibid

166 No equipment: ibid

166 lack of transparency and narrow
focus: Phil Miller, 'Too narrow'
inquiry into British complicity in
1984 Amritsar raid', *Open Democracy*,
31 January 2014

166 reveal a far greater role: Sean O'Neill,
'Files on Sikh massacre are withdrawn
'to hide SAS role', *The Times*, 4
November 2016; Kevin Rawlinson,
'Sikh campaigners seek release of UK
files on Golden Temple assault', *The
Guardian*, 29 December 2016

167 calls urging the government:
'Government urged to set up public
inquiry into 1984 Amritsar massacre',
National Union of Journalists, 12 June
2014; 'British Sikh MPs seek inquiry
into UK's role in Operation Bluestar',
NDTV, 29 July 2017

19. THE LIVING DEAD

169 had been convicted for killing Sikhs:
'Only 442 convicted for 1984 riots:
government', *The Times of India*,
1 May 2013; 'India: no justice for
1984 anti-Sikh bloodshed', *Human
Right Watch*, 29 October 2014

169 Convictions for riot-related offences
amounted to 412: 'Only 442
convicted for 1984 riots: government',
The Times of India, 1 May 2013

169 not one officer has been prosecuted:
'India: No Justice for 1984 Anti-Sikh

Bloodshed', *Human Right Watch*, 29
October 2014; Tusha Mittal, 'A pack
of wolves in khaki clothing', *Tehelka*,
25 April 2009

169 nobody was ever prosecuted for rape:
'India: no justice for 1984 anti-Sikh
bloodshed', *Human Right Watch*, 29
October 2014

170 a vicious cycle of inter-generational
sufferin: Bobby Friction,
'Assassination: when Delhi burned',
BBC Radio 4, 31 October 2014

170 Both were hanged: David Devadas
& Vipul Mudgal, 'End of the road',
India Today, 31 January 1989

170 tens of thousands of survivors: Sanjay
Suri, 1984: *The Anti-Sikh Violence and
After*, 2015, p 20

170 'internally displaced persons': *1984
Carnage in Delhi*, November 1992, p 7

170 abandoned their devastated homes:
Harpreet Kaur, *The Widow Colony:
India's Unsettled Settlement*, 2009;
Sanamdeep Singh Wazir, 'Revisiting
Widows' Colony 30 years after the
Sikh massacre', *Amnesty International
India*, 12 March 2015

170 The Widow Colony: *1984 Carnage in
Delhi*, November 1992, p 2; Harpreet
Kaur, *The Widow Colony: India's
Unsettled Settlement*, 2009

170 often the main breadwinners: Harsh
Mander, 'Barefoot - Lingering
memories', *The Hindu*, 23 April 2011

170 'between cold bitterness': Barbara
Crossette, 'The Sikh's Hour of
Horror, Relived After 5 Years', *The
New York Times*, 7 September 1989

170 the after-effects of the trauma: Professor
Swaran Preet Singh, 'The assassination
of Indira Gandhi: I was there', *The
University of Warwick*, 2014

170 sought solace in alcohol and drugs: Harsh Mander, 'Barefoot - Lingering memories', *The Hindu*, 23 April 2011

171 turning to crime: Pritha Chatterjee, 'Boys of Tilak Vihar are seen as useless...I don't blame them', *The Indian Express*, 3 November 2014

171 a deliberate campaign: Jarnail Singh, *I Accuse... The Anti-Sikh Violence of 1984*, 2011, p 121

171 two hundred youths have lost their lives: ibid

171 five people were killed: Rone Tempest, 'Sikhs, Hindus Fight in New Delhi; 5 Die, 45 Hurt', *Los Angeles Times*, 27 July 1986

171 Police arrested 1,500 people: G. G. LaBelle, 'Army Alerted, 1,500 Arrested as Violence Hits New Delhi', *Associated Press*, 2 December 1986

171 'The drunken youth': Pheroze L. Vincent, 'Sikhs find it hard to forget the trauma of the 1984 riots', *The Hindu*, 8 November 2014

171 'That's why I am ashamed': ibid

171 '1984 Bhool gaye?': 'Sikh Family brutally attacked in Delhi, attacker '1984 Bhool gaye, Sallo Yaad Karwata hoon', *Punjabi Bolo*, 8 October 2013

172 not provided with jobs: 'Their battle for survival is far from over', *Tribune India*, 30 October 2012

172 equivalent to £125: GNI per capita, Atlas method (current US$), converted to pounds sterling using FXTop.com and XE.com

172 in respect of those killed: *1984 Carnage in Delhi*, November 1992, p 25

172 approximately £10,000: converted to pounds sterling using XE.com

172 average income of around £400: GNI per capita, Atlas method (current US$), converted to pounds sterling using FXTop.com and XE.com

172 following the release of the Nanavati Commission's report: Manoj Mitta and Harvinder Phoolka, *When a Tree Shook Delhi*, 2007, p 206

172 widows had to prove their links: 'Their battle for survival is far from over', *Tribune India*, 30 October 2012

172 they had lost their entire lives: ibid

172 approximately £460: converted to pound sterling using XE.com

172 average income was £291: GNI per capita, Atlas method (current US$), converted to pounds sterling using FXTop.com and XE.com

172 approximately £3,000: converted to pound sterling using XE.com

172 average income of £998: GNI per capita, Atlas method (current US$), converted to pounds sterling using FXTop.com and XE.com

172 by 2013: 'Life after 1984 anti-Sikh riots: 29 years of struggle', *Youtube*, posted by 'TehelkaTV', 1 May 2013

172 'every year, on the 1984 anniversary': Pritha Chatterjee, 'Boys of Tilak Vihar are seen as useless...I don't blame them', *The Indian Express*, 3 November 2014

172 Author, activist and filmmaker: Gurcharan Singh, 'Scorched White Lilies of '84', review in *Institute of Sikh Studies*, January 2011

173 'Lots of people came to us: 'Life after 1984 anti-Sikh riots: 29 years of struggle', *Youtube*, posted by 'TehelkaTV', 1 May 2013

173 but no one comes back: Meena

Radhakrishna, 'Urban Denotified Tribes: Competing Identities, Contested Citizenship', *Economic and Political Weekly*, 22 December 2007, p 59

173 trace their ancestry back: Madhu Kishwar, 'Gangster Rule', *Manushi*, 1985

173 finally relocating to Delhi: 'Two thousand people out of the 3,000 Sikhs which were killed selectively belonged to banjara community', Haribhau Rathod's submission in Parliament, Lok Sabha, Synopsis of Debates, Proceedings other than Questions and Answers, Wednesday, August 10, 2005, cited in Meena Radhakrishna, 'Urban Denotified Tribes: Competing Identities, Contested Citizenship', *Economic and Political Weekly*, 22 December 2007, p 59

173 they do not live in Punjab: Sanjay Suri, 1984: *The Anti-Sikh Violence and After*, 2015 p 32

173 the political outcome: ibid

174 plan to exact revenge: C. G. Manoj, 'Rajiv Gandhi didn't take calls from President after 1984 riots broke out', *The Indian Express*, 30 January 2014

174 I have no right to intervene': Patwant Singh, 'Affidavit of Prominent Persons', *Justice Nanavati Commission of Inquiry*, 2005, at *Carnage '84*

174 'What have they done?': Shyam Bhatia, *Bullets and Bylines*, 2016, p 47

174 awarded bravery medals: Manoj Mitta and Harvinder Phoolka, *When a Tree Shook Delhi*, 2007, p 87

174 Sikh ceremonial honours on Tytler: Jarnail Singh, *I Accuse... The Anti-Sikh Violence of 1984*, 2011, p 93

174 and Bhagat: Hartosh Singh Bal, 'Secular Nonsense on 1984', *Open*, 5 September, 2013

174 to bribe and apply pressure: '1984 riots: 'Sikh bodies seek action against Sajjan Kumar, Hanspal', *India Today*, 15 April 2011

174 not been involved in the massacres: Ketki Angre, 'Am not a court, but Tytler was not involved in 1984 riots: Amarinder Singh', *NDTV*, 21 April 2014

174 concede the involvement: Khushwant Singh, *Captain Amarinder Singh: The People's Maharaja - An Authorized Biography*, 2017, Chapter 48: 2014: Battleground Amritsar

175 'Mr. Speaker, Sir': 'PM's intervention during the debate in Lok Sabha on motion for adjournment on need to take action against persons indicated by Nanavati Commission', Lok Sabha, *Press Information Bureau, Government of India*, 11 August 2005

175 'We had no hands': ibid

175 the limiting misnomer: 'Kanhaiya Kumar under fire for remarks on 1984 anti-Sikh riots', *The Economic Times*, 29 March 2016

176 score cheap political goals: Hartosh Singh Bal, 'The wilful ignorance of a new generation of 'liberals' shields the Congress from its culpability in the 1984 massacres', *The Caravan*, 2 April 2016

176 deliver an impassioned election speech: 'Rahul Gandhi Speech in Public Rally at Kherli (Alwar) Rajasthan on Oct 23, 2013', *Youtube*, posted by 'Indian National Congress', 23 October 2013

176 'Is it true, that you and your party men': 'Narendra Modi rakes up anti-Sikh riots to counter Rahul Gandhi', *DNA*, 25 October 2013

176 Rahul Gandhi spoke about 1984: 'Frankly Speaking With Rahul

Gandhi - Full Interview: Arnab Goswami Exclusive Interview', *Youtube*, posted by 'Times Now', 27 January 2014

176 'everything it could to stop the riots': ibid

177 'There is a process': ibid

177 the quest for justice: 'Rahul Gandhi on 1984 anti-Sikh riots victim: I am with them in their fight for justice', *The Indian Express*, 12 September 2017

177 he and his wife were gunned down: Dilip Bobb, 'In cold blood', *India Today*, 15 August 1985

177 members of an armed Sikh group: 'SGPC honours kin of Vaidya's assassins', *The Tribune*, 9 October 2008

177 guarded by 2,000 armed personnel: Prabhu Chawla and Sumit Mitra, 'Hit list: living in fear', *India Today*, 30 September 1985

178 a corruption scandal: 'In death, Gandhis make up with Arun Nehru', *The Times of India*, 27 July 2013

178 the second highest number of votes: 'East Delhi Parliamentary Constituency (Lok Sabha) Election Results - 1984', *Maps of India*

178 the onset of dementia: Manoj Mitta and Harvinder Phoolka, *When a Tree Shook Delhi*, 2007, p 187

178 furnishing his legacy: 'HKL Bhagat is dead', *The Hindu*, 30 October 2005

178 the taint of the allegations: Manoj Mitta and Harvinder Phoolka, *When a Tree Shook Delhi*, 2007, p 164

178 one of the largest wins: General Election 2004, 'State-wise results', Outer Delhi Constituency, 30 August 2005

178 forced to resign: Sujay Mehdudia, 'Sajjan Kumar quits as Rural Development Board chief', *The Hindu*, 12 August 2005

178 the hurling of a shoe: Pallavi Polanki, 'Delhi polls: son of 1984 riots accused Sajjan Kumar gets Congress ticket', *Firstpost*, 16 November 2013

178 a Congress hopeful: Jiby Kattakayam, 'Sajjan Kumar acquitted, 5 others convicted in 1984 riot case', *The Hindu*, 30 April 2013

179 a state ravaged by the anti-Sikh violence: Damini Nath, 'Sajjan Kumar, Hooda bat for Cong in Bawana', *The Hindu*, 8 August 2017

179 An appeal against the 2013 acquittal: 'Tell us at what times FIRs were lodged against Sajjan Kumar, HC asks SIT', *Hindustan Times*, 23 February 2017

179 first in 2007 and then in 2009: 'India: No justice for 1984 anti-Sikh bloodshed', *Human Rights Watch*, 29 October 2014

179 'a string of charges': Ritu Sarin, 'CBI chief gave Tytler a clean chit, his officers had said prosecute him', *The Indian Express*, 26 April 2009

179 decided to give Tytler a 'clean chit': ibid

179 to be appointed as a governor: Sundeep Dougal, 'Jagdish Tytler: a recap', *Outlook*, 10 April 2013

179 ordered to reopen the case: 'India: No justice for 1984 anti-Sikh bloodshed', *Human Rights Watch*, 29 October 2014

179 there was 'sufficient evidence': Sreenivasan Jain, '1984 riots: CBI may have come under pressure to give Jagdish Tytler a clean chit, reveals ex-official', *NDTV*, 5 February 2014

179 'not credible reasons: ibid

179 'no recollection of Mr Tytler': Sunetra Choudhury, 'Amitabh Bachchan Says he can't recall Jagdish Tytler at Delhi's Teen Murti', *NDTV*, 5 June 2015

179 he 'vehemently' denied: 'When Amitabh Bachchan spoke about allegations against him in the 1984 anti-Sikh riots', *The News Minute*, 25 February 2015

180 'boasted of having met the Prime Minister': 'Jagdish Tytler got clean chit after meeting Manmohan Singh', *The Economic Times*, 3 June 2015

180 'the investigating conducted': ibid

180 as a 'valued colleague': 'PM's intervention during the debate in Lok Sabha on motion for adjournment on need to take action against persons indicated by *Nanavati Commission*', Lok Sabha, *Press Information Bureau, Government of India*, 11 August 2005

180 evidence was found to be 'vague': *Nanavati Commission*, 2005, at *Carnage '84*, p 141

180 India's minister of urban development: 'Kamal Nath', *World Economic Forum*

180 the Protem Speaker: Akash Deep Ashok, 'Pro tem Speaker: all you need to know about this parliamentary post', *India Today*, 4 June 2014

180 forced to resign: 'Kamal Nath resigns as Congress general secretary in charge of Punjab', *Live Mint*, 15 June 2016

180 Nath remains a senior figure: Rajendra Sharma, 'Chouhan to cross swords with Kamal Nath in Chhindwara campaign', *The Times of India*, 4 August 2017

180 'Congress leaders had planned the riots': *1984 Carnage in Delhi*, November 1992, pp 12–13

180 found credible evidence against him: G. T. Nanavati, *Justice Nanavati Commission of Inquiry 1984 (Anti-Sikh Riots)*, Volume One, 2005, p 144

180 despite there being evidence: 'The action not taken report', *Outlook*, 8 August 2005

180 heralding the era: 'Narasimha Rao - a reforming PM', *BBC*, 23 December 2004

180 quelling of militancy in Punjab: Prem Shankar Jha, 'Quiet goes the Don', *Outlook*, 17 January 2005

181 a 'cash-for-votes' scandal: Luke Harding, 'India's ex-leader gets jail term for bribing MPs', *The Guardian*, 13 October 2013

181 he was finally acquitted: Nirnimesh Kumar, 'Narasimha Rao acquitted in Lakhubhai Pathak case', *The Hindu*, 23 December 2003

181 she forgave the murderers: Sundanda Mehta, 'The quality of mercy: restorative justice has started to make its impact in India', *The Indian Express*, 24 August 2015

181 'If the 1984 victims had received justice': 'Life after 1984 anti-Sikh riots: 29 years of struggle', *Youtube*, posted by 'TehelkaTV', 1 May 2013

20. Truth, Justice & Reconciliation

183 a number of issues and rising intolerance: 'India: events of 2016', *Human Rights Watch*, 2017

184 the 13th most dangerous country: Nandini Rathi, 'Gauri Lankesh's murder puts focus on press freedom,

climate of impunity towards journalists', *The Indian Express*, 9 September 2017

184 paying the ultimate price: 'Gauri Lankesh: Indian journalist shot dead in Bangalore', *BBC*, 6 September 2017

184 The Indian government: 'India', *Human Rights Watch*, 2017

184 Khalra was a human rights activist: 'India: A Mockery of Justice: The case concerning the 'disappearance' of human rights defender Jaswant Singh Khalra severely undermined', *Amnesty*, 31 March 1998

185 Tortured and shot dead: Ram Narayan Kumar & Amrik Singh, *Reduced to Ashes: The Insurgency and Human Rights in Punjab, Final Report: Volume 1*, 2003, pp 9–10

185 highlighting to the wider world: 'India: events of 2016', *Human Rights Watch*, 2017

185 ranked the worst G20 country: Katherine Baldwin 'Canada best G20 country to be a woman, India worst - TrustLaw poll', via *Wikipedia*, 13 June 2012

185 especially the 680 million: Richard Dobbs and Anu Madgavkar, 'Five Myths About India's Poverty', *Huffington Post*, no date

185 22 million cases languish: Vidhi Doshi, 'India's long wait for justice: 27m court cases trapped in legal logjam', *The Guardian*, 5 May 2016

185 quality and number of judges: 'Pendency of cases', 'Judiciary of India', *Wikipedia*

186 temporary bodies authorised by the state: Priscilla B. Hayner, 'Truth Commissions: a Schematic Overview', *International Review of the Red Cross*, 88, 862, p 295

187 the cultural, historical and social contexts: David K. Androff, 'Truth and Reconciliation Commissions (TRCs): An International Human Rights Intervention and Its Connection to Social Work', *British Journal of Social Work*, 2010, 40, p 1965

187 move a nation forward: Eric Brahm, 'What is a Truth Commission and Why Does it Matter?', *Peace and Conflict Review*, 3, 2, 2009, p 5

187 a restorative or retributive form: David K. Androff, 'Truth and Reconciliation Commissions (TRCs): An International Human Rights Intervention and Its Connection to Social Work', *British Journal of Social Work*, 2010, 40, p 1965

187 some have recommended: Priscilla B. Hayner, 'Truth Commissions: a Schematic Overview', *International Review of the Red Cross*, 88, 862, p 296

187 Truth and Reconciliation Commission in Peru: 'Truth Commission: Peru 01', *United States Institute of Peace*, 1 December 1995

187 openly named culprits: Priscilla B. Hayner, 'Truth Commissions: a Schematic Overview', *International Review of the Red Cross*, 88, 862, p 296

187 Commission for Truth and Reconciliation in South Africa: 'Truth Commission: South Africa', *United States Institute of Peace*, 1 December 1995

187 set-up a truth commission: Jean Lambert, Caroline Lucas, Matti Wuori and Alima Boumediene-Thiery, 'Written declaration on the deaths of Sikh civilians in Panjaab and India in 1984', *European Parliament*, 19 April 2004

187 They will first have to: Bhavna Vij-Aurora, Twenty Years After', *The Indian*

Express, 2 May 2004, quoted in Jaskaran Kaur, *Twenty Years of Impunity*, 2006, p 126

189 saw it as a 'neutral' term: Naresh Puri, 'Sajjan Kumar acquitted in 1984 anti-Sikh riot case', *BBC Asian Network*, 1 May 2013

189 refused to engage with: Hartosh Singh Bal, 'The wilful ignorance of a new generation of 'liberals' shields the Congress from its culpability in the 1984 massacres', *The Caravan*, 2 April 2016

190 'rape and killing-by-incineration': Martha C. Nussbaum, *The Clash Within: Democracy, Religious Violence, and India's Future*, 2007, p 23

190 a 'spontaneous' outburst: 'Kristallnacht: A Nationwide Pogrom', *United States Holocaust Memorial Museum*, 9–10 November 1938

190 two victims did manage to testify: 'For first time, 1984 Sikh victims testify before United Nation panel', *The Indian Express*, 9 November 2014

190 a number of genocidal massacres: Pradyot Lal, NK Bhoopesh, Anurag Tripathi, 'A Festering Sore on Indian Democracy', *Tehelka*, 11 April 2015

191 India's main criminal code: Abraham Joseph, 'India is in breach of its obligations to the genocide convention', *The Wire*, 2 May 2017

191 'In the absence of such': Ibid

191 "misguided"; 'unreal and exaggerated': Anirudh Bhattacharyya, 'Ontario passes motion calling 1984 riots genocide, India says move misguided', *Hindustan Times*, 8 April 2017; Ajay Banerjee, 'Ontario resolution on '84 riots 'unreal, exaggerated', Canada told', *The Tribune*, 18 April 2017

191 Rajnath Singh acknowledged: 'Rajnath called 1984 killings 'genocide', now MEA objects when Canada does the same', *The Wire*, 7 April 2017

191 'India's denial of the 1984 pogrom': Abraham Joseph, 'India is in breach of its obligations to the genocide convention', *The Wire*, 2 May 2017

192 resulting in mass protests across India: 'Delhi gang rape: protests go viral nationwide, unstoppable public outpouring as gang rape victim dies', *The Economic Times*, 29 December 2012

192 punishments for perpetrators: Mrinal Satish, 'Forget the chatter to the contrary, the 2013 rape law amendments are a step forward', *The Wire*, 22 August 2016

192 violent crimes against women: 'India 2016/2017', *Amnesty International*, 2017

192 For the perpetrators: Zainab Hawa Bangura, 'Statement by the special representative of the Secretary-General on sexual violence in conflict', *UN*, 17 April 2013

193 A system which permits: 'India: No Justice for 1984 Anti-Sikh Bloodshed', *Human Rights Watch*, 29 October 2014

194 the strength of recent arms sales: Alice Ross, 'UK approved £283m of arms sales to Saudis after airstrike on Yemen funeral', *The Guardian*, 23 July 2017

194 Operation Blue Star: Peter Walker, 'Sikhs demand inquiry into claims of British role in 1984 Amritsar attack', *The Guardian*, 13 January 2014

194 We must always take sides: Elie Wiesel, 'Acceptance Speech, The Nobel Peace Prize', *Nobel Prize*, 10 December 1986

194 8,000 Muslims: 'Bosnians, world
leaders converge on Srebrenica
to remember victims', *Radio Free
Europe/Radio Liberty*, 10 July 2015

Bibliography

1. BOOKS

Ahluwalia, Meenakshi. *Assassination of Rajiv Gandhi*. New Delhi: Mittal Publications, 1991.

Anand, Reema. *Scorched White Lilies of 84*. New Delhi: Rupa India, 2009.

Andreopoulos, George J. *Genocide: Conceptual and Historical Dimensions*. University of Pennsylvania Press, 1997.

Babbar, Gurcharan Singh. *Government-organised Carnage*, November 1984. New Delhi: Babbar Publications, 1998.

Badami, Anita Rau. *Can You Hear the Nightbird Call?* Delhi: Penguin Books, 2006.

Banerjee, Ashish. 'Comparative Curfew: Changing Dimensions of Communal Politics in India', in *Mirrors of Violence*, ed Veena Das. London: Oxford University Press, 1990.

Bedi, Rahul Kuldip. 'Politics of a Pogrom' in *The Assassination and After*, eds Arun Shourie et al. New Delhi: Roli Books, 1985.

Bhanwar, Harbir Singh. *Diary De Panne*. Amritsar: Nanak Singh Pustak Mala, 1999.

Bhowmik, Someswar. 'Film censorship in India: Deconstructing an incongruity', in *Indian popular cinema: a narrative of cultural change*, eds K. Moti Gokulsing and Wimal Dissanayake. Stoke-on-Trent: Trentham, 2004.

Bose, Sugata & Jalal, Ayesha. *Modern South Asia: History, Culture, and Political Economy*. 2nd ed. New York: Routledge, 2004.

Brass, Paul R. *The Politics of India - A New Cambridge History of India*. Cambridge: Cambridge University Press, 1990.

Butalia, Urvashi. *The Other Side of Silence: Voices From the Partition of India*. North Carolina: Duke University Press, 2000.

Chakravarti, Uma and Haksar, Nandita. *Delhi Riots: Three Days in the Life of a Nation*. New Delhi : Lancer International, 1991.

Crossette, Barbara. *India: Facing the Twenty-First Century*. Indianapolis: Indiana University Press, 1993.

Dalrymple, William. *City of Djinns*. New Delhi: Penguin Books, 2005.

Das, Veena (ed). *Mirrors of Violence: communities, riots and survivors in South Asia*. Oxford: Oxford University Press, 1990.

————. *Life and Words: Violence and the Descent into the Ordinary*. Berkeley: University of California Press, 2007.

Destexhe, Alain. *Rwanda and Genocide in the Twentieth Century*. London: Pluto Press, 1995.

Dobhal, Harsh (ed). *Writings on Human Rights, Law and Society in India: A Combat Law Anthology. Human Rights Law Network*. New Delhi: Human Rights Law Network, 2011.

Fear, John. *Exclusive Pedigree: My life in and out of the Brethren*. ed Robert Fear. Rukia Publishing, 2016. Kindle ed.

Forrest, Duncan, Smith, Sally Verity & Malcolm, S. *Lives Under Threat: a study of Sikhs coming to the UK from the Punjab*. 2nd ed. London: Medical Foundation, 1999.

Gaur, K. D. *Textbook on the Indian Penal Code*. Delhi: Universal Law Publishing, 2011.

Gopal, S. (ed). *Selected works of Jawaharlal Nehru, Volume 4*. Delhi: Jawaharlal Nehru Memorial Fund, 1987.

Gossman, Patricia. *Punjab in Crisis: Asia Watch Report*. New York: Human Rights Watch, 1991.

Grewal, Jyoti. *Betrayed by the State: the anti-Sikh pogrom of 1984*. New Delhi: Penguin India, 2007.

Grewal, Manraj. *Dreams after Darkness, a Search for a Life Ordinary under the Shadow of 1984*. New Delhi: Rupa & Co, 2004.

Grover, Vrinda. 'The Elusive Quest for Justice: Delhi 1984 to Gujarat 2002', in *Gujarat: Thwe Making of a Tragedy*, ed Siddharth Varadarajan, pp 355–88. New Delhi: Penguin Books India, 2002.

Guha, Ramachandra. *India After Gandhi*. London: MacMillan, 2007.

Gupte, Pranay. *Mother India: A Political Biography of Indira Gandhi*. Delhi: Penguin Books India, 2009.

Hajari, Nisid. *Midnight's Furies: The Deadly Legacy of India's Partition*. Boston: Houghton Mifflin Harcourt, 2015.

Hansen, Thomas Blom. *Wages of Violence: Naming and Identity in Postcolonial Bombay*. Princeton: Princeton University Press, 2001.

Heine, Heinrich. *Almansor: A Tragedy (1821)*. Quoted in Thomas Pfau. *Romantic Moods: Paranoia, Trauma, and Melancholy, 1790–1840*. Baltimore: JHU Press, 2005.

Henham, Ralph and Behrens, Paul (eds). *The Criminal Law of Genocide*. London: Routledge, 2007.

Hewitt, Vernon Marston. *International Politics of South Asia*. Manchester: Manchester University Press, 1992.

Hundert, Gershon. *Yivo Encyclopaedia of Jews in Eastern Europe*. New Haven: Yale University Press, 2008.

Jeffrey, Robin. *What's Happening to India?: Punjab, Ethnic Conflict, and the Test for Federalism*. Basingstoke: Macmillan, 1994.

Joyce, James. *Ulysses*. London: Penguin Classic, 2000.

Kapur, Vikram (ed). *1984: In Memory and Imagination – Personal Essays and Stories on the 1984 Anti-Sikh Riots.* Bhopal: Amaryllis, 2016.

Kaur, Harminder. *1984: Lessons from History: intrigue and conflict in centre Sikh relations.* New Delhi: Corporate Vision, 2010.

Keay, John. *Midnight's Descendants: South Asia from Partition to the Present Day.* London: William Collins, 2014.

Kiernan, Ben. *Blood and Soil: A World History of Genocide and Extermination from Spartan to Darfur.* New Haven: Yale University Press, 2007.

Kumar, Keval J. *Mass Communication in India.* 4th ed. Mumbai: Jaico Publishing House, 2010. Kindle ed.

Kumar, Ram Narayan. *Terror in Punjab: Narratives, Knowledge and Truth.* Delhi: Shipra Publications, 2008.

———, Singh, Amrik, Agrwaal, Ashok & Kaur, Jaskaran. *Reduced to Ashes: The Insurgency and Human Rights in Punjab Final Report: Volume One (1).* Kathmandu: South Asia Forum for Human Rights, 2003.

Kuper, Leo. *Genocide: Its Political Use in the Twentieth Century.* New Haven: Yale University Press, 1983.

Lustig, Robin. *Is Anything Happening?: My Life as a Newsman.* London : Biteback Publishing, 2017. Kindle ed.

Mackinnon, Catharine A. *Are Women Human?: And Other International Dialogues.* Cambridge: Harvard University Press, 2007.

Mahmood, Cynthia Keppley. *Fighting for Faith and Nation.* Philadelphia: University of Pennsylvania Press, 1996.

———. *One More Voice!: Perspectives on South Asia.* Bloomington: Xlibris, 2012.

Markovits, Claude. 'The End of the British Empire in India', in *A History of Modern India: 1480-1950,* ed Claude Markovits, pp 469–97. London: Anthem, 2002.

Mehta, Ved. *Rajiv Gandhi and Rama's Kingdom.* New Haven: Yale University Press, 1996.

Messervy, General Sir Frank. Quoted in Colonel F.T. Birdwood, forward to *The Sikh Regiment in The Second World War.* East Sussex: Naval & Military Press, 1953.

Mitta, Manoj & Phoolka, H.S. *When a Tree Shook Delhi.* New Delhi: Roli Books, 2007.

Mojzes, Paul. *Balkan Genocides: Holocaust and Ethnic Cleansing in the Twentieth Century.* Lanham: Rowman & Littlefield Publishers, 2015.

Moore, Charles. *Margaret Thatcher: The Authorized Biography, Volume Two: Everything She Wants.* London: Allen Lane, 2015. Kindle ed.

Mukerjee, Madhusree. *Churchill's Secret War: The British Empire and the Ravaging of India during World War II.* New York: Basic Books, 2010.

Mukherjee, Aditya (ed). *A Centenary History of the Indian National Congress, Volume V: 1964-84.* New Delhi: Academic Foundation, 2011.

Mukherjee, Pranab. *The Turbulent Years: 1980-1996.* New Delhi: Rupa Publications India, 2016.

Mukhopadhyay, Nilanjan. *Sikhs: The Untold Agony of 1984.* New Delhi: Tranquebar Press, 2015.

Nandy, Ashis. 'The Politics of Secularism', in *Mirrors of Violence:*

Communities, riots and survivors in South Asia, ed Veena Das, pp 69–93. Oxford: Oxford University Press, 1990.

Nayar, Kuldip & Singh, Khushwant. *The Tragedy of Punjab: Operation Bluestar and after.* New Delhi: Vision Books, 1984.

———. *Beyond the Lines: An Autobiography.* New Delhi: Roli Books, 2012. Kindle ed.

Nayar, Pramod. K. *Writing Wrongs: The Cultural Construction of Human Rights in India.* London: Routledge, 2012.

Nehru, Jawaharlal. 'Lahore Bulletin. 9 January 1930'. Quoted in Usman Khalid. *Authentic voices of South Asia.* London: London Institute of South Asia, 2005, p 138.

Nugent, Nicholas. *Rajiv Gandhi – Son of a Dynasty.* London: BBC Books, 1990.

Nussbaum, Martha C. *The Clash Within: Democracy, Religious Violence, and India's Future.* Cambridge: Harvard University Press, 2007.

Orwell, George. *Nineteen Eighty-Four.* London: Martin Secker & Warburg Ltd, 1949.

Pearsall. Judy (ed). *New Oxford Dictionary of English.* Oxford: Oxford University Press: 1998.

Pettigrew, Joyce. *The Sikhs of the Punjab: Unheard Voices of State and Guerrilla Violence.* London, Zed Books, 1995.

Prunier, Gérard. *The Rwanda Crisis: History of a Genocide.* 2nd ed. Kampala: Fountain Publishers Limited, 1999.

Ranganathan, Maya and Rodrigues, Usha M. *Indian Media in a Globalised World.* New Delhi: Sage, 2010.

Rao, Amiya, Ghose, Aurobindo &

Pancholi, N. D. *Truth about Delhi Violence: Report to the Nation.* New Delhi: Citizens for Democracy, 1985.

Rao, Amiya, et al. *Report to the Nation: Oppression in Punjab.* Bombay: Hind Mazdoor Kisan Panchayat, 1985.

Robertson, Geoffrey. *An Inconvenient Genocide: Who Now Remembers the Armenians?* London: Biteback Publishing, 2014.

Rushdie, Salman. *Imaginary Homelands: Essays and Criticism 1981-1991.* London: Vintage, 2010. Originally published 1991 by Granta Books.

———. *Joseph Anton: a memoir.* London: Random House, 2012.

Sandhu, Amandeep. *Roll of Honour.* New Delhi: Rupa Publications, 2012.

Schabas, William A. *Genocide in International Law: The Crime of Crimes.* Cambridge: Cambridge University Press, 2009.

Schmidt, Karl J. *An atlas and survey of South Asian history : India, Pakistan, Bangladesh, Sir Lanka, Nepal, Bhutan.* New Delhi : Vision Books, 1999.

Sebald, W. G. (translated by Michael Hulse). *Vertigo.* New York: New Directions, 2001.

Singh, Harjinder. *Reflection on 1984.* Walsall: Akaal Publishers, 2014.

Singh, Jarnail. *I Accuse…: the anti-Sikh violence of 1984.* Gurgaon: Penguin Books, 2011.

Singh, Jaspreet. *Helium.* London: Bloomsbury, 2013.

———. *November: Selected Poems.* Calgary: Bayeux Arts, 2017.

Singh, Khushwant. *Captain Amarinder Singh: The People's Maharaja - An Authorized Biography.* London: Hay

House, 2017. Kindle ed.

Singh, Khushwant. *My Bleeding Punjab.* New Delhi: UBS Publishers, 1992.

———. *The History of The Sikhs, Volume 2: 1839-1988.* Oxford: Oxford University Press, 2001.

———. *The End of India.* New York: Penguin Books, 2003.

Singh, Nazer. *Guru Granth Sahib Over to the West: Idea of Sikh scriptures translations 1810-1909.* New Delhi: Commonwealth Publishers, 2005.

Singh, Patwant. *The Sikhs.* London: John Murray, 1999.

Singh, Pritam. *Political economy of the Punjab: an insider's account.* New Delhi: MD Publications, 1997.

———. *Federalism, Nationalism and Development: India and the Punjab Economy.* London: Routledge, 2008.

Singh, Sangat (foreword by Prof. Noel Q. King). *The Sikhs in History.* Amritsar: Singh Bros, 2010.

Singh, Sarbpreet & Kaur, J. Mehr. *Kultar's Mime: Stories of Sikh children who survived the 1984 Delhi massacre.* CreateSpace Independent Publishing Platform, 2016.

Singh, Tavleen. *Durbar.* Gurgaon: Hachette India, 2017. Kindle ed.

Sitapati, Vinay. *Half-Lion: How P.V Narasimha Rao Transformed India.* New Delhi: Penguin Books, 2016.

Smith, Sheamus. *Off Screen: A Memoir.* Dublin: Gill Books, 2007.

Suresh, Hosbet. *All Human Rights are Fundamental Rights.* Allahabad: Universal Law Publishing Co Ltd, 2010.

Suri, Sanjay. *1984: The Anti-Sikh Violence and After.* Noida: HarperCollins, 2015.

Swami, Subramaniam. *Creating a Martyr. Imprint.* July 1984.

Tambiah, Stanley J. 'Reflections on Communal Violence in South Asia', in *Perspectives on Modern South Asia: A Reader in Culture, History, and Representation,* ed Kamala Visweswaran, pp 177–86. Chichester: Blackwell Publishing, 2011.

Tarlo, Emma. *Unsettling Memories: Narratives of the Emergency in Delhi.* Berkeley: University of California Press, 2003.

Tatla, Darshan Singh. *The Sikh Diaspora: The Search For Statehood.* London: UCL Press, 1999.

Thapar, Romesh. *These Troubled Times.* Bombay: Popular Prakashan, 1986.

Tharoor, Shashi. *India from Midnight to the Millennium.* London: Penguin, 2012.

Thompson, Allan (ed). *The Media and the Rwanda Genocide.* Ottawa: Pluto Press, 2007.

Vasishth, Saroj. *Kala November - The Carnage of 1984.* Calcutta: Rupa & Co, 1995.

Zamindar, Vazira Fazila-Yacoobali. *The Long Partition and the Making of Modern South Asia: Refugees, Boundaries, Histories.* New York: Columbia University Press, 2010.

2. JOURNALS

Ahmed, Saifuddin. 'The Role of the Media during Communal Riots in India: A Study of the 1984 Sikh Riots and the 2002 Gujarat Riots'. *Media Asia,* 37, 2, January 2010, pp 103–11. researchgate.net

Androff, David K. 'Truth and Reconciliation Commissions (TRCs):

An International Human Rights Intervention and Its Connection to Social Work'. *British Journal of Social Work*, 40, 2010, pp 1960–77. watermark.silverchair.com

Baixas, Lionel. 'The Anti-Sikh Pogrom of October 31 to November 4, 1984'. *Online Encyclopedia of Mass Violence*, 9 June, 2009. sciencespo.fr

Baxi, Pratiksha. 'Adjudicating the Riot: Communal Violence, Crowds and Public Tranquility in India'. *Domains (Special Issue): Riot Discourses*, 3, 2007, pp 70–105. academia.edu

Brahm, Eric. 'What is a Truth Commission and Why Does it Matter?'. *Peace and Conflict Review*, 3, 2, 2009, pp 1–14. review.upeace.org

Chakravarti, Uma. 'Long Road to Nowhere: Justice Nanavati on 1984'. *Economic & Political Weekly*, 40, 35, 2005, pp 3790–95. epw.in

Hayner, Priscilla B. 'Truth Commissions: a Schematic Overview'. *International Review of the Red Cross*, 88, 862, June 2006, pp 295–310. icrc.org

Mehta, Parvinder. 'Repressive Silences and Shadows of 1984: Erasures, Omissions, and Narrative Crisis'. *Sikh Formations*, 6, 2, 2010, pp 153–75. tandfonline.com

Radhakrishna, Meena. 'Urban Denotified Tribes: Competing Identities, Contested Citizenship'. *Economic and Political Weekly*. 42, 51, 22–28 December 2007, pp 59–64.

Rajeshwari, B. 'Communal Riots in India: A Chronology (1947–2003)'. *Institute of Peace and Conflict Studies Research Papers*, March, 2004, pp 1–33. nagarikmancha.org

Russell-Brown, S. L. 'Rape as an Act of Genocide'. *Berkeley Journal of International Law*, 21, 2, 2003, pp 350–74. scholarship.law.berkeley.edu

Saluja, Anshu. 'Shadows of 1984: Exploring the Communal Question'. *Social Action*, 65, 2, 2015, pp 162–78. researchgate.net

3. NEWSPAPERS & MAGAZINES

'1st top judge with Z-category cover'. *The Times of India*. 29 August 2017. pressreader.com

'84 riots: probe sought into soldiers' death'. *The Tribune*. 14 April 2014. tribuneindia.com

'1982: High On Drama'. *India Today*. 2 July 2007. indiatoday.intoday.in

'1984 anti-Sikh riots were genocide, says Home Minister Rajnath Singh'. *The Economic Times*. 26 December 2014. economictimes.indiatimes.com

'1984 riots not comparable with post-Godhra violence: Amartya Sen'. *The Times of India*. 18 December 2013. timesofindia.indiatimes.com

'1984 riots: Sikh bodies seek action against Sajjan Kumar, Hanspal'. *India Today*. 15 April 2011. indiatoday. intoday.in

'1984 riots: witness pressurised to save Sajjan Kumar'. *India Today*. 14 April 2011. indiatoday.intoday.in

'A Canadian reporter is arrested in Amritsar'. *The New York Times*. 12 November 1984. nytimes.com

'A method in the madness'. *Outlook*. 11 August 2005. outlookindia.com

Agnihotri, Amit. 'Sanjay Gandhi was much misunderstood, says President Pranab Mukherjee in memoir'. *India Today*. 30 January 2016. indiatoday. intoday.in

Aiyar, Swaminathan. 'Financial story of our independence'. *The Times of India*. 17 August 2003. timesofindia. indiatimes.com

Akbar, M.J. 'Interview with Rajiv Gandhi'. *Sunday Magazine*. 10 March 1985.

Anshuman, Kumar. 'Arun Nehru: a business honcho who rose and fell due to his astuteness'. *India Today*. 26 July 2013. indiatoday.intoday.in

Arora, Sakshi. 'Gurdwaras became the first target, the last refuge'. *The Times of India*. 2004. info.indiatimes. com/1984/

'Arun Nehru passes away'. *The Indian Express*. 26 July 2013. indianexpress.com

'As it happened: Congress leaders petition President over 'rising intolerance'. *The Times of India*. 3 November 2015. timesofindia.indiatimes.com

Ashok, Akash Deep. 'Pro tem Speaker: all you need to know about this parliamentary post'. *India Today*. 4 June 2014. indiatoday.intoday.in

Ashraf, Ajaz. 'Narasimha Rao's role in anti-Sikh riots: evidence his supporters missed'. *Outlook*. 28 October 2016. outlookindia.com

———. 'Lest we forget: what five eminent Sikhs and a former prime minister witnessed during the 1984 riots'. *Scroll*. 31 October 2016. scroll.in

Badhwar, Inderjit. 'Serious setbacks'. *India Today*. 30 April 1986. indiatoday.intoday.in

Bal, Hartosh Singh. 'Secular nonsense on 1984'. *Open*. 5 September 2013. openthemagazine.com

———. 'The shattered dome'. *The Caravan*. 1 May 2014. caravanmagazine.in

———. 'Sins of commission'. *The Caravan*. 1 October 2014. caravanmagazine.in

———. 'The wilful ignorance of a new generation of 'liberals' shields the Congress from its culpability in the 1984 massacres'. *The Caravan*. 2 April 2016. caravanmagazine.in

Banerjee, Ajay. 'Ontario resolution on '84 riots 'unreal, exaggerated', Canada told', *The Tribune*, 18 April 2017. tribuneindia.com

Basu, Deep. 'Beant Singh: the man who killed Indira Gandhi!'. *India Opines*. (no date). indiaopines.com

Baweja, Harinder. 'I felt like a Jew in a Nazi camp'. *Tehelka*. 20 August 2005. tehelka.com

———. '1984 victim brings alive Sajjan Kumar's riot act'. *Hindustan Times*. 29 April 2012. hindustantimes.com

Bevins, Anthony. 'Nelson Mandela: from 'terrorist' to tea with the Queen'. *The Independent*. 8 July 1996. independent. co.uk

Bhatia, Ramaninder K. 'Killers' motive was 'revenge' at Hondh Chillar [mentions FIR]'. *The Times of India*. 24 Febuary 2011. timesofindia. indiatimes.com

Bhattacharyya, Anirudh. 'Ontario passes motion calling 1984 riots genocide, India says move misguided'. *Hindustan Times*. 8 April 2017. hindustantimes.com

'Bir Devinder questions silence of minorities' minister, NCM, NHRC on Hond'. *The Times of India*. 25 February 2011. timesofindia. indiatimes.com

Bobb, Dilip. 'In cold blood'. *India Today*. 15 August 1985. indiatoday.intoday.in

Brelis, Dean. 'After Indira's death, her

daughter-in-law Maneka hungers to head the Gandhi dynasty'. *People*. 26 November 1984. people.com

Brown, Will. 'It's a Spartan life at 'the Eton of India'. *The Spectator*, 18 March 2017 spectator.co.uk

'California Assembly describes 1984 riots as 'genocide'. *The Times of India*. 22 April 2015. timesofindia.indiatimes.com

Caplan, Gerald. 'Who killed the president of Rwanda?'. *Pambazuka*. 21 January 2010. pambazuka.org

Chatterjee, Pritha. 'Boys of Tilak Vihar are seen as useless…I don't blame them'. *The Indian Express*. 3 November 2014. indianexpress.com

Chauhan, Neeraj. 'Police had shielded 1984 rioters'. *The Times of India*. 31 January 2014. timesofindia.india-times.com

Chawla, Prabhu. 'New entrants: the Sanjay men'. *India Today*. 31 January 1980. indiatoday.intoday.in

Chawla, Prabhu and Mitra, Sumit. 'Hit list: living in fear'. *India Today*. 30 September 1985. indiatoday.intoday.in

'Civil rights group says ruling Congress Party was behind anti-Sikh riots'. *The Guardian*. 30 January 1985

'Civilian authorities were unwilling to deploy army during 1984 riots: A.S. Brar'. *Outlook*. 29 July 2002. outlook-india.com

Claiborne, William & Sun, Lena. 'Indira Gandhi cremated in Hindu ritual'. *The Washington Post*. 4 November 1984. washingtonpost.com

'Cobrapost sting claims police didn't check 1984 rioters'. *The Hindu*. 22 April 2014. thehindu.com

Crossette, Barbara. 'Mob's wrath brings death to Sikh area'. *The New York Times*. 4 November 1984. nytimes.com

———. 'The Sikh's hour of horror, relived after 5 years'. *The New York Times*. 7 September 1985. nytimes.com

Dayal, Sakshi. '1984 anti-Sikh riots, 32 years later: 'They called my family out, burnt them alive'. *The Indian Express*. 30 June 2016. indianexpress.com

'Delhi cops, govt 'colluded' during 1984 anti-Sikh riots: Sting operation'. *The Times of India*. 22 April 2014. timesofindia.indiatimes.com

'Delhi gang rape: protests go viral nationwide, unstoppable public outpouring as gang rape victim dies'. *The Economic Times*. 29 December 2012. economictimes.indiatimes.com

'Delhi Police kept eyes "closed" during 1984 anti-Sikh riots: CBI'. *India Today*. 31 March 2012. indiatoday. intoday.in

'Delhi polls: 1984 riots accused Tytler, Sajjan Kumar on Cong election committee?'. *Firstpost*. 5 November 2014. firstpost.com

'Delhi polls: son of 1984 riots accused Sajjan Kumar gets Congress ticket'. *Firstpost*. 16 November 2013. firstpost.com

Devadas, David and Mudgal, Vipul. 'End of the road'. *India Today*. 31 January 1989. indiatoday.intoday.in

Doshi, Vidhi. 'India's long wait for justice: 27m court cases trapped in legal logjam'. *The Guardian*. 5 May 2016. theguardian.com

Dougal, Sundeep. 'Jagdish Tytler: a recap'. *Outlook*. 10 April 2013. outlookindia.com

'Dutch bounty hunters preyed on Jews during Holocaust, study shows'.

The Times of Israel. 19 April 2013. timesofisrael.com

Endrst, James. 'A look at the mystery of India's independence: Rushdie's 'riddle' unfolds in documentary'. *Los Angeles Times*. 7 July 1989. articles. latimes.com

Fera, Ivan. 'The Enemy Within'. *Illustrated Weekly*. 23 December 1985.

'For first time, 1984 Sikh victims testify before United Nation panel'. *The Indian Express*. 9 November 2014. indianexpress.com

Gahilote, Prarthana, '1984 riots: R K Anand says he's sorry, recalls 25 yrs ago, Gurbani helped start his car!'. *The Indian Express*, 19 April 2004. expressindia.indianexpress.com

'Gandhi, seeking sympathy vote, calls early election'. *Los Angeles Times*. 14 November 1984.

Ghosal, Aniruddha. 'Often in records, no entries about police movements'. *The Indian Express*, 3 November 2014. indianexpress.com

Ghosh, Amitav. 'The Ghosts of Mrs Gandhi'. *New Yorker*. July 1985.

Goodwin, Stephen. 'Tory MP says party biased against Asians'. *The Independent*, 28 October 1995. independent.co.uk

Gupta, Bhabani Sen. 'Rajiv Gandhi: Image building'. *India Today*. 30 April 1985 indiatoday.intoday.in

Gupte, Pranay. 'At Sikh shrine, worried and deep anger'. *The New York Times*. 5 November 1984. nytimes.com

Haksar, Nandita, 'Memories of 1984'. *Mainstream Weekly*. 2 November 2014, mainstreamweekly.net

Hamlyn, Michael. 'Journalists removed from Amritsar: army prepares to enter Sikh shrine'. *The Times*. 6 June 1984.

_____. 'Sikhs butchered in mob attacks on trains to Delhi'. *The Times*. 3 November 1984. 8t4files.wordpress.com

_____. 'Opposition leaders blame Congress Party for violence against Sikhs'. *The Times*. 8 November 1984. 8t4files.wordpress.com

Harding, Luke. 'India's ex-leader gets jail term for bribing MPs'. *The Guardian*. 13 October 2013. theguardian.com

Hazarika, Sanjoy. 'News from Punjab: how New Delhi curbs what is reported'. *The New York Times*. 13 June 1984. nytimes.com

'Hindu mobs attack Sikhs'. *Los Angeles Times*. 7 May 1985. latimes.com

'H. K. L. Bhagat cremated'. *The Hindu*. 31 October 2005. thehindu.com

'HKL Bhagat is dead'. *The Hindu*. 30 October 2005. thehindu.com

Hundal, Sunny. 'Operation Blue Star: 25 years on'. *The Guardian*. 3 June 2009. theguardian.com

'In death, Gandhis make up with Arun Nehru'. *The Times of India*. 27 July 2013. timesofindia.indiatimes.com

'Jagdish Tytler got clean chit after meeting Manmohan Singh'. *The Economic Times*. 3 June 2015. economictimes. indiatimes.com

Jaitly, Ashok. 'Their demeanour was frighteningly casual'. *Outlook*. 19 October 2009. outlookindia.com

Jha, Prem Shankar. 'Quiet Goes The Don'. *Outlook*. 17 January 2005. outlookindia.com

'Kanhaiya Kumar under fire for remarks on 1984 anti-Sikh riots'. *The Economics Times*. 29 March 2016. economic-times.indiatimes.com

Kattakayam, Jiby. 'Sajjan Kumar acquitted, 5 others convicted in 1984 riots case'. *The Hindu*. 30 April 2013. thehindu.com

———. 'Sajjan Kumar got 'benefit of doubt'. *The Hindu*. 2 May 2013. thehindu.com

Kesavan, Mukul. 'What about 1984?'. *The Telegraph*. 26 July 2013. telegraphindia.com

Khullar, Mridu. 'India's 1984 anti-Sikh riots: waiting for justice'. *Time Magazine*. 28 October 2009. content. time.com

Kumar, Nirnimesh. 'Narasimha Rao acquitted in Lakhubhai Pathak case'. *The Hindu*. 23 December 2003. thehindu.com

Lal, Amrith. '40 years on, those 21 months of Emergency'. *The Indian Express*. 20 July 2015. indianexpress.com

Lal, Pradyot, Bhoopesh, N.K. & Tripathi, Anurag. 'A festering sore on Indian democracy'. *Tehelka*. 11 April 2015. tehelka.com

Lamba, Nikita. 'Have 1984 anti-Sikh riots evidences been destroyed?'. *Tehelka*. 13 April 2015. tehelka.com

Langer, Avalok. '1984. Riots in Pataudi. Not a whisper escaped'. *Tehelka*. 12 March 2011. tehelka.com

'Leading police official replaced in New Delhi'. *The New York Times*. 11 November 1984. nytimes.com

Maliakan, Joseph. '1984 riots in Trilokpuri: 'bodies of hundreds of Sikhs were scattered'. *The Indian Express*. 3 November 2014. indianexpress.com

Malik, K. N. 'Do NRIs need a minister? In any case, Tytler is a wrong choice'. *Tribune India*. 17 August 2004.

tribuneindia.com

'Maken pardons father's killer'. *Deccan Herald*. 10 May 2004. archive. deccanherald.com

Mander, Harsh. 'Barefoot - Lingering memories'. *The Hindu*. 23 April 2011. thehindu.com

———. 'Delhi's indifference to 1984 riots led to other massacres.' *Hindustan Times*. 13 December 2014. hindustantimes.com

Mani, V.S. 'Needed, a law on genocide'. *The Hindu*. 10 April 2002. thehindu.com

Manoj, C.G. 'Rajiv Gandhi didn't take calls from President after 1984 riots broke out'. *The Indian Express*. 30 January 2014. indianexpress.com

Markham, James M. 'Rajiv Gandhi and Sikhs meet and he offers reassurances'. *The New York Times*. 7 November 1984. nytimes.com

———. 'Anti-Sikh whirlwind: where did it come from?'. *The New York Times*. 16 November 1984. nytimes.com

Massey, Reginald. 'Amrita Pritam'. *The Guardian*. 4 November 2005. theguardian.com

Mehta, Sunandà. 'The quality of mercy: restorative justice has started to make its impact in India'. *The Indian Express*. 24 August 2015. indianexpress.com

Mitta, Manoj. 'Shielding the politicians'. *India Today*. 15 September 1993. indiatoday.intoday.in

———. 'Rao told me to protect friends'. *The Indian Express*. 9 August 2005. indianexpress.com

Mitta, Manoj & Phoolka, H.S. 'The case against Kamal Nath'. *Outlook*. 8 April 2010. outlookindia.com

Mittal, Tusha. 'A pack of wolves in khaki

clothing'. *Tehelka*. 25 April 2009. tehelka.com

_____. 'Bhagat's men offered me Rs 25 lakh'. *Tehelka*. 25 April 2009. tehelka.com

'Model, Gandhi bahu, Modi's minister: Maneka's fight against dynasty'. *Firstpost*. 27 May 2014. firstpost.com

Naithani, Shobhita. 'I don't think justice will come.' *Tehelka*. 25 April 2009. tehelka.com

_____. 'I lived as a queen. Now, I'm a servant'. *Tehelka*. 25 April 2009. tehelka.com

Narayan, Shalini. 'Trilokpuri: once upon a riot', *The Indian Express*, 2 November 2014. indianexpress.com

'Narendra Modi: a man of some of the people'. *The Economist*. 18 December 2013. economist.com

Nath, Damini. 'RTI query reveals cops destroyed FIRs of 1984 riots'. *The Hindu*. 13 April 2015. thehindu.com

Ndahiro, Kennedy. 'Dehumanisation: How Tutsis were reduced to cockroaches, snakes to be killed'. *The New Times*. 13 March 2014. newtimes.co.rw

'No love between police and public'. *Deccan Herald*. 26 April 2015. deccanherald.com

O'Neill, Sam. 'Files on Sikh massacre are withdrawn 'to hide SAS role'. *The Times*. 4 November 2016. thetimes.co.uk

'Only 442 convicted for 1984 riots: government'. *The Times of India*. 1 May 2013. timesofindia.indiatimes.com

Pandya, Haresh. 'Jagjit Singh Chauhan, Sikh militant leader in India, dies at 80'. *The New York Times*, 11 April 2007. nytimes.com

Phoolka, H.S. '30 yrs of commissions & omissions'. *The Tribune*. 2 November 2014. tribuneindia.com

Portillo, Michael. 'Britain had to change, Margaret Thatcher had the courage to make it happen'. *The Guardian*. 14 April 2013. theguardian.com

Rao, Amiya. 'When Delhi burnt'. *Economic and Political Weekly*. 8 December 1984. epw.in

'Rahul Gandhi on 1984 anti-Sikh riots victim: I am with them in their fight for justice'. *The Indian Express*. 12 September 2017. indianexpress.com

Ramesh, Randeep. 'Jagjit Singh Chauhan'. *The Guardian*. 10 April 2007. theguardian.com

Rathi, Nandini. 'Gauri Lankesh's murder puts focus on press freedom, climate of impunity towards journalists'. *The Indian Express*. 9 September 2017. indianexpress.com

Rawlinson, Kevin. 'Sikh campaigners seek release of UK files on Golden Temple assault'. *The Guardian*. 29 December 2016. theguardian.com

'Rights group disappointed with SIT re-probing 1984 riots case'. *Hindustan Times*. 22 March 2017. hindustantimes.com

Ross, Alice. 'UK approved £283m of arms sales to Saudis after airstrike on Yemen funeral'. *The Guardian*. 23 July 2017. theguardian.com

Sahu, Priya Ranjan. 'Former chief justice Ranganath Mishra passes away'. *Hindustan Times*. 14 September 2012. hindustantimes.com

'Sajjan Kumar, Hooda bat for Cong in Bawana'. *The Hindu*. 8 August 2017. thehindu.com

'Sajjan Kumar quits as Rural Development Board chief'. *The Hindu*. 12 August 2005. thehindu.com

'Sajjan Kumar resigns from Delhi govt post'. *Outlook*. 11 August 2005. outlookindia.com

Sarin, Ritu, 'CBI chief gave Tytler a clean chit, his officers had said prosecute him'. *The Indian Express*. 26 April 2009. archive.indianexpress.com

Sharma, Rajendra. 'Chouhan to cross swords with Kamal Nath in Chhindwara campaign'. *The Times of India*. 4 August 2017. timesofindia. indiatimes.com

Sharma, Rajnish. 'Sikh riots: BJP names figure in records'. *Hindustan Times*. 2 February 2002. Retrieved from kractivist.org

Sharmal, Amaninder Pal. '30 years on, book on 1984 victims still banned'. *The Times of India*. 3 February 2014. timesofindia.indiatimes.com

'SGPC honours kin of Vaidya's assassins'. *The Tribune*. 9 October 2008. tribuneindia.com

Shrivastava, Aseem. 'The winter of Delhi, 1984'. *Counterpunch*. 10 December 2005. counterpunch.org

'Shoot-at-sight orders in Delhi, other cities'. *The Indian Express*. 2 November 1984.

'Sikh family injured in Sonepat acid attack'. *Hindustan Times*. 7 October 2013. hindustantimes.com

Singh, Ajmer & Khan, Etmad A. 'Carnage 84: The ambushing of witnesses'. *Tehelka*. 8 October 2005. tehelka.com

———. 'HKL Bhagat: a witness won over'. *Tehelka*. 8 October 2005. tehelka.com

Singh, Indarjit. 'Faith and reason: how to turn religious beliefs into a nuclear explosion'. *The Independent*. 22 May 1998. independent.co.uk

Singh, I. P. 'Man who exposed Hondh Chillar loses job'. *The Times of India*. 13 March 2011. timesofindia. indiatimes.com

———. 'Report on '1984 Sikh genocide' to be submitted to UN Secretary General'. *The Times of India*. 10 October 2014. timesofindia.india-times.com

———. 'H S Phoolka sends list of 50 Sikh armymen killed in November 1984, seeks relief for kin'. *The Times of India*. 6 November 2014. timesofindia.indiatimes.com

Singh, Jaspreet. 'Thomas Bernhard in New Delhi'. *The New York Times*. 22 July 2013. india.blogs.nytimes.com

———. 'Sifting through the ashes of a charred history'. *Open*. 9 November 2013. openthemagazine.com

Singh, Khushwant. 'Biased view'. *India Today*. 31 August 1994. indiatoday. intoday.in

———. 'Oh, that other Hindu riot of passage'. *Outlook*. 15 November 2004. outlookindia.com

———. 'Victory to the mob'. *Outlook*. 22 August 2005. outlookindia.com

Singh, Kuldip. 'Obituary: Girilal Jain'. *The Independent*, 20 July 1993. independent.co.uk

Singh, Simran Jeet. 'It's time India accept responsibility for its 1984 Sikh genocide'. *Time*. 30 October 2014. time.com

'Soldiers killed in 1984 riots: ex-servicemen to approach court'. *The Indian Express*. 2 November 2008. archive. indianexpress.com

Srivastava, Mihir. 'Tytler said he'll finish my family'. *Tehelka*. 29 March 2008. tehelka.com

Stevens, William K. 'Gandhi, slain, is succeeded by son'. *The New York Times.* 1 November 1984.

_____. 'Indian Army Goes into 9 Cities as Anti-Sikh Battling Flares; throngs file by Gandhi's bier'. *The New York Times.* 2 November 1984. nytimes.com

Tejpal, Tarun J. 'Christianity didn't damage India like Islam'. *Outlook.* 15 November 1999. outlookindia.com

'Tell us at what times FIRs were lodged against Sajjan Kumar, HC asks SIT'. *Hindustan Times.* 23 February 2017. hindustantimes.com

Tempest, Rone. 'Sikhs, Hindus fight in New Delhi; 5 die, 45 hurt'. *Los Angeles Times.* 27 July 1986. articles.latimes.com

Thapar, Romesh. 'When the state collapses…'. *Illustrated Weekly of India.* 23 December 1984. nov1984.org

'The action not taken report'. *Outlook.* 8 August 2005. outlookindia.com

'The day India killed its own'. *The Indian Express.* 31 October 2004 archive. indianexpress.com

'The violent aftermath'. *India Today.* 30 November 1984. indiatoday.intoday.in

'Their battle for survival is far from over'. *The Tribune.* 31 October 2012. tribuneindia.com

Thukral, Gobind. 'The press and stress'. *India Today.* 15 July 1984. indiatoday. intoday.in

'Tories split over immigration'. *Gadsden Times.* 13 October 1983. news.google. com/newspapers

'Unreasonable cuts diluted impact of '31st October': Producer'. *Darpan Magazine.* 24 October 2016. darpan-magazine.com

'US refuses to declare 1984 anti-Sikh riots as Genocide'. *The Times of India.* 2 April 2013. timesofindia.indiatimes.com

Varadarajan, Siddharth. 'Moral indifference as the form of modern evil'. *The Hindu.* 12 August 2005. thehindu.com

Venkatraman, Latha. "A' for Amu'. *The Hindu Business Line.* 6 January 2005. thehindubusinessline.com

Vincent, Pheroze L. 'The scars remain'. *The Hindu.* 8 November 2014. thehindu.com

'VS links Rajiv to Sikh riots, Anderson escape'. *The Times of India.* 5 July 2010. timesofindia.indiatimes.com

Walker, Peter. 'Sikhs demand inquiry into claims of British role in 1984 Amritsar attack'. *The Guardian.* 13 January 2014. theguardian.com

'Was it a communal riot?'. *Outlook.* 11 August 2005. outlookindia.com

Watt, Nicholas, Burke, Jason and Deans, Jason. 'Cameron orders inquiry into claims of British role in 1984 Amritsar attack'. *The Guardian.* 14 January 2014. theguardian.com

Weaver, Mary Anne. 'India's warring "ayatollah" faced commando siege'. *The Sunday Times.* 4 March 1984

'Westland chopper deal Achilles heel in UK-India ties'. *Business Standard.* 18 July 2015. business-standard.com

4. OTHER MEDIA

'1984: Rajiv Gandhi wins landslide election victory'. *BBC.* (no date). bbc.co.uk

'1984 riots: Tytler gets clean chit from CBI'. *Rediff.* 2 April 2009. rediff.com

'3 convicted for lynching family in 1984 anti-Sikh riots'. *Rediff.* 26 March 2007. rediff.com

Agal, Renu. 'Justice delayed, justice denied'. *BBC News*. 11 August 2005. bbc.co.uk

Alah, Yoginder K. 'Rajiv Gandhi and the story of Indian Modernization'. *Livemint*. 19 May 2013. livemint.com

Angre, Ketki. 'Am not a court, but Tytler was not involved in 1984 riots: Amarinder Singh'. *NDTV*. 21 April 2014. ndtv.com

'Army admits 34 soldiers killed in '84 anti-Sikh riots'. *Discrimination & National Security Initiative Blog*. 24 October 24, 2008. korematsu. blogspot.co.uk

Aulakh, Jasneet. 'Sikh and Hindu Resistance in the 1984 Anti-Sikh Pogrom'. *University of Southern California*. 2012. dornsife.usc.edu

Baldwin, Katherine. 'Canada best G20 country to be a woman, India worst - TrustLaw poll'. Thomson Reuters Foundation News. 13 June 2012. Accessed via wikipedia.org/wiki/ Women_in_India

Bedi, Rahul. 'Indira Gandhi's death remembered'. *BBC*. 1 November 2009. bbc.co.uk

Bhatt, Sheela. 'The trial of Kamal Nath'. *Rediff*. 9 August 2005. rediff.com

'Bhattacharya, Sumit. 'If Fahrenheit 9/11 can, so can Amu'. *Rediff*. 10 January 2005. rediff.com

'British actor Peter Ustinov said on French television Wednesday', *UPI*. 31 October 1984. upi.com

'British Sikh MPs seek inquiry into UK's role in Operation Bluestar'. *NDTV*. 29 July 2017. ndtv.com

Bose, Sarmila. 'The many British connections to massacres of Sikhs'. *Al Jazeera*. 28 March 2014. aljazeera.com

Chakravarti, Uma and Haksar, Nandita. *The 1984 Archive*. 1984livinghistory.org

'Chapter 84: An investigation into the anti-Sikh riots in Delhi'. *Cobrapost*. 1 July 2016. cobrapost.com

Chhibber, Devika. 'Rediscovering the phantoms of 1984'. *Zee News*. 7 November 2009. zeenews.india.com

Choudhury, Sunetra. 'Amitabh Bachchan Says he can't recall Jagdish Tytler at Delhi's Teen Murti'. *NDTV*. 5 June 2015. ndtv.com

Choudhury, Sunetra, Pandey, Sidharth & Bhatt, Abhinav. '1984 anti-Sikh riots case reopened against Jagdish Tytler'. *NDTV*. 11 April 2013. ndtv.com

'Congress leader 'incited' 1984 anti-Sikh riots'. *BBC India*. 23 April 2012. bbc.co.uk

'Delhi bus gang rape: Sonia Gandhi visits hospital'. *BBC*. 19 December 2012. bbc.co.uk

Dobbs, Richard and Madgavkar, Anu. 'Five myths about India's poverty'. *Huffington Post*. (no date). huffington-post.com

Ghai, R. '1984 survivors: The people that time forgot'. *Madhyamam*. 29 October 2012. yespunjab.com

'Gauri Lankesh: Indian journalist shot dead in Bangalore'. *BBC*. 6 September 2017. bbc.co.uk

'Helicopter deal: India's jinxed Westland saga'. *Rediff*. 20 February 2013. rediff.com

'High ranking Sikh army officers were killed in 1984 Sikh genocide'. *Panthic*. 20 December 2012. panthic.org

'History of Indian Television'. *India Netzone*. 10 January 2015. indianet-zone.com

'How do you define genocide?'. *BBC*. 17 March 2016. bbc.co.uk

'India Congress leader 'incited' 1984 anti-Sikh riots'. *BBC*. 23 April 2012. bbc.co.uk

'Indira Gandhi's 'confidant' Lord Swraj Paul was reliable source of information to Margaret Thatcher'. *News World India*. 19 July 2015. www.newsworldindia.in

'Indira Gandhi's death remembered'. *BBC*. 1 November 2009. bbc.co.uk

Islam, Shamsul. 'RSS ideologue Nana Deshmukh condoned the massacre of Sikhs in 1984'. *Countercurrents*. 29 October 2013. countercurrents.org

Jain, Girilal. 'Editorial: identify and punish'. *Girilal Jain Archive*. 7 November 1984. girilaljainarchive.net

Jain, Sreenivasan. '1984 riots: CBI may have come under pressure to give Jagdish Tytler a clean chit, reveals ex-official'. *NDTV*. 5 February 2014. ndtv.com

Jain. Sreenivasan (with inputs from Niha Masih, Tanima Biswas). 'Truth vs hype: 1984 riots - political complicity, aborted justice'. *NDTV*. 8 February 2014. ndtv.com

Jolly, Schona. 'Thirty years on, still no justice for India's Sikhs'. *The Huffington Post*. 31 December 2014. huffingtonpost.co.uk

Joseph, Abraham. 'India is in breach of its obligations to the genocide convention'. *The Wire*. 2 May 2017. thewire.in

'Kamal Nath resigns as Congress general secretary in charge of Punjab. *Livemint*. 15 June 2016. livemint.com

Kapoor, Coomi. 'How Indira Gandhi gagged the media during Emergency'. *Daily O*. 14 June 2015. dailyo.in

Kaufman, M. 'Circumstantial Evidence Keeps Sikh on Death Row'. *Philly*. January 1989.

Kaur, Gunisha & Singh, Simran Jeet. 'Remembering the massacre of Sikhs in June of 1984'. *The Huffington Post*. 3 August 2013. huffingtonpost.com

Kaur, Mallika, Neelam, Kaur Harpreet & Kaur, Kirpa. 'Sikh feminism and SAFAR'. *Guernica*. 12 December 2014. guernicamag.com

Kothari, Rajni 'Genocide - 1984: The How and Why of it All'. *Angelfire*, 1994. angelfire.com

LaBelle, G. G. 'Army alerted, 1,500 arrested as violence hits New Delhi'. *Associated Press*. 2 December 1986.

'Liberal Canadian leader seeks to silence the voice of 1984 Sikh victims'. *Panthic*. 4 June 2010. panthic.org

Malhi, Bhupinder. 'What a young army officer saw in '84 riots'. *NDTV*. 3 February 2014. ndtv.com

Mander, Harsh. 'If Sardarji had been alive...' How anti-Sikh lynch mobs changed Lachmi's life on October 31, 1984'. *Scroll.in*. 31 October 2016. scroll.in

Miller, Phil. "Too narrow' inquiry into British complicity in 1984 Amritsar raid'. Open *Democracy*. 31 January 2014. opendemocracy.net

Mitta, Manoj. 'Too late in the day for giving closure to 1984 anti-Sikh crimes'. *Rediff*. 4 November 2014. rediff.com

———. 'Not just Kanhaiya, even JNU. Historians went soft on Congress for 1984 violence'. *The Wire*. 6 April 2016. thewire.in

'Narendra Modi rakes up anti-Sikh riots to counter Rahul Gandhi'. *DNA*. 25 October 2013. dnaindia.com

'No harm in involving Tytler, Sajjan Kumar in Delhi polls: Sheila Dikshit'. *WorldNews Network.* 5 November 2014. wn.com

North, Andrew. 'Delhi 1984: India's Congress party still struggling to escape the past'. *BBC.* 18 February 2014. bbc.co.uk

'NRI Jasbir, key witness, San Francisco'. *NRI Press.* 20 December 2007. nriinternet.com

Nussbaum, Martha C. & Myers, Joanne. *Interview on The Clash Within: Democracy, Religious Violence, and India's Future.* Transcript. Carnegie Council. 3 May 2007. carnegiecouncil.org

"Old fox' Bhagat passes away'. *Rediff.* 29 October 2005. rediff.com

'Rajiv Gandhi cleared over bribery'. *BBC.* 4 February 2004. bbc.co.uk

'Rajnath called 1984 killings 'genocide', now MEA objects when Canada does the same'. *The Wire.* 7 April 2017. thewire.in

Satish, Mrinal. 'Forget the chatter to the contrary, the 2013 rape law amendments are a step forward'. *The Wire.* 22 August 2016. thewire.in

'Serb 'Adolf' innocent of genocide'. *BBC.* 5 July 2001. bbc.co.uk

Sharma, Mihir, S. 'Modi, myths and man'. *Business Standard.* 21 January 2013. business-standard.com

Singh, Hardeep. 'The Thatcher-Gandhi papers: Operation Bluestar's bitter legacy 30 years on'. *Left Foot Forward.* 19 February 2014. leftfootforward.org

Singh, Lord (Indarjit). 'Religion and religious freedom in international diplomacy'. *Network of Sikh Organisations.* 19 October 2016. nsouk.co.uk

Sharma, Sudesh. 'Burned, paralyzed and after 25 yrs on bed victim dies without seeing any justice'. *NRI Internet.* 17 February 2009. nriinternet.com

Singh, Professor Swaran Preet Singh. 'The assassination of Indira Gandhi: I was there', *The University of Warwick,* 2014. warwick.ac.uk

'Sikh family brutally attacked in Delhi, attacker "1984 bhool gaye, sallo yaad karwata hoon".' *Punjabi Bolo.* 8 October 2013. punjabibolo.wordpress.com

'Sikh family on train attacked, young Sikh girl stripped and assaulted'. *Panthic.* 20 April 2013. panthic.org

Singh, Sarbpreet. '1984: The semantics of genocide and the bugbear of Khalistan'. *The Huffington Post.* 19 April 2017. huffingtonpost.com

Soriano, Rueda. 'Manipulation of language as a weapon of mind control and abuse of power in 1984'. *Rocio's Blog.* 28 October 2010. rorueso.blogs.uv.es

Suri, Sanjay. 'In Kamal Nath, Congress finds a dubious general for Punjab'. *CNN-News18.* 14 June 2016. news18.com

'The five Ks'. *BBC.* 29 September 2009. bbc.co.uk

'The Machete'. *Imaging Genocide.* 2017. genocide.leadr.msu.edu

'Truth Commission: Peru 01'. *United States Institute of Peace.* 13 July 2001 – 28 August 2003. www.usip.org

'Truth Commission: South Africa'. *United States Institute of Peace.* 1 December 1995. usip.org

Walia, Amarjit Singh. 'I lived through the Sikh riots and 30 years later, I'm not ready to forgive or forget'. *Quartz India.* 31 October 2014. qz.com

Watson, Tom. 'Blog: Margaret Thatcher's interest in aiding Operation Bluestar',

NDTV, 15 January 2014. ndtv.com

Weaver, Mary Anne. 'Sikhs and Hindus in Punjab show rare unity in protest over wheat'. *The Christian Science Monitor.* 30 May 1984. csmonitor.com

_____. 'Sikh-Hindu clash tests Mr. Gandhi; violent backlash could build pressure for independent Sikh nation'. *The Christian Science Monitor.* 5 November 1984. csmonitor.com

'We had no choice: Indira Gandhi told Margaret Thatcher on Operation Bluestar'. *NDTV.* 4 February 2014. ndtv.com

'We will not forget you'. *My Malice and Bias.* 25 October 2016. malicethoughts.blogspot.co.uk

'When Amitabh Bachchan spoke about allegations against him in the 1984 anti-Sikh riots'. *The News Minute.* 25 February 2015. thenewsminute.com

5. ONLINE ARTICLES & RESOURCES

Amnesty International India. '31 Years and waiting: an era of injustice for the 1984 Sikh massacre'. *Amnesty International India.* September 2016. amnesty.org.in

Annan, Kofi. 'May we all learn and act on the lessons of Srebrenica'. *United Nations.* 11 July 2005. un.org

'Appeals Chamber Judgement in the Case the Prosecutor v. Radislav Krstic'. *International Criminal Tribunal.* 19 April 2004. icty.org

Arora, Aditya. P. 'Genocide - An Indian Perspective'. Amoolya Khurana (ed). *Lawctopus,* 2015. lawctopus.com

Bangura, Zainab Hawa. 'Statement by the special representative of the Secretary-General on sexual violence in conflict'. *United Nations.* 17 April 2013. un.org

_____. 'Sexual violence in Conflict'. *Department for International Development,* 12 November 2013. dfid.blog.gov.uk

Bedi, Puneet. *1984 Living History.* 4 June 2014. 1984livinghistory.org

'Bosnians, world leaders converge on Srebrenica to remember victims'. *Radio Free Europe/Radio Liberty.* 10 July 2015. rferl.org

'Convention on the Prevention and Punishment of the Crime of Genocide'. *United Nations Human Rights.* (no date). ohchr.org

Delhi Diary. 'Credible evidence that he played a role in organizing the communal attacks'. Cable 08 New Delhi 790. *WikiLeaks,* 14 March 2014. wikileaks.org

Delhi Sikh Gurdwara Management Committee. *Written arguments on behalf of Delhi Sikh Gurdwara Management Committee to Justice R.N. Misra.* (no date). carnage84.com

Directorate of Intelligence of the Central Intelligence Agency (CIA). *India and the Sikh challenge.* March 1987. cia.gov

'East Delhi Parliamentary Constituency (Lok Sabha) Election Results – 1984'. *Maps of India.* mapsofindia.com

Eng, Kok-Thay. (n.d.). 'Redefining genocide'. *Genocide Watch.* genocide-watch.org

Ensaaf & Human Rights Watch. *Protecting the killers - a policy of impunity in Punjab, India.* 17 October 2007. hrw.org

'Foreign Secretary and Angelina Jolie address military conference'. *Foreign & Commonwealth Office and The Rt Hon William Hague.* 28 March 2014. gov.uk

FXTop online currency converter. fxtop.com

Gill, Gauri. *1984*. November 2014. gaurigill.com

'GNI per capita, Atlas method (current US$)'. India. *The World Bank*. data. worldbank.org

'Government urged to set up public inquiry into 1984 Amritsar massacre'. *National Union of Journalists*. 12 June 2014. nuj.org.uk

Hynes, Andy. 'Everett Rovers 3 St Albans 2'. *Everett Rovers FC*. 20 November 2016. everettroversfc.co.uk

'India'. *Human Rights Watch*. 2017. hrw.org

'India 2016/2017'. *Amnesty International*. 2017. amnesty.org

'India: a mockery of justice: the case concerning the "disappearance" of human rights defender Jaswant Sing Khalra severely undermined'. *Amnesty International*. 31 March 1998. amnesty.org

'India: bring charges for newly discovered massacre of Sikhs'. *Human Rights Watch*. 25 April 2011. hrw.org

'India enters new political territory'. *Lubbock Avalanche-Journal*. 12 June 2004. lubbockonline.com

'India: events of 2016'. *Human Rights Watch*. 2017. hrw.org

'India: no justice for 1984 anti-Sikh bloodshed'. *Human Rights Watch*. 29 October 2014. hrw.org

'Indian Response to European Motion on 1984'. *A Blog by Ensaaf*. 2 May 2004. blogs.harvard.edu

'International Covenant on Civil and Political Rights'. *United Nations Human Rights*. (no date). ohchr.org

'Jean Paul Akayesu. ICTR-96-4'. *United Nations Mechanism for International Criminal Tribunals*. 1 June 2001. unictr.unmict.org

'Judiciary of India'. *Wikipedia*. wikipedia.org

Kagan, Sophia. 'The "media case" before the Rwanda Tribunal: The Nahimana et al. appeal judgement'. *The Hague Justice Portal*. 24 April 2008. hague-justiceportal.net

'Kamal Nath'. *World Economic Forum*. weforum.org

Kaur, Jaskaran. *'Twenty Years of Impunity: The November 1984 Pogroms of Sikhs in India'*. Portland: Ensaaf. October 2006. ensaaf.org

Kishwar, Madhu. 'Gangster Rule: The massacre of the Sikhs'. *Manushi*. 1985. manushi-india.org

———. 'In the Name of Secularism and National Unity: How Congress Engineered the 1984 Pogroms'. *Manushi*. manushi.india.org

'Kristallnacht: a nationwide pogrom'. *United States Holocaust Memorial Museum*. 9–10 November 1938. ushmm.org

Lambert, Jean. Lucas, Caroline. Wuori, Matti. and Boumediene-Thiery, Alima. 'Written declaration on the deaths of Sikh civilians in Panjaab and India in 1984'. 32/2004. *European Parliament*. 19 April 2004. europarl. europa.eu

Lok Sabha, Press Information Bureau, Government of India. *PM's intervention during the debate in Lok Sabha on motion for adjournment on need to take action against persons indicated by Nanavati Commission*. 11 August 2005. pib.nic.in

'Manmohan Singh a True Statesman in Reacting to Sikh Riot Report'. Cable 05DELHI6310_a. *WikiLeaks*. 12

August 2005. wikileaks.org

Miliband, David. *Reply to Jeremy Dear, General Secretary, National Union of Journalists.* Letter. 13 January 2010. 8t4files.wordpress.com

Miller, Phil. 'Revealed: SAS advised 1984 Amritsar raid'. *Stop Deportations.* 13 January 2014. stopdeportations. wordpress.com

Nagrik Ekta Manch volunteers. 'Those Who Remain…'. *Manushi.* January 1985. manushi-india.org

Noble, L. 'Burning Books'. *Cambridge University Library website.* (no date). lib.cam.ac.uk

'Outer Delhi Constituency results'. General Election 2004. *Election Commission of India.* 30 August 2005. eci.nic.in

'Parliamentary Committees'. *Indian Parliament.* (no date). parliamentofin-dia.nic.in

'Pendency of cases'. *Wikipedia.* wikipedia.org

'Press Conference leaving for India (Mrs Gandhi's funeral)'. *Margaret Thatcher Foundation.* 2 November 1984. margaretthatcher.org

'Rae Bareli Lok Sabha Elections and Results 2014'. Elections.in.

'Reality demands: documenting viola-tions in Kosovo 1999'. *International Crisis Group.* 27 June 2000. cms. crisisgroup.org

'Service record of Wing Commander Manmohan Bir Singh Talwar'. *Bharat Rakshak, IAF.* bharat-rakshak.com

Singh, Gurcharan. 'Review of Scorched White Lilies of '84'. *Institute of Sikh Studies.* January 2011. sikhinstitute.org

Singh, Jaspreet. 'Golden Temple 1947, 1984, 2014'. *Montréal Serai.* 27

September 2014. montrealserai.com

Singh, Parvinder. *1984 Sikhs' Kristallnacht.* UK: Network of Sikh Organisations, 2009. ensaaf.org

Stanton, Gregory. H. 'The ten stages of genocide'. *Genocide Watch.* 2013. genocidewatch.org

Swire, Hugh. *Reply to Michelle Stanistreet, General Secretary, National Union of Journalists.* Letter. 20 July 2014. 8t4files.wordpress.com

'Terry Dicks: an 80s Tory Politician'. *The Thatcher Crisis Years.* 29 December 2012. thatchercrisisyears.com

Trial Chamber. *International Criminal Tribunal for the former Yugoslavia (ICTR).* 1998. icty.org

'UK Government involvement in the attack on the Golden Temple and its failure to respect the human rights of Sikh in Genocide of 1984'. *Network of Sikh Organisations.* 9 February 2014. nsouk.co.uk

Wazir, Sanamdeep Singh. 'Revisiting Widows' Colony 30 years after the Sikh massacre. *Amnesty International India.* 12 March 2015. amnesty.org.in

Wiesel, Elie. 'Acceptance Speech'. *The Nobel Peace Prize.* Oslo City Hall, Norway. 10 December 1986. nobel-prize.org

Wilton Park. *The G8 makes landmark dec-laration on preventing sexual violence.* 19 April 2013. wiltonpark.org.uk

XE Online currency converter. xe.com

6. Reports

1984 Carnage in Delhi: A Report on the Aftermath. People's Union for Democratic Rights. November 1992. unipune.ac.in

Justice Denied: A Critique of the Misra Commission Report on the Riots in November 1984. People's Union for Democratic Rights & People's Union for Civil Liberties. April 1987. unipune.ac.in

Rao, Amiya, et al. *Oppression in Punjab: Report to the Nation.* New Delhi: Citizens for Democracy, 1985. unipune.ac.in

Report on 1984 Sikh Genocide. Sikhs for Justice. Submitted to UN Secretary General, November 2013. referendum2020.org

Sikri Report. New Delhi: Citizens' Commission, 1984. Available at carnage84.com

Who are the Guilty? Report of a Joint Inquiry into the Causes and Impact of the Riots in Delhi from 31 October to 10 November. Delhi: Jointly published by the People's Union for Democratic Rights & People's Union for Civil Liberties, 1984. pucl.org

7. OTHER MEDIA

i. Radio

Friction, Bobby. 'Assassination: when Delhi burned', *BBC Radio 4*, 31 October 2014. bbc.co.uk

DJ Nihal. 'Sajjan Kumar acquitted in 1984 anti-Sikh Riots case'. *BBC Asian Network.* 1 May 2013. bbc.co.uk

ii. Films and Documentary

BBC footage of the mobs, 1–3 November 1984.

Bose, Shonali. *Amu.* Film. Delhi: Jonai Productions, 2005.

Eastern Eye. TV programme. Channel 4: London Weekend Television. 1985.

Courtesy of ITV Archive.

ITN News footage of the mobs, 1–3 November 1984.

Kaur, Harpreet. *The Widow Colony: India's Unsettled Settlement.* Documentary Film. Delhi, 2009. thewidowcolony.com

Pasricha, Teenaa Kaur. *1984, When the Sun Didn't Rise.* Documentary Film. June 2017. whenthesundidntrise. wordpress.com

Rushdie, Salman. *The Riddle of Midnight.* Documentary Film. Antelope South for Channel 4, 1988. bfi.org.uk

Sharat, Raju. *Divided We Fall: Americans In The Aftermath.* Film. USA: New Moon Productions, 2001.

8. ONLINE VIDEOS

'1984 After the Darkness'. *YouTube*, 1:36:18. Posted by 'Sikh Research Institute (SikhRI)'. 5 June 2016. youtube.com

'1984 Anti Sikh Pogrom'. *YouTube*, 20:36. Posted by 'Pav Singh'. 27 July 2013. youtube.com

'1984: The Anti-Sikh Propoganda [sic] Tapes'. *YouTube*, 53:32. Posted by '1984MemorialProject'. 30 May 2012. youtube.com

'Babbar on 84'. *YouTube*, 57:31. Posted by 'Sikh Channel Delhi Unit'. 13 February 2014. youtube.com

'Chapter 84: Introduction'. *YouTube*, 10:45. Posted by 'Cobra Post'. 21 April 2014. youtube.com

'Frankly Speaking with Amitabh Bachchan'. *YouTube*, 1:14:06. Posted by 'Times Now'. 30 May 2015. youtube.com

'Frankly Speaking With Rahul Gandhi - Full Interview | Arnab Goswami Exclusive Interview'. *YouTube*, 1:20:03. Posted by 'Times Now'. 27 January 2014. youtube. com

'Life after 1984 anti-Sikh riots: 29 years of struggle'. *YouTube*, 15:37. Posted by 'TehelkaTV'. 1 May 2013. youtube.com

'Living-Jeevit History-Itihaas'. *YouTube Channel*. youtube.com

'Margaret Thatcher's disgust at Sikhs-1984, funeral of Indira Gandhi', *YouTube*, 1:22. Posted by 'Sikh2Inspire'. 3 February 2014. youtube.com

'Rahul Gandhi Speech in Public Rally at Kherli (Alwar) Rajasthan on Oct 23, 2013'. *YouTube*, 24:13. Posted by 'Indian National Congress'. 23 October 2013. youtube.com

'Rajiv Gandhi exposed by Advo. H S Phoolka: Video of Boat Club Speech (Nov. 19, 1984) released'. *YouTube*, 4:51. Posted by 'SikhSiyasat'. 20 November 2015. youtube.com

'The Last Killing'. YouTube, 23:01. Posted by 'Ensaaf'. 22 May 2014. youtube.com

'The Newshour Direct: Ram Jethmalani'. *YouTube*, 10:21. Posted by 'Times Now'. 28 May 2013. youtube.com

'Elie Wiesel Acceptance Speech'. *Online Video*, 18:00. Oslo City Hall, Norway. 10 December 1986. nobelprize.org

9. Talks

Brass, Paul R. 'On the Study of Riots, Pogroms, and Genocide.' *Prepared for the Sawyer Seminar. Session on Processes of Mass Killing.*

The Center for Advanced Study in the Behavioral Sciences, Stanford University, 6–7 December 2002. faculty.washington.edu

10. Interviews by author

Lord Indarjit Singh, April 2017

Professor Swaran Preet Singh, 21 February 2015

11. Government Records & Publications

i. India

Ahooja, R.K. *Ahooja Committee Report*. New Delhi: Ministry of Home Affairs, 1987. carnage84.com

Central Government Act. 'Article 25(2) (b)'. *The Constitution of India*. 1949.

Government of India. *White Paper on the Punjab Agitation*. New Delhi: Government of India Press, 1984.

Jain, J. D. and Aggarwal, D. K. *Jain Aggarwal Report*. Delhi: Government of India Publications, 1993. carnage84.com

Justice Ranganath Misra Commission of Inquiry. *Misra Commission Report*. Sirhind Mandi: Takshila Publications, 1987. carnage84.com, witness84.com

Kishori vs State (Nct) Of Delhi. *Supreme Court of India*. December 1999. indiankanoon.org

Mittal, Kusam Lata. *Kusum Lata Mittal Commission of Inquiry*. Delhi: Government of India Publications, 1990. carnage84.com

Nanavati, G. T. *Justice Nanavati Commission of Inquiry 1984 (Anti-Sikh*

Riots). Report Volumes One and Two.
New Delhi: Ministry of Home
Affairs, 2005. mha.nic.in

ii. *United Kingdom*

Churchill, Winston Spencer.
'Amendment of Road Traffic
Act, Committee Stage'. House of
Commons. 23 June 1976. Quoted in
Sydney Bidwell *The Turban Victory*,
London: Sikh Missionary Society,
1987. sikhmissionarysociety.org

Heywood, Jeremy. 'Allegations of UK
involvement in the Indian operation at
Sri Harmandir Sahib, Amritsar 1984'.
Cabinet Office. 4 February 2014. gov.uk

'Letter concerning UK's involvement
in attack on Golden Temple'. 10
Downing Street. Found on Sikh
Council UK website. 6 and 23
February 1984. sikhcounciluk.org

The National Archives. *INDIA. UK/
Indian Relations: Situation in Punjab;
Activities Of Sikh Extremists; Proposed
Visit To UK By Rajiv Gandhi In June
1985; Part 4.* Ref: PREM 19/1536. 5
March 1984–22 May 1985. Released
16 July 2015.

Dr Jagjit Singh Chauhan. BBC Radio 4
programme 'World at One'. 12 June
1984.

Letter from Indira Gandhi to Margaret
Thatcher. Dated 14 June 1984.

Letter from Lord Aldington to Margaret
Thatcher. Dated 4 January 1985.

Letter from Stuart Young, Chairman of
the BBC, to Pushkar Johari, Acting
High Commissioner in the UK.
Dated 14 June 1984.

Letter from Mehtab Singh, Chairman of
KNO to Margaret Thatcher. Dated 18
June 1984.

Telegram from Sir Geoffrey Howe to

Indira Gandhi conveying Margaret
Thatcher's words. Dated 30 June 1984.

Note of a meeting between Margaret
Thatcher, Sir Robert Wade-Gery and
Lord Swraj Paul in New Delhi. Dated
4 November 1984.

Meeting between Margaret Thatcher and
Rajiv Gandhi in Moscow. Dated 13
March 1985.

The National Archives. *Conclusions of
Cabinet Meetings 24–41 (1984).* Ref:
CAB 128/79.
28 June 1984 - 13 December 1984.
Released 3 January 2014.

'Conclusions of a meeting of the Cabinet
at 10 Downing Street'. 8 November
1984.

'Conclusions of a meeting of the Cabinet
at 10 Downing Street'. 15 November
1984.

'Conclusions of a meeting of the Cabinet
at 10 Downing Street'. 22 November
1984.

Hansard (hansard.millbanksystems.com)

'China'. House of Commons, vol 156, c
965–67. 12 July 1989.

'Foreign Affairs and Overseas
Development'. House of Commons,
vol 67, c 324. 9 November 1984.

'Golden Temple, Amritsar'. House of
Commons, vol 65, c 111. 30 July 1984.

'India'. House of Commons, vol 139 c
484. 31 October 1988.

'India', House of Commons, vol 169, c
1333–40. 22 March 1990.

'India (Sikh Community)'. House of
Commons, vol 140, cc 718–26. 11
November 1988.

'John McDonnell maiden speech to
Parliament'. House of Commons,

c 734. 6 June 1997. publications.
parliament.uk

'Motor-cycle crash-helmets (religious
exemption) bill'. House of Commons,
vol 374, cc 1055–69. 4 October 1976.

'Mrs. Indira Gandhi'. House of
Commons, vol 65, cc 1297–99. 31
October 1984.

'Mrs Kuldip Kaur'. House of Commons,
vol 107 cc 1504–15. 19 December
1986.

'Sikh Demonstrations'. House of
Commons, vol 62, cc296-7w. 22 June
1984.

'Sikh Demonstration (London)'. House
of Commons, vol 61, c 602. 15 June
1984.

'Sikhs in India (Human Rights)'. House
of Commons, vol 199, cc 1241–48. 29
November 1991.

12. Affidavits

*i. Misra Commission of Inquiry, 1987 (see
carnage84.com)*

Affidavits submitted by Prominent Persons

Aseem Srivastava son of (s/o) Umesh
Srivastava.

Ashok Jaitly s/o Hari Ram.

Dinesh Mohan s/o Raties Mohan.

Jaya Srivastava w/o Umesh Srivastava.

Munish Sanjay Suri s/o B. N. Suri.

N. D. Pancholi s/o D. R. Pancholi.

Parabhjiv Miglani s/o A.S. Miglani.

Poonam Mutreja daughter of (d/o)
Amarnath.

Rahul Kuldip Bedi s/o Kuldip Chand.

Rajiv Lechan s/o Dr A. V. Sharma.

Ram Bilas Paswan s/o Juman Paswan.

Ravi Chopra s/o B. D. Chopra.

Smitu Kothari s/o Rajni Kothari.

V. Khosla s/o D. P. Khosla.

Vasant Sabharwal s/o Dr Satish.

Others

Ajit Singh s/o Boorh Singh

Amrik Singh.

Smt. Balwant Kaur.

Bua Singh.

Cham Kaur.

Didar Singh, Kiran Gardens.

Gurbachan Singh, Nangloi.

Inder Singhs s/o Sardar Basan Singh.

Jagjit Singh, Kiran Gardens.

Jatan Kaur.

Miss Jasbir Kaur, Gammon Colony.

Moti Singh, Sultanpuri.

Narinder Singh, Gammon Colony.

Padmi Kaur.

Prof. Madhu Dandavate.

Raj Kumar, Palam Colony.

Sadora Singh.

Subedar Balwant Singh, near
Sagarpur.

Sukhan Singh Saina, Shakarpur.

Tehmi Devi.

Group Captain Manmohan Bir Singh
Talwar.

ii. The Nanavati Commission of Inquiry,
2005 (see carnage84.com)

Affidavits submitted by Prominent Persons

Lt. Gen (Retd) J. S. Aurora.

Kamni Jaiswal.

Khuswant Singh.

Madan Lal Khurana.

Madhu Kishwar.

Patwant Singh.

Rahul Kuldip Bedi.

Ranjit Singh Narula.

Shanti Bhushan.

Swami Agniwesh.

Others

K. R. Malkani.

Kuldip Singh Bhogal.

Amar Singh, Yamna Vihar.

Bhagwani Bai.

Dara Singh.

Davinder Singh.

Gurmeet Singh, s/o S. Mohan Singh.

Harnam Singh, Mangolpuri.

Monish Sanjay Suri.

Mukhtiar Singh.

Pratap Singh, DIG, BSF (Retired).

Ram Jethmalani.

Satu Singh s/o Sunder Singh.

Surinder Singh.

Vrinda Grover.

Wazir Singh s/o S. Dharam Singh.

Index

A note about the Author

PAV SINGH was born in Leeds, England, the son of Punjabi immigrants. As a member of the Magazine and Books Industrial Council of the National Union of Journalists he has been instrumental in campaigning on the issues surrounding the 1984 massacres.

In 2004, he spent a year in India researching the full extent of the pogroms (from which members of his extended family narrowly escaped) and the subsequent cover-up. He met with survivors and witnessed the political fall-out and protests following the release of the flawed Nanavati Report into the killings. His research led to the pivotal and authoritative report *1984 Sikhs' Kristallnacht*, which was first launched in the UK Parliament in 2005 and substantially expanded in 2009. In his role as a community advocate at the Wiener Library for the Study of the Holocaust and Genocide, London, he curated the exhibition 'The 1984 Anti-Sikh Pogroms Remembered' in 2014 with Delhi-based photographer Gauri Gill.

www.8t4files.wordpress.com
@Parvinder66

Also by
Kashi House

THE TARTAN TURBAN
In Search of Alexander Gardner

THE GOLDEN TEMPLE OF AMRITSAR
Reflections of the Past (1808-1959)

WARRIOR SAINTS
Four Centuries of Sikh Military History (Vol. 1)

KASHI HOUSE CIC is a media and publishing social enterprise focused on the rich history and culture of the Sikhs and the Punjab region (in both India and Pakistan). For further details of our books, prints and events visit:

kashihouse.com
facebook.com/kashihouse
twitter.com/kashihouse

www.kashihouse.com